To Jessie and Josh, who teach us something new about media every day

The New Media Environment

An Introduction

Andrea L. Press and Bruce A. Williams

A John Wiley & Sons, Ltd., Publication

This edition first published 2010
© 2010 Andrea L. Press and Bruce A. Williams

Blackwell Publishing was acquired by John Wiley & Sons in February 2007. Blackwell's publishing program has been merged with Wiley's global Scientific, Technical, and Medical business to form Wiley-Blackwell.

Registered Office
John Wiley & Sons Ltd, The Atrium, Southern Gate, Chichester, West Sussex, PO19 8SQ, United Kingdom

Editorial Offices
350 Main Street, Malden, MA 02148-5020, USA
9600 Garsington Road, Oxford, OX4 2DQ, UK
The Atrium, Southern Gate, Chichester, West Sussex, PO19 8SQ, UK

For details of our global editorial offices, for customer services, and for information about how to apply for permission to reuse the copyright material in this book please see our website at www.wiley.com/wiley-blackwell.

The right of Andrea L. Press and Bruce A. Williams to be identified as the authors of this work has been asserted in accordance with the UK Copyright, Designs and Patents Act 1988.

Library of Congress Cataloging-in-Publication Data
Press, Andrea Lee.
    The new media environment : an introduction / Andrea L. Press and Bruce A. Williams.
        p. cm.
    Includes bibliographical references and index.
    ISBN 978-1-4051-2767-7 (hardcopy : alk. paper) – ISBN 978-1-4051-2768-4 (pbk. : alk. paper)   1. Internet–Social aspects.   2. Information technology–Social aspects.
3. Mass media–Social aspects.   I. Williams, Bruce Alan.   II. Title.
    HM851.P73 2010
    302.23′1–dc22

                                                                                    2010004723

A catalogue record for this book is available from the British Library.

Set in 10 on 12.5pt Galliard by Toppan Best-set Premedia Limited
Printed in Singapore by Ho Printing Singapore Pte Ltd

01   2010

Contents

Acknowledgements   viii

1. Introduction: Modern Life Is a Media Experience   1

    A Tale of Two Hurricanes   2
    What Is a Media Environment?   8
    The Importance of Changing Media Environments   10
        The electronic media   12
    Media in the Twenty-First Century: What Has Changed?   16
        The age of the internet   19
    Conclusion   21

2. Ownership and Control in the New Media Environment   26

    Patterns of Media Ownership and Control   26
    Ownership and Control of the Media: Assumptions and
        Realities   32
        Alternative models of media ownership   35
        Who owns the media?   37
        Ownership and control in a global context   46
    Does It Matter? The Consequences of Concentration and
        Conglomeration   48
        The argument for market-driven media   48
        The argument against market-driven media   49
        What this means today   55
    Conclusion   56

3. Media and Democracy   63

    Introduction   63
    Changing Media Environments and Changing Democratic
      Politics   68
      Why nervous liberals are still with us: The enduring
        problem of propaganda   71
      John Dewey and the reconstruction of media and
        democratic politics   74
      Empirical research: How do media actually affect
        citizens?   75
      Television and the "Age of Broadcast News"   79
    Politics in the New Media Environment   84
    Conclusion   87

4. Studying Popular Culture: Texts, Reception, and Cultural
      Studies   91

    Introduction: Hollywood and Representations of Reality   91
    Media Studies and the Study of Reception: A Brief
      History of Its Methods and Findings   101
    Conclusion   107

5. Studying Inequalities: Class, Gender, Race, and Sexuality
      in Media Studies   112

    A Critical Perspective on Inequality in Media Studies   112
      The Frankfurt School   116
      Cultural studies   116
      Media studies research findings on class, gender, race,
        and sexuality   119
    Gender in Media Studies Research: Are Gender Roles
      Culturally Reproduced?   124
      Film and gender: Issues of reception and
        representation   128
      Television and gender: Issues of reception and
        representation   132
    Media and Race   136
    Sexuality   144
    Conclusion   148

Contents   vii

6. Studying Media Texts and Their Reception in the New
        Media Environment   156

    Transformative Images in the New Media Environment   160
        Globalization and the new shape of media identities   162
    Media Reception Research in the New Media Environment   163
        Global reception in the new media environment   167
    Gender, Race, Sexuality, and Social Class Inequality in
        New Media Reception: A New Study   169
    New Studies: Gender and Social Class Identities in the
        New Media Environment   173
    Politics, Media Impact and Use, and the New Media
        Environment   178
    Old and New Media in the Individualized Media
        Environment: The New Media Environment Is Never
        Just New Media   181
        Bias in old media and new   182
        Civic engagement in the new media environment   184
    Americans and Political Discussion: How the New Media
        Environment Is Changing the Civic Landscape   184
    Conclusion   187

7. Conclusion   194

    We Are Living in a Mediated Age   194
    The Complexity of Our Relationship With the Media   196
    Human Agency in Media Decisions and Directions   198
    In Closing: The Case of the RFID   202

Index   205

Acknowledgements

Our main debt in writing this book is to our students, both the undergraduate and graduate students that we have taught over our years as professors in the communications and media fields. We'd particularly like to thank the undergraduate and graduate students at the University of Virginia and the University of Illinois. Their curiosity and love of the field of media has kept us working hard to hone the arguments which form the crux of this book. Those two institutions generously supported the work for this book by providing research stipends, leave time, and research and secretarial assistance. We'd also like to thank the Department of Media and Communications at the London School of Economics, which provided a wonderful academic home during two separate sabbaticals. We are grateful to the National Science Foundation for funding one of the studies we discuss in chapter 6, and to the Research Board of the University of Illinois for funding the other.

Thanks are due as well to a number of our colleagues who have made obvious and not so obvious contributions to this book. Dale Bauer, Clifford Christians, Nick Couldry, Michael Delli Carpini, Tamar Liebes, Sonia Livingstone, Melanie Loots, Maria Mastronardi, Bob McChesney, and Dan Schiller deserve particular mention. Our colleagues in the new Media Studies Department at the University of Virginia – Hector Amaya, Aniko Bodroghkozy, Robert Kolker, Jennifer Petersen, and Siva Vaidhyanathan – have provided one of academia's most joyful and collegial homes. This certainly facilitated the manuscript's completion. Special thanks are owed to our graduate students at the University of Virginia and the University of Illinois, in particular Tatiana Omeltchenko, Camille Johnson-Yale, and Joy Pierce, who served as assistants at various stages of the research that informed this manuscript. Judith McPeak and Bonnie Howard deserve enormous gratitude for their dedicated administrative support. An anonymous reviewer of the manuscript was extremely help-ful. And finally, our editorial staff at Blackwell, including our copyeditor Cheryl Adam, our acquisitions editor Jayne Fargnoli, and Margaret Morse and Joanna Pyke, kept the project running smoothly to completion.

Final thanks are due to our children, Jessica Press-Williams and Joshua Press-Williams, who teach us far more about media (and everything else) than we are able to teach them. This book is dedicated to them with all our love and admiration (and now, get OFF that computer Josh!).

Chapter 1

Introduction
Modern Life Is a Media Experience

Why study the media? The answer is so obvious that many academics and educators overlook its paramount importance. Media are key to everyday life in the twenty-first century. But more than that, media are the lens through which we experience the world and what we take to be the reality of that world.

Any quick observation of today's children will uncover the central importance of media in constituting, not simply influencing, their lives. Our 15-year-old daughter gets up in the morning and turns on her computer and radio at the same time. While text messaging her friends before school, she downloads new songs to her MP3 player. When she comes home and turns to homework, it is done on the computer while she keeps track of her friends on the social-networking site Facebook.

Our 11-year-old son rises early so that he has a couple of hours to play his computer games before the structure of school keeps him from them for at least a few hours. When we ask him why he loves to play with computers, he says that playing with other kids is more fun, but when they are not around, computers are almost as fun and almost as interactive, especially when he plays games online. They are much more fun, in fact, than the possibilities that old media hold for him. Watching TV or reading books is too passive, in his opinion. It scarcely needs pointing out that both children will often see video or watch TV as part of their daily school routine. And so their day goes.

For both of us, often the first act in the morning is to check e-mail and see what has come in. This act of turning on a computer also lets us check the day's *New York Times*. In the interim we might turn on the radio and listen to National Public Radio, either the news or the music station. A walk to the front door gets us the print version of *The Washington Post*. Before any of the four of us are fully awake, we are immersed in media: old and new, print and electronic, audio and video, passive and interactive, and synchronous and asynchronous.

This is only one family's habits, but habits that are increasingly common in the United States. Internet service providers (ISPs), which used to see traffic increase only with the start of the workday, now find that it takes off "like a rocket ship" at 7 a.m. as adults and children go online as soon as they wake up (Stone 2009). The experience of living life betwixt and between media use is quickly becoming one of the universal conditions of life, certainly in the developed and developing worlds, crossing cultural, social class, and racial lines.[1] It is this ubiquity of the media in the modern world that we seek to show to our readers, as we describe the new academic field of media studies and what it has to offer to all of us as we negotiate modern life. We address both how the ever-presence of the media affects all dimensions of our lives, and how the *way* media are always present has changed dramatically over the last few decades.

A short comparison helps us to move beyond our particular family and our particular moment in the history of media to emphasize in a very general way how media operate to structure our experience, and how dramatically the role of media has changed over the last century.

A Tale of Two Hurricanes

The hurricane slammed into the United States packing winds of over 145 mph, slightly down from the Category 5 levels it registered over open water. While evacuation warnings had been circulating for days and wealthy neighborhoods emptied, other residents, predominantly poor and black, stayed behind. Hours later, when the storm had passed, it seemed at first that the damage from wind and rain would be serious, but far from catastrophic. Sadly, that was not to be the case. Earthen dikes erected to contain a huge lake gave way. As floodwaters rose, desperate people sought safety in the attics and on the rooftops of their submerged homes. Thousands of people died in one of the worst natural disasters in American history.

Government response was slow and insufficient, as state and local authorities were rapidly overwhelmed and the federal government seemed nowhere to be found. The fact that the dead were disproportionately poor and black raised questions of racism in both evacuation and rescue efforts. While these issues were quickly forgotten by the white community and the wider society, they remain a source of bitterness in the black community.

This description might be about Hurricane Katrina hitting the Gulf Coast in 2005, with which we are all familiar (because most of us followed it in the media), but it actually describes a hurricane that hit Florida in 1928.[2] Sometimes called the "Forgotten Hurricane," it left 2,500 dead and is the second deadliest hurricane in American history, behind only the 1900 Galveston hurricane, which killed 8,000. By way of contrast, the death toll for Katrina is estimated at around 1,600. Considering the similarities and differences between the hurricanes of 2005 and 1928 helps introduce many of the central points we want to make about media studies in the rest of this book.

First and perhaps most significantly, consider the vast differences in the state of the media in 1928 compared to 2005. Katrina was tracked from satellites and searcher planes in continuous contact with the US Weather Service, which then almost instantaneously transmitted storm information to the public via radio, television, the Internet, and other forms of communication. Updates on the direction and intensity of the storm were continuous and close to real time. Directions on preparing for the storm and, ultimately, evacuation orders could easily be communicated from authorities to the anxious citizens in Katrina's path.[3] Information about the storm and preparations for its landfall were not limited to those living in Katrina's path, but rather were instantly transmitted to a worldwide audience.

Consider the very different state of telecommunications in 1928. Information about the 1928 storm was sporadic, often inaccurate, and usually hopelessly outdated. Ships at sea transmitted wireless information about the storm when they could (i.e., when not being swamped or sunk). Most data came from telegraph and wireless ground stations based on reports from local weather stations on the Atlantic islands that were devastated by the storm before it hit Florida. At one point, the Weather Service "lost" the storm when communication facilities were destroyed in Puerto Rico. The inability to accurately track the storm greatly increased the number of dead and injured in Florida. When the hurricane did not appear for hours after people expected it (based on outdated and inaccurate warnings), they left their places of shelter so that when the storm did hit, many were in vulnerable positions.

Even the notion of "warning" must be examined in light of the vast differences in media between 1928 and today. We take it for granted that once vital information is known to authorities, it will be rapidly disseminated via widely available media channels. In 1928, such channels either did not exist (e.g., television, mobile phones, and the Internet) or were available to only a very few (e.g., telephone and radio). Hurricane warnings were sent through newspapers (as a result, they came hours or even days too late), telephone (in one Florida town, there was only one phone, whose owner had to go from house to house trying to warn his 400 neighbors), radio (again, only available to a small proportion of Floridians), or flags flown from the tops of public buildings. Most Floridians, especially those who were poor and lived in rural communities, were outside the reach of any channels of mass communication and had to rely on word of mouth spread from family to family.

Organizing prompt relief to a stricken area is a life-and-death issue: the more rapid the response, the more lives can be saved. In 1928 local governments ceased to operate due to the storm, and no information about its impact was available to the Florida state government for over a day. The federal government was in the dark for longer than that.[4]

Information about the storm was slow to reach any kind of wider audience. The first article about the storm did not appear in *The New York Times* until September 18, two days after it hit Florida. Even then, the initial facts reported were highly inaccurate (it was first estimated that 24 had drowned around Lake Okeechobee). In subsequent days, the estimated death toll continued to rise (it reached 800 in a front-page *Times* story on September 21). Somewhat ironically, by the time accurate information about the magnitude of the catastrophe became available, the story had ceased to be front-page news. A *Times* story reporting that an estimated 2,500 might have died (close to what we now believe was the storm's toll) appeared on September 22, but was printed on page 10 of the newspaper. By September 28, a story about the storm's aftermath was on page 38.

In general, newspaper coverage of this enormous catastrophe was sporadic outside of the stricken area. This could not contrast more with the extended focus on Hurricane Katrina in all the forms of media we take for granted today – television, radio, the Internet, and print. While in 1928 someone who lived outside the stricken area might pay virtually no attention to the event, this was not so for the media event that took place in 2005. By a "media event," we mean an occurrence that commands the attention of all of the media – print and electronic, including the Internet. Such an event calls a virtual "time-out" from ordinary life, more or less requiring that we pay attention. September 11, the death of Princess Diana, and the invasion of Iraq were all media events. The concept of a media event is essential to understanding the role of media in modern life and is a key concept in the media studies literature.[5]

Although comparing the 1928 and 2005 hurricanes highlights dramatic improvements in the way information is produced and disseminated, this does not mean that changes in telecommunications led to improvements in other areas of American society. When, for example, it came to issues of race and class, many aspects of the two hurricanes were remarkably similar and illustrate important continuities in American society between 1928 and the present. These continuities, despite dramatic changes in specific features of telecommunications technology, illustrate how media *both* influence and are influenced by the structures that shape society.

Like the rest of US society, the American media have, at best, a checkered record when it comes to dealing with issues of racial and economic inequality. Yet, one of the most striking aspects of media coverage of Katrina was that with cameras and journalists reporting live from the scene, powerful images and stories of the degree to which most victims were poor and black were unavoidable. As CNN commentator Jack Cafferty said, race has become "the big elephant in the room" (Daily Kos 2005).

These sorts of comments and the emotional stories coming out of New Orleans highlighting the plight of the black and poor residents left behind in the city's evacuation prompted a national dialogue (if only a brief one) about the plight of the black underclass in many American inner cities. It raised questions about how even evacuation plans, by relying primarily on residents owning their own automobile, inevitably left many poor city residents behind. Likewise, those forced to rely on the increasingly overwhelmed and horrific public facilities, like the New Orleans Superdome, were almost entirely poor and black. No such national conversation was sparked by media coverage of the 1928 storm.

Although this blatant disparity in the treatment of the rich and poor seemed shocking to journalists and many viewers in 2005, had the hurricane of 1928 not been forgotten, it would have been much clearer that such inequality in the face of natural disaster has a long history. In the 1928 storm, race and class were important determinants of who survived and who perished. Of the 2,500 fatalities, an estimated three quarters were black (mostly farmers and migrant farm workers who worked and lived north and south of the dike that gave way). In contrast, the overwhelmingly rich and white community of Palm Beach suffered few fatalities due to, among other things, better access to what information was available (not a digital divide, but a communications–information divide).

In both cases, rescue and recovery efforts similarly raised questions about race and class. In the Katrina case, many accused the federal government of responding slowly due to the poverty and race of the victims. In 1928, coffins were reserved for white victims, while most black victims were buried in unmarked mass graves. Similarly, many black survivors were forced at gunpoint to work at recovery efforts. Given the magnitude of the storm and the horrors of its aftermath, Eliot Kleinberg (2003), author of a definitive book about the 1928 hurricane, asks whether this catastrophe would have faded so completely from public memory had the victims been overwhelmingly white.

One reason for the degree to which the 1928 hurricane was "forgotten" has to do with the ways in which the media system has been and continues to be dominated by issues of concern to middle-class white Americans. This is true for the news as well as the myriad forms of popular entertainment that help shape the consciousness and attention of most Americans. Given the ways in which issues of race and class are addressed– or, more accurately, ignored– it is not surprising that the conditions of poor black Americans could be ignored as easily in 2005 as they had been in 1928.

At the same time, popular culture in some of its forms can serve as a repository for the memories and concerns lost to the mainstream media (Lipsitz 2001). While much media attempt to construct a picture of white, middle-class life as the norm for America, some forms of popular culture can also reflect and appeal to smaller ethnic, racial, gendered, or classed audiences. For instance, memories of the forgotten hurricane remain for readers of the celebrated 1937 novel *Their Eyes Were Watching God* by Zora Neale Hurston, an acclaimed black writer who was born in Florida. And, as mentioned above, although the memory of the 1928 storm has faded for the general public, bitterness about the differential treatment of blacks lingers in the black families who still live in the devastated towns. Evidence of the longevity of this bitterness is evidenced by protests that led mass gravesites to be marked with memorials in 2002. (See Figure 1.1.)

In short, the story of these two hurricanes highlights several of the points we shall emphasize throughout this book. First, and most

Figure 1.1. Two different ways the "Forgotten Hurricane" is remembered. On the left, Zora Neale Hurston's *Their Eyes Were Watching God*; and on the right, the plaque erected in 2002 to honor the African-American flood victims buried in mass graves.

significantly, the media matter. The contours of the media environment in which we live determine what we know about the world; indeed, in large part they determine our understanding of reality. In the extreme, access to media can be a matter of life or death. It is clear that access to telephones and radio in 1928 determined who would live and who would die. The vast differences between the plights of poor blacks and wealthy whites in 1928 were at least partially because the latter had access to the newest communication technologies. This is no less true today. As we increasingly organize modern life on the assumption that everyone will have access to the newest forms of media, lack of access can have dire consequences.[6]

Second, the new media environment within which we live has fragmented audiences in ways that were unimaginable even 25 years ago – the mass audience of the heyday of television is a thing of the past. New forms of communications technology mean that we increasingly consume a media diet unique to each of us – what we watch, listen to, and think about (and when) differs widely across different segments of the public (Turow 1997, 2006; Sunstein 2001). While there may be groups of people who were concerned with the plight of inner-city blacks, or the impact of climate change on hurricanes, these folks could attend to media meeting their interest without ever encountering the much broader public, who knew little and (perhaps) cared less about these issues. Consequently, when media events occur that focus all the myriad forms of media on the same subject – whether Hurricane Katrina, the terrorist attacks of 9/11, or a presidential campaign – they become rare moments of public dialogue about vital questions usually ignored by the vast majority of media outlets and the audiences who use them.

Finally, although media matter, it is important to see that they are not all that matters. By focusing on issues of racial, class, and gender inequality, we are reminded that some social problems and issues endure, despite the dramatic changes in media with which we all live. Before moving on to a closer examination of today's media and the ways in which they differ from the media of the recent and distant past, we first highlight several of the key concepts we will be using throughout the book.

What Is a Media Environment?

In media studies, we define the "media environment" as both the specific communications technology in use (e.g., personal computers, newspapers, and television) and the social, political, and economic structure within which these technologies are used (e.g., how media outlets are owned, how individuals actually use them for a wide range of purposes, and the government regulations that affect them). This is vital, since to understand media, we need to know much more than the characteristics of the specific technologies available and in use. As we saw from the example of the 1928 hurricane, knowing that both radio and telephone were available tells us little about the ways they were used in a crisis, since they were differentially available to segments of the population depending on economic and racial inequalities.

So media studies scholars draw from other fields in both the social sciences and humanities. Sociology, political science, and economics help us discuss the different types of contexts within which media operate. For example, sociologists help us to define the social context of the media by giving us a theoretical and empirical understanding of institutions like the family, schools, the government, and the church; media operate within and on all of these social structures. In addition, these institutions are the source of values and attitudes that affect the way we think about and use media in our everyday lives. Issues like what television shows are considered appropriate for children, whether the Internet is safe or dangerous, and who should buy Internet access at home – all of these issues are affected by social attitudes and values, which sociologists study.

Political science focuses on the institutions of government and the play of power, examining how political decisions are made and the forces that affect the political system, like voting, political activism, campaigning, political parties, and so on. The political process affects the working of media institutions in that it determines regulations and laws within which they operate. At the same time, media also play a leading role in bringing information to the public about the political process itself, in enabling participation and organization, and in other ways as well. When it comes to elections, for example, Americans receive virtually all of their information about the long campaign – from information during the primary season to each party's convention to the actual campaign itself to the outcome of voting on Election Night – through media of one sort or another, from older forms like television, radio, and newspapers to newer forms like the Internet and cell phones.

At the same time, policy decisions made by the political system shape the nature of those various media channels and the types of information that flow through them. So, for example, since policy makers in the 1930s created a privately owned and advertiser-driven media system, in contrast to the public broadcasting models of many western democracies, candidates are forced to raise large amounts of money to pay for campaign ads, with obvious consequences for the role of money in politics (McChesney 1993; Hallin and Mancini 2004).

Economics gives us the tools to analyze the financial structure of media organizations, and a critical perspective on the way the government chooses to allow them to make profits (e.g., through advertising or subscription), how much concentration of ownership will be allowed, and so on. The comparative economic perspective that media studies offers is particularly useful in making sense of the constraints and possibilities characterizing different approaches to ownership and control of media in different nations.

Media studies scholars also draw on disciplines like English, film studies, and anthropology to understand the meaning that might be attached – by authors, critics, and viewers/readers – to any particular media text. They do this to grasp the complexity of analyzing and understanding these issues. Especially influential have been those scholars working in the interdisciplinary tradition defined as "cultural studies." Most generally, we learn from this body of literature that culture is best understood as the ways in which individuals, groups, and societies struggle to "make meaning." Media are central to the making of culture.

Although we draw on other disciplines, we still argue that media studies constitutes a unique and vital discipline in its own right. All disciplines borrow from each other – imagine trying to study sociology without drawing on the insights of psychology or trying to understand politics without also understanding history. Media studies is a distinct discipline to the extent that it places the media environment at the center of its focus. It insists that media are a primary feature of modern society and central to any sophisticated analysis of life in the twenty-first century.

The Importance of Changing Media Environments

The significance of the media environment (or more generally, the dominant form of communication that characterizes a society) is best illustrated at times when the media environment is changing. As Marshall McLuhan argued, "[C]hanges in broader communication cultures alter the very structure of human consciousness" (1964).

What does it mean to say that changes in the media environment alter the very structure of human consciousness? It is hard to see these changes when we are living in the media environment we are trying to analyze – something like a fish trying to describe water. So, before considering more recent and familiar changes, especially the transition from print to electronic culture, an example from a much earlier change is especially useful to illustrate the profound transformations McLuhan describes.

Eric Havelock (1903–88), an influential classicist, was the first to argue that the transition from oral to written cultures between the sixth and fourth centuries BC fundamentally altered human thought and, in the case of the Greeks, the course of Western civilization. His ideas were a strong influence on media scholars, including McLuhan. In *ABC: The Alphabetization of the Western Mind*, Illich and Sanders (1988) illustrate how the transition between oral and written culture altered the ways people understood reality, how they understood themselves, and how they organized their societies. For example, while we are used to thinking of memory as a library (where our brain stores discrete pieces of information that we retrieve, much as we take books off library shelves and open them to the specific sections) or a computer (where our brain processes information and stores it for retrieval later, much as a computer stores and retrieves information saved on its hard drive), such an understanding could not, of course, precede the invention of libraries or computers.

> Like words and text, memory is a child of the alphabet. Only after it had become possible to fix the flow of speech in phonetic transcription did the idea emerge that knowledge – information – could be held in the mind as a store. Today, we take this idea so completely for granted that it is hard for us to reconstruct an age when recollection was not conceived as a trip into the cellar to pick up stores, or a look into a ledger to verify an entry. Since the fourth century B.C., memory has been conceived as such a deposit that can be opened searched and used. [Yet,] it is now clear that a purely oral tradition knows no division between recollecting and doing. (Illich and Sanders 1988, 54)

It is worth remembering that, just as many intellectuals today believe that a decline in reading and an increase in reliance on television and computers are "dumbing down" today's young people, so too did teachers once believe that moving from oral to print cultures was having a negative impact on their students' abilities. Plato, "the first uneasy man of letters," was anguished by the effect that the alphabet was having on his pupils. "Their reliance on silent, passive texts could not but narrow the stream of their remembrance, making it shallow and dull" (Illich and Sanders 1988).

How are you reading this book? Likely you are sitting somewhere by yourself and silently concentrating on the text. It is very unlikely that you are reading aloud. Yet, when writing and print were only beginning to emerge as the dominant form of communication, silent reading was not yet possible. Because in an oral tradition there is no separation between recollecting and doing or performing, reading could only be done out loud. Indeed, libraries did not become places of silence until around the thirteenth century.

In his history of reading, Alberto Manguel tells the story of St. Augustine's bewilderment in 383 AD at finding that Ambrose, the bishop of Milan, was reading in silence.

> "When [Ambrose] read," said Augustine, "his eyes scanned the page and his heart sought out the meaning, but his voice was silent and his tongue was still. Anyone could approach him freely and guests were not commonly announced, so that often, when we came to visit him, we found him reading

like this in silence, for he never read aloud." Eyes scanning the page, tongue held still: that is exactly how I would describe a reader today, sitting with a book in a café.

To Augustine, however, such reading manners seemed sufficiently strange for him to note them in his Confessions. The implication is that this method of reading, this silent perusing of the page, was in his time something out of the ordinary, and that normal reading was performed out loud. Even though instances of silent reading can be traced to earlier dates, not until the tenth century does this manner of reading become usual in the West. (1997, 51)

In fundamental ways, the dominant form of communication carries with it many assumptions about the world around us – indeed, communication constructs reality itself. Reality and the mode of communication through which we perceive reality are not two distinct entities, but rather the former constructs the latter. So, the development and spread of print culture precipitated fundamental changes in how societies could be organized, how the state would be organized, and how individuals would define themselves and their relationship to others. For example, the basic principle on which the United States was founded – that government powers are limited by a contract – is, obviously, dependent on a written Constitution.

Our point here is not to provide a thorough analysis of the changes that followed on the rise of print culture. Rather, we use this example to emphasize how communication structures virtually everything around us, even our most basic notions of what constitutes reality. In order to understand the implications of a new media environment, we need to analyze the ways it structures our own reality. The tools of media studies are, we believe, the best way to make these structuring principles visible and to examine their significance.

The electronic media

Just as the emergence of writing and printing altered the oral cultures of the world, so too did the emergence, beginning in the middle of the nineteenth century, of electronic communication and new forms of visual media that transformed the existing print culture.[7] The emergence of the telegraph, for example, changed forever the way people thought about time and space. With the telegraph, for the first time ever, information traveled more rapidly than the speed of the fastest physical transportation (a train, for example), thus breaking the connection between communication and transportation (Carey 1988).

As an example of how strange, even miraculous, this seemed at the time, consider that the telegraph set off a craze for consulting psychics who claimed to talk to the dead. It seemed no less remarkable that we could communicate with the dead than it did that messages could be transmitted without material form, instantaneously across vast differences (Peters 2001).

We now turn to the changes wrought by the transition from print to electronic cultures by exploring television, a centrally important medium from the middle of the twentieth century onward. A wonderful place to begin is with Neil Postman's influential book *Amusing Ourselves to Death*, first published in 1985. Focusing on the transition from print to electronic media, the book highlights the unique characteristics of a culture dominated by television and other visual, electronic media. This book allows us to see what was important about such a media environment, and so prepares us for exploring the media environment in which we live today.[8] The key issue is how any particular media environment, with its own peculiar mix of telecommunications technologies, operating within and on economic, political, and social institutions, structures our vision of the world, affects the operation of democracy, and sets the boundaries for what we see as "natural" and inevitable.

Signaling the significance of media to our most basic understanding of the world, Postman (1985) argues that to talk seriously of television (or any other dominant form of communication) is to talk of epistemology ("the theory or science of the method or grounds of knowledge"): "Television has been, in the second half of the twentieth century, our society's principle way of knowing about itself." What does he mean by this? Simply that our knowledge about the world, our basic notion of truth, depends on the particular medium that dominates our culture.

Television is a visual medium and, at a most basic level, reinforces the idea that seeing is believing. It is also a mass medium, based on communications from the few (those who control what goes over the air waves) to the many (the mass audience sitting at home watching). "The Age of Television," as we shall see, was a media environment characterized by a limited number of authoritative sources of information about the world – three broadcast networks and a single newspaper in most towns and cities. This environment contrasts with early typographic America (the late eighteenth to late nineteenth centuries), where there were many more outlets, including direct experience, for information that was more focused on the local environment and hence about fewer things in a smaller number of places.

Some of the implications of television's influence seem obvious to us. When it comes to politics, for example, because they must communicate with the public in a visual medium, politicians must be attractive. This effect of television was demonstrated in the very first televised presidential debates in 1960 between John F. Kennedy and Richard Nixon. Kennedy, young, handsome, and with a nice tan from campaigning in California, stood in stark visual contrast to Nixon, who was looking haggard as a result of recovering from a knee injury and refusing makeup. Citizens who listened to the debate on radio tended to see Nixon as the winner, while those who watched the exact same debate on television tended to see Kennedy as the winner (Museum of Broadcast Communications n.d.).

Similarly, the commercial style becomes the style we expect all issues to be dealt with, be they health, politics, or personal. This style involves messages delivered in seconds-long bits, rapid cutting, and the avoidance of detailed or sophisticated argumentation. As political debate has adopted rapid cutting and arresting images to compete for the fickle attentions of the audience, it is reduced to brief sound bites by opposing talking heads, rather than the extended oratory Postman (1985) describes as typifying nineteenth-century political debate.[9] For example, between 1968 and 2004, the length of sound bites allotted to presidential candidates on the network news broadcasts shrank from 48 to 8 seconds (Hallin 1998). Postman argues that in the Age of Typography (i.e., the stretch from the widespread adoption of the printing press to the rise of electronic media in the early twentieth century), discourse in America was generally "serious, coherent, and rational," while in the Age of Television it became "shriveled, absurd … and dangerous."

On television, pictures are an integral, necessary part of the process of storytelling, and this is what gives television its particular power. "Seeing is believing" for the public: this has been a theme in the history of media coverage of current events. In the case of the 2003 American invasion of Iraq, we are continually learning the power of this aphorism, as we struggled to understand the connection between the reality of the war and the story told in televised images. Of course, television is not the only communications technology responsible for the increasing significance of the image. The rise of photographic representation in the mid-nineteenth century, first in the medium of photography and then with the development of movies at the very end of the nineteenth century, predated television. Both photography and movies introduced a higher level of truth, or so it was initially thought, to media representations.[10]

The rise of a new dominant form of communication does not, of course, eliminate older forms – people did not stop speaking when they started reading and writing. However, while these older forms remain, they too are changed. In the Age of Television, the logic of a visual medium like television intrudes into all areas of the media environment, including the printed word.

> [T]here are still readers and there are many books published, but the uses of print and reading are not the same as they once were; not even in schools, the last institutions where print was thought to be invincible. They delude themselves who believe that television and print can coexist, for coexistence implied parity. There is no parity here. Print is now merely a residual epistemology, and it will remain so, aided to some extent by the computer, and newspapers and magazines that are made to look like television screens. (Postman 1985: 28)

Even oral communication is altered by television. Consider the university lecture. It is an ancient way for teachers to convey information to students, but while it still survives today, it has been transformed by the rise of television. When one of us first started teaching, we were advised by an older colleague that our students were used to the rhythms of television. Therefore, to be successful, our lectures had to imitate that rhythm – 10 minutes and a commercial, 10 minutes and a commercial. That is, we were to provide a small bit of information (the 10 minutes) and then break the lecture up with a joke, an anecdote, or a brief bit of interaction with students (the commercial). Today, we have gone much further, routinely using PowerPoint slides, video clips, and so on. We now mimic the rhythms of the music video.

By this logic, the media environment of the last half of the twentieth century was an all-encompassing system, influencing virtually everything in the societies in which it was deployed. As Postman argues,

> There is no audience so young that it is barred from television. There is no poverty so abject that it must forgo television. There is no education so exalted that it is not modified by television. And most important of all, there is no subject of public interest – politics, news, education, religion, science, sports – that does not find its way to television. Which means that

all public understanding of these subjects is shaped by the biases of television. (1985: 78)

While Postman sees the rise of television as a kind of fall from the grace of print culture, we need not reach the same judgment to see that it did constitute a profound change in the media environment and so the rest of society. For example, Postman celebrates the Lincoln–Douglas debates as an exemplar of nineteenth-century political debate. Yet, Gary Wills (2006) notes that Lincoln himself was impressed by the impact of the telegraph and absorbed its impact on the way we communicate. It is no accident that it is the Gettysburg Address, only 237 words long and influenced by the demands for brevity of the telegraph, which became the greatest and most influential speech in American history. Wills notes that other nineteenth-century figures saw the advantages of brevity and directness introduced by the telegraph. As Mark Twain noted, "Few souls are saved after the first 20 minutes of a sermon."

Do we still live in the Age of Television? Is the development of the Internet, satellite communication, and so on just an extension of television – "television on steroids," as Postman wrote? We would like to argue that, writing before the full influence of the Internet was clear, Postman was wrong. A change is now occurring that is every bit as profound as the change from typography to television. It is this enormous, ongoing change that we discuss in the next section. Given the ways in which changes in media both over the long run, as in the case of the shift from oral to written and then to electronic media environments, or in the shorter run, as in the case of the two hurricanes, alter much of what we take for granted in our society, the changes we chronicle in the next section can be expected to exert significant and profound effects.

Media in the Twenty-First Century: What Has Changed?

To simply list the developments in communications that have occurred over the last 25 years is to be reminded of how radically different the media environment of the early twenty-first century is from what preceded it. Here we focus on the specific technological changes which have taken place, but it is important to remember that these changes occurred in the context of broader social, political, and economic changes. These include the end of the Cold War, the accelerated emergence of a global economy, and the changing status and voice of formerly marginalized groups – people of color, women, and gays (we return to this topic in the next chapter).[11]

Alterations in the media environment are influenced by and, in turn, influence these broader social, economic, and political dynamics. We saw this in the example of the two hurricanes when the media environment interacted with the structures of racial inequality in the United States to influence who survived and who did not. While racial inequality remains a significant issue, the media environment of the twenty-first century, unlike the one of 1928, made visible these racial disparities to the wider nation and so prompted a national conversation about the plight of the poor, primarily African-American residents of New Orleans.

Some figures indicate the dramatic changes in the media environment over the last two and a half decades. In 1982, the first year for which we could find figures, fewer than 2 million personal computers were sold in the United States. By 2004 annual sales had grown to 178 million, with three quarters of US households having at least one personal computer by 2008 ("Examine the Home Computers" 2008). In 1982 the average home received approximately 10 television channels, only 21 percent of American homes had a VCR, and the Internet and mobile phones were for all intents and purposes nonexistent. By 2006 the average number of channels received had increased to over 100, approximately 90 percent of homes had VCRs or DVD players, and approximately three in four US households had an Internet connection (50 percent of which were high-speed connections); and by 2008, over three quarters of adult Americans had a cell phone or portable digital assistant (PDA).[12] The result of these developments has been unprecedented access to mediated information and the speed at which it is acquired, as well as greater variation than at any point in history in the form, content, and sources of this information.

Television, of course, remains an important medium, but it has been changed in fundamental ways over the last 25 years. During the era when the number of television stations was limited, content was quite similar across channels. Each network broadcast similar programming designed to attract the largest audience possible. During prime time the usual fare was dramas and comedies, with the preceding hour almost universally devoted to local and national news.

Today, the dramatic increase in the number of available media channels has shattered this arrangement. As recently as 1980 the average number of stations viewed per week was under six, with over eight hours a week devoted to each. By 2003, however, the average viewer watched 15 channels a week, devoting only 3.4 hours to each. Thus, while Americans are watching more television than ever before, the range of what they are watching is greater, and the audience for any particular program smaller. The impact of this increased competition is illustrated by a single example:

> When *Seinfeld* was the number one program in America in 1995, it had a big share of audience. But that share of audience 20 years earlier, in 1975, would not have placed it in the top 20 shows on TV. It would have been the 21st most popular show in the United States in 1975. (Pruitt 2000: 15)

Fragmentation of television audiences can also be seen in television news. Although the news was once dominated by the three networks, in 2003 there were more "regular viewers" of cable national news (68 percent) than of the nightly national news on ABC, CBS, and NBC (49 percent combined).[13] At a time when television programmers frantically compete for the attention of the young, the median age for network news is over 60, and their share of the most prized segment of the audience (18-to-49 year olds) has declined in the last 10 years from 46 to 29 percent (Kurtz 2002).[14] The audience for cable news is also aging: the average age of viewers of Headline News is 54, and CNN's average is 64 (Rutenberg 2001).

Media scholars such as Joseph Turow (1997, 2006) and James Webster and Patricia Phalen (1997) note that shifts in communication technology alter several fundamental expectations about media audiences and media content. The notion of a mass audience, at least as defined in the latter half of the twentieth century, is quickly being abandoned as networks and their competitors vie for audience share by marketing to different segments of the population. As a result, networks such as WB, Fox, ABC, MSNBC, and Lifetime (and their advertisers) seek to maximize differences in an effort to develop unique identities and "brand" loyalty. Developing within the greater consciousness of differing cultural identities based on race, ethnicity, gender, age, sexual preference, religious beliefs, and ideology, the result of this change in communication technology and the media's response to it has been a more fragmented audience and greater diversity in genres and content.

Further complicating this picture is the growing ability of viewers to control much of the mediated information they receive, though even here the line between true control and manipulation is a fine one. Television now serves as a portal to other forms of media through increasingly common technology such as DVD players, digital video recorders, and video game players. While significant in and of themselves, even these figures underestimate the full amount of audience fragmentation. For example, in 1980 fewer than half of all households had multiple televisions, while this figure had increased to 74 percent by 1996.[15] These and related technological developments are changing the way in which television is watched, altering the relationship between content producers and consumers.

Consider the growth of a seemingly mundane technological device – the remote control. This simple innovation made it possible to shift easily between channels, between real-time programming and pre-recorded programming on a DVD player, or even between television and the Internet, all without ever getting up from the couch: the remote control made the "couch potato" possible. As recently as 1985, only 29 percent of all households had a remote control, while by 1996 they were almost universal (94 percent). Far more revolutionary are new technologies such as digital video recording (DVR) systems like TiVo, which in July 2008 were in over 20 million homes. These systems allow viewers to automatically record and play back television shows based on personal preferences and schedules.

The age of the Internet

As dramatic as changes in television have been over the past two decades, they pale in comparison to the impact of the Internet. As noted above, fully three quarters of US households had Internet access by 2006, and half had high-speed connections in their homes. On any given day in 2007, nearly three quarters of adult Americans with an Internet connection went online. By 2007 nearly three in four Americans over the age of 18 used the Internet, and (in 2008) 85 percent of those between the ages of 12 and 17 at least "occasionally" used the Internet (Pew Internet and American Life Report 2008).

The diverse, extensive, and fluid nature of Internet use is matched by the content and form of the information created and provided. For example, consider the home page of Yahoo, the most popular Internet portal (Yahoo's audience is 500 million hits a month). One of every two Internet users visits a Yahoo-branded site at least once a month, and

Yahoo boasts 3.8 billion page views a day (Boulton 2006). The page contains a bewildering combination of information: there are links to "news," business, sports, and celebrity and popular culture stories. There are also recipes, weather, e-mail links, advertisements, and so forth. Unlike technology in earlier eras, however, the Yahoo home page and other portals (such as Google) serve as gateways *for* millions of people around the world, and *to* any one of a billion Web pages of varying topics, sources, genres, and points of view.[16] Hyperlinks on this, and other, Web pages further fragment the audience as viewers follow the links that most interest them: even when two people hit the same page, they are unlikely to actually view the same content.

Numerous other examples highlight the ways in which the Internet challenges the assumptions of the Age of Television described by Postman. The growing phenomenon of Web logs (blogs) is eroding the distinction between producers and consumers of media and even between elites and the broader society. For celebrities like Britney Spears, Tiger Woods, and Lindsey Lohan, the ability of anyone with a cell phone camera or Internet connection to circulate embarrassing images and controversial claims of scandalous behavior have dramatically reduced the ability to maintain a carefully crafted public persona distinct from private behavior. In chapter 3 we discuss the ways in which bloggers have become key players in the political process, challenging the dominance of professional journalists and political elites.

Other aspects of the Internet further complicate the information environment and the struggle for control of it. Chat groups and online discussions provide new venues for fans to discuss television shows, music, and movies; for patients to discuss their illness and the medical profession; for citizens to directly discuss public issues; and so on. Nonmainstream and/or international websites serve as alternative sources of information and opinion on social, political, and economic issues, challenging the gatekeeping functions of the older media producers. Networks of political and social activists use the Web to mount virtual and real-world opposition to traditional political elites or create alternative spaces for discussing issues ignored by mainstream media and elites.[17]

Overall, this new media environment challenges elites – political, social, and economic – by providing communication channels for ordinary citizens to directly produce and access information about political, social, and economic life, bypassing both traditional and new media gatekeepers entirely. For example, the ubiquity of cell phones and other small handheld video devices, coupled with the ease of uploading information, has led to numerous websites devoted to allowing almost anyone to post their own media messages. The most popular of these sites, YouTube, provides a forum for all categories of information, from popular music to political rants to clever and not-so-clever spoofs. In some cases, this capability has reinforced the ability of citizens to challenge the authority of even the most authoritarian regimes. In 2009, for instance, cell phones captured images of a young Iranian woman bleeding to death after being shot by pro-government militias. The video circulated rapidly throughout the world and helped gain international support for protesters challenging the fairness of the Iranian elections.

Of course traditional political, economic, cultural, and media elites are also using – and in many ways still dominating – the Internet.[18] Iran and China, for example, maintain extensive facilities for censoring and monitoring the Internet activities of their citizens. But in doing so, they are changing the way they interact with the public, further eroding the tenets of the Age of Television. In addition, new elites – from upstart independent filmmakers, musicians, and journalists to representatives of nonmainstream ideological perspectives, to new media players such as Google, Yahoo, and Microsoft – are vying for control of the media environment. In short, while the Internet has changed, and will continue to change, the way in which information is disseminated and used, the ultimate shape of the "Age of the Internet" is unclear.

Conclusion

In this chapter we have begun to explain how media studies can help us make sense of the mediated world within which we all live. We have shown how changes in the media environment, both over a relatively brief period of time (e.g., 1928–2005) and over much longer time periods (e.g., the transition from oral to print and then from print to electronic media cultures), influence virtually everything about the world within which we live, from the structure of our consciousness to who will live and who will die in the face of natural disasters. These examples demonstrate that media matter and that changes in media must be at the center of our understanding of changes in the world around us. Consequently, it seems clear that the changes of the last two and a half decades will have similarly profound effects on our world in the twenty-first century. The rest of the book explores how media studies can help us understand and critically analyze those changes.

Notes

1. It is, of course, important to remember that much of the world, and indeed many in the United States, do not share this life experience. Yet, even then, the lack of access to the full panoply of media is understood as an impediment to full participation in society, whether local, national, or global.
2. Our discussion of the hurricane of 1928 is drawn from the wonderful book by Eliot Kleinberg, *The Black Cloud: The Great Florida Hurricane of 1928* (New York: Carroll & Graf, 2003).
3. The wisdom and fairness of these evacuation plans comprise, of course, a very different issue. As we note below, they failed to take into account the very different access to transportation of the average middle-class car owner and poorer inner-city residents without private means of transport.
4. Even then, the differences between 2005 and 1928 are stark. President Calvin Coolidge's response, in the absence of federal agencies like the Federal Emergency Management Administration (FEMA), was to call for citizens to make contributions to the Red Cross and other voluntary organizations.
5. We provide an extended discussion of media events in chapter 3.
6. This echoes the argument of the great sociologist Max Weber, who observed that modern society – what he called "rational-legal society" – transforms wants into needs. That is, as the mass production of a wide variety of goods and services addresses the wants of mass markets, society itself becomes organized on the assumption that everyone will have these goods and services. To that extent, they are no longer wants, but needs.
7. It is important to note that much else was changing besides forms of communication during this period. For example, as historians and social scientists have long noted, in the United States, from the middle of the nineteenth century onward, the development of industrial capitalism, modern transportation systems, immigration, and the like transformed a predominantly rural society into a predominantly urban one. However, in a brief book like this, we are more interested in highlighting the dramatic role that changes in the dominant forms of media had in this transformation.
8. As we shall see, there is much debate over whether and in what sense, as media scholar Elihu Katz put it, "Television is over," and has been superseded by a fundamentally different "Age of the Internet."
9. A sound bite is defined as the length of uninterrupted speech allowed to a person.

10. Matthew Brady's famous Civil War photographs, first publicized in 1862, ushered in new expectations that this new medium could provide us direct and, paradoxically, unmediated access to reality. Yet, it turns out that many of the shots of the dead on the battlefield were actually carefully posed by the photographers. So, while it was assumed that pictures couldn't lie, these pictures did – a paradox that remains with us to this day as we attempt to unpack what is real and what is not in the representations we daily confront on television, in newspapers, and elsewhere.

11. For a more detailed treatment of the relationship between these broader shifts and changing communication technologies, see Williams and Delli Carpini (forthcoming, chap. 3), on which the rest of this chapter is largely based.

12. Figures are from *Statistical Abstract of the United States, 1999* (Bureau of the Census 1999) and *TV Dimensions 2004* (Media Dynamics, 2004). Internet statistics from WebSiteOptimization.com (n.d.).

13. Percentages total more than 100 percent because survey respondents could be regular viewers of more than one news source.

14. One need only consider the advertisements that aired during the first commercial break of the *CBS Evening News* on June 14, 2001, to conclude that news is a genre that increasingly appeals only to older Americans: Zantac 75 heartburn relief medication, air freshener, Viagra, Caltrate (a calcium supplement that "helps reduce colon polyps and osteoporosis"), Centrum vitamin supplement for heart disease, and an ad for the Mitsubishi Gallant that had as its theme a song with the lyrics, "I wish I knew what I know now when I was young."

15. All audience figures are from Nielson Media Research (n.d.).

16. As of August 2005, Yahoo (2005) indexed 19.2 billion Web pages.

17. These networks span the political spectrum from Moveon.com on the left to the conservative FreeRepublic.com on the right.

18. Consider, for instance, that Google bought YouTube for $1.65 billion. The deep pockets of Google have meant a crackdown on the posting of copyrighted and/or libelous videos.

References

Boulton, Clint. 2006. "Yahoo's earning message to Google: We're bigger than you are." http://googlewatch.eweek.com/content/archive/yahoos_earnings_message_to_google_were_bigger_than_you.html.

Bureau of the Census. 1999. *Statistical abstract of the United States, 1999.* Washington, D.C.: Author.

Carey, James. 1988. *Communication as culture.* New York: Routledge.

Daily Kos. 2005. "Jack Cafferty on CNN." September 1, www.dailykos.com/story/2005/9/1/155317/6225.

"Examine the Home Computers–US." 2008. Reuters, February 22, www.reuters.com/article/pressRelease/idUS130720+22-Feb-2008+BW20080222.

Hallin, Daniel C. 1998. "Sound bite news." In *Do the media govern? Politicians, voters, and reporters in America*, edited by Shanot Iyengar and Richard Reeves. New York: Sage.

Hallin, Daniel C., and Paolo Mancini. 2004. *Comparing media systems: Three models of media and politics.* Cambridge: Cambridge University Press.

Hurston, Zora Neale. 1937. *Their eyes were watching god.* New York: Harper & Row.

Illich, Ivan, and Barry Sanders. 1988. *ABC: The alphabetization of the popular mind.* San Francisco: North Point Press.

Kleinberg, Eliot. 2003. *Black cloud: The great Florida hurricane of 1928.* New York: Carroll & Graf.

Kurtz, Howard. 2002. "Troubled times for network evening news." *Washington Post*, March 10, p. A1.

Lipsitz, George. 2001. *Time passages: Collective memory and American popular culture.* Minneapolis: University of Minnesota Press.

Manguel, Alberto. 1997. *A history of reading.* New York: Penguin.

McChesney, Robert Waterman. 1993. *Telecommunications, mass media, and democracy: The battle for the control of U.S. broadcasting, 1928-1935.* New York: Oxford University Press.

McLuhan, Marshall. 1964. *Understanding media: The extensions of man.* New York: McGraw-Hill.

Media Dynamics. 2004. *TV dimensions 2004.* Nutley, N.J.: Media Dynamics.

Museum of Broadcast Communications. N.d. "The Kennedy-Nixon presidential debates, 1960." www.museum.tv/archives/etv/K/htmlK/kennedy-nixon/kennedy-nixon.htm.

Nielson Media Research. N.d. "Media practice: Extract more value from your audiences and properties." http://en-us.nielsen.com/tab/industries/media.

Peters, John Durham. 2001. *Speaking into the air: A history of the idea of communication.* Chicago: University of Chicago Press.

Pew Internet and American Life Report. 2008. *America's online pursuits.* Philadelphia: Pew Charitable Trust.

Postman, Neil. 1985. *Amusing ourselves to death: Public discourse in the age of show business.* New York: Viking.

Pruitt, Gary. 2000. *Roadmap 2005: National vs. regional journalism strategies for a successful future.* Philadelphia: Pew Center for Civic Journalism.

Rutenberg, Jim. 2001 "CNN aims at young viewers as it revamps news format." *New York Times*, August 5, p. A1.

Stone, Brad. 2009. "Coffee can wait: Day's first stop is online." *New York Times*, August 10.

Sunstein, Cass. 2001. *republic.com*. Princeton, N.J.: Princeton University Press.

Turow, Joseph. 1997. *Breaking up America: Advertisers and the new media world.* Chicago: University of Chicago Press.

Turow, Joseph. 2006. *Niche envy: Marketing discrimination in the digital age.* Cambridge, M.A.: MIT Press.

WebSiteOptimization.com. N.d. "US broadband penetration jumps to 45.2% – US Internet access nearly 75%: March 2004 bandwidth report." www. websiteoptimization.com/bw/0403/.

Webster, James, and Patricia F. Phalen. 1997. *The mass audience: Rediscovering the dominant model.* Mahwah, N.J.: Laurence Erlbaum, 1997.

Williams, Bruce A., and Michael X. Delli Carpini. Forthcoming. *After the news: Media regimes and American democracy in the new information environment.* New York: Cambridge University Press.

Wills, Gary. 2006. *Lincoln at Gettysburg: The words that remade America.* New York: Simon & Schuster.

Yahoo. 2005. "Our blog is growing up, and so has our index." www.ysearchblog. com/2005/08/08/our-blog-is-growing-up-and-so-has-our-index/.

Chapter 2

Ownership and Control in the New Media Environment

Patterns of Media Ownership and Control

Imagine that you're getting ready to travel to China and you'll be spending a week in Beijing. It will be the first time you've ever been to that country and, quite naturally, you want to learn all you can before you go. So you do what many folks do today: you go online. (Of course, this presumes you have access to the Internet and a connection speed that does not lead to more frustration than information.)

You do several Google searches to figure out what to see when you're in the Chinese capital and, eventually, wind up entering the phrase "Tiananmen Square." Table 2.1 lists the first page of results from this search. A careful and critical perusal of these results tells us a great deal about the new media environment, in terms of both what has changed and, equally important, what has not changed. This example sets the context for the rest of our discussion in this chapter about the significance of understanding patterns of media ownership and control.

First, consider the ease with which you can access this information. Just 15 years ago, before the growth of the Internet and World Wide Web, you would have most likely traveled to a bookstore or library and read through tourist guides, many of which would have been years old. Or, using snail mail, you would have had to order information that might take weeks to arrive. Today, without leaving your room, you are able to access a wide range of sources in a matter of seconds (again, depending on connection speed). Many of these sources would have been updated within the last few days, or even hours. Many of us now take it for granted that up-to-the-minute information will be at our fingertips, but it is worth noting that such ease of access to constantly updated information from

Table 2.1. First Page of Google Results for Search Term "Tiananmen Square"

Subject	Web Address
1. **Tiananmen Square** protests of 1989; from Wikipedia, the Free Encyclopedia	http://en.wikipedia.org/wiki/ **Tiananmen_Square**_protests_ of_1989
2. **Tiananmen Square**; from Wikipedia, the Free Encyclopedia "**Tiananmen Square** is the large plaza near the center of ..."	http://en.wikipedia.org/wiki/ **Tiananmen_Square**
3. BBC ON THIS DAY | 4 | 1989: Massacre in **Tiananmen Square** "The Chinese army storms a mass demonstration in **Tiananmen Square**, killing several hundred people."	http://news.bbc.co.uk/onthisday/ hi/dates/stories/june/4/ newsid_2496000/2496277.stm
4. **Tiananmen**, 1989 "The blood shed in **Tiananmen Square** has come to symbolize the triumph of the spirit over brute force."	www.christusrex.org/www1/sdc/ **tiananmen**.html
5. **Tiananmen Square**: Beijing: China. "Information on **Tiananmen Square** in Beijing, with pictures."	www.travelchinaguide.com/ attraction/beijing/tianan.htm
6. **Tiananmen Square**: 360-Degree Virtual Tour – Beijing, China "The name in Chinese, Yiheyuan, means garden of restful peace. It served as a suburban pleasance for emperors, a place in the countryside yet near the ..."	www.thebeijingguide.com/ **tiananmen_square**/index.html
7. **Tiananmen Square**; The Declassified History, 1989 "Useful collection of documents providing a US perspective of the events surrounding the Chinese government's use of heavily armed military forces against ..."	www.gwu.edu/~nsarchiv/NSAEBB/ NSAEBB16/index.html
8. Beijing **Tiananmen**: ChinaVista "The **Tiananmen Square** in the center of Beijing is said to be the biggest **square** in the world."	www.chinavista.com/experience/ **tiananmen**/main.html

Table 2.1. *Continued*

Subject	Web Address
9. Frontline: The Gate of Heavenly Peace "**Tiananmen Square** is a 'theme park' of the Chinese Revolution and 20th-century Chinese history."	www.pbs.org/wgbh/pages/frontline/gate/
10. Beijing Attractions: **Tiananmen Square**, Tian'an Men Tower, Mao … "**Tiananmen Square**, the largest city **square** in the world, is a mixture of a lofty monument, a magnificent tower, solemn halls and a great museum."	www.beijingtrip.com/attractions/**square**.htm
11. News archive results for **Tiananmen Square**	
1989	"Chinese Citizens Block Troops From Reaching Central **Square**; For 2nd Time, …" *Washington Post*
1997	"At **Tiananmen Square**, Exuberance Is Reined In" *New York Times*
1998	"CLINTON IN CHINA: THE SITE; Clinton, in Beijing **Square**, May Tread on the Ghosts" *New York Times*

Source: Google.com, September 17, 2007.

sources around the world was unimaginable only 15 years ago. Indeed, it is this miraculous immediate access to diverse information that accounts for much of the excitement about the new media environment.

Second, consider the different types of references on the list. Some of the links (links 5, 6, 8, and 10) are to sites of interest to tourists, likely what you were searching for. However, there are even more links related to the student-led democratic protests in 1989 that culminated in the Tiananmen Square massacre (see links 1–4, 7, and 9, and the articles under 11). Had you not known about these events, or only vaguely recalled them, your search put you a click away from finding out about them. Had you gone to the bookstore or library and stayed in the travel section, it is unlikely you would have been confronted quite so bluntly with information on a significant political issue. The degree to which we encounter information we were not specifically looking for (what we might call "serendipity") is an important characteristic of any media systems. Some scholars argue that being forced to engage with information and perspectives on topics with which you might not be familiar, or eager to seek out, is an important feature of a well-functioning public sphere and a prerequisite for an informed citizenry (Sunstein 2007). How well Internet searches, in particular, and broader features of the new media environment, more generally, serve this public purpose is an important, but often overlooked, topic.[1]

Third, consider the different sources of information on this list. Some of the links are to fairly conventional sources: the British Broadcasting Corporation (BBC) (link 3), the Public Broadcasting System (PBS) (link 9), and "The Beijing Guide," a tourist guide (link 6). However, the first two links to the online user-created encyclopedia Wikipedia bear comment. The entries in this encyclopedia are written and edited by the users themselves. Readers can correct mistakes, object to distortions or biases in stories, and generally enter into the process of creating knowledge.

In chapter 1, we illustrated the impact of a changing media environment on many of the fundamental characteristics of a society. Now consider that, although encyclopedias have existed for centuries, Wikipedia and other sites like it show the potential, for better or worse, of the Internet (and new media, more generally) to generate new models for the creation of knowledge (Sunstein 2006, 2007; Tapscott and Williams 2006; and, for a very critical view of this phenomenon, Keen 2007).

Fourth, note how many of the links are to the websites of traditional news outlets: PBS (link 9), the BBC (link 3), *The New York Times*, and *The Washington Post* (link 11, news archive). Is the Internet really providing us with new sources of information if much of what we find, and even more importantly the most trusted and used information, is produced, albeit on a different platform, by media outlets that have been around for a very long time and simply recycle stories produced for other media (e.g., television or newspapers)? Many commentators either celebrate or criticize the degree to which the Internet undercuts the authority of traditional elites and allows a broad range of people to create and disseminate all kinds of information. But how new and different is what we read on the Internet, especially since most research finds that users almost never click past the first one or two pages of search results?

Fifth, what about the links to sources that are, indeed, unfamiliar? Consider link 5, a website that provides a pictorial history of the Tiananmen Square massacre, links to a petition campaign,[2] and so forth. Closer perusal reveals that link 5 is run by ChristusRex.org, which according to other Internet sources is an "unofficial" Vatican website. What difference does it make that this site is run by a group supportive of the Catholic Church, an institution quite hostile to the Chinese government? Whose responsibility, if anyone's, is it to make the source of information transparent? Without such transparency, is it possible to critically evaluate the information we obtain?

Our sixth, and final question, looks past the results on the screen to what is "under the hood," so to speak: how does a search engine work? Why do we get these particular links and not another list? What sort of a company is Google, and how does it operate (Vaidhyanathan forthcoming)? How does Google's search engine differ from other search engines? How does Google make money off its search operations? According to its own corporate home page,

> As a business, Google generates revenue by providing advertisers with the opportunity to deliver measurable, cost-effective online advertising that is relevant to the information displayed on any given page. This makes the advertising useful to you as well as to the advertiser placing it. We believe you should know when someone has paid to put a message in front of you, so we always distinguish ads from the search results or other content on a page. We don't sell placement in the search results themselves, or allow people to pay for a higher ranking there. (Google 2009)

While this is quite clear (and, arguably, consistent) with Google's corporate mantra, "Don't be evil," it also begs a number of questions raised by blogger Josh McHugh: "Should Google play ball with repressive foreign governments? Refuse to link users to 'hate' sites? Punish marketers who artificially inflate site rankings? Fight the Church of Scientology's attempts to silence critics? And what to do about the cache, Google's archive of previously indexed pages?" (2003).

Another set of questions interrogates Google's approach to the privacy of those who use its search engine and other services: what about the information it collects about your searches? Can Google sell this information? Does it, and should it? Finally, given that Google is the most popular search engine and that search engines are now the primary gatekeepers for information gathering on the Internet, what, if any, public obligations does Google have? Should these obligations be determined by government through public policy or by the corporate leaders at Google? If it should be determined by governments, then which ones?

This last question raises another concern often overlooked when we go online: does it make any difference where we are and what Internet service provider (ISP) we use when we search Google or use the Web? What role does government regulation play in the way the Internet operates? What requirements are placed on the companies that we rely on to access it? For example, if you were to wait until you actually got to China and tried your search, the results might be considerably different. It turns out that the People's Republic of China maintains an extensive, sophisticated, and effective filtering system for blocking access to websites that deal with topics deemed objectionable by the state (Zittrain and Edelman 2003). So, your search in China would likely not list Wikipedia, PBS, BBC, *New York Times*, or *Washington Post* links. And, even if the links showed up, they would likely be blocked and inaccessible from China. Indeed, every 30 minutes or so, a cartoon of two young police officers would pop up to remind you that your Internet activities are being monitored and provide a link to the authorities where you can report suspicious activities by other Web users (Figure 2.1). So, despite the seemingly placeless nature of the Internet, evoked in terms like "virtual reality" or "cyberspace," it turns out that where you access the Internet from and the government policies there make a great deal of difference.

Finally, what role does the cooperation of telecommunications companies like Google, Time Warner, AOL, or Cisco Systems play in the censorship efforts of the Chinese government (Schiller 2007)? Are the software and hardware that allow censorship to operate used only by the Chinese government, or are they used in other governments, including the United States?[3]

Our brief discussion of searching Google for information on Tiananmen Square previews the issues we will be dealing with in this chapter:

- How are media companies organized, owned, and operated?
- What difference, if any, do such patterns have on the content of media we actually receive?
- How different, if at all, are new media when it comes to the relationship between ownership and content?
- What difference does government policy make?

Figure 2.1. Chinese reminder that your Internet activities are being monitored. *Source*: www.uberreview.com.

By focusing on questions like these, media studies moves us beyond simply using (and being used by) media to understanding them. True media literacy and effective citizenship now depend on such an understanding.

Ownership and Control of the Media: Assumptions and Realities

When we think about the new media environment – the Internet, cable and satellite television, digital video recordings, MP3 players, cell phones, and the like – it is easy to get caught up in the sense of wonder we feel as each new technology is placed in our hands (if we are able to afford them). Indeed, much public and scholarly discussion focuses on the impact that this or that new communications technology will have on our lives. For example, as we write, the impact of Twitter[4] on various aspects of American life – from its impact on teen attention span to the propriety of senators and representatives Twittering during President Obama's address to Congress and the nation – is being vigorously debated and satirized across the media landscape (from newspapers to blogs to *The Daily Show*).

Less recognized are the sets of assumptions about media that underlie such discussions. Too often, when focusing on specific new products and technologies, we unthinkingly assume what is called "technological determinism": that there is something inherent in the features of a particular technology that inevitably leads (or has led) to specific changes in our lives. Media studies cautions us to be skeptical about such easy assumptions.

As an example, the combination of the Internet's interactivity, the wide availability of personal computers, and high-speed access is often claimed to have profound impacts on the way social, political, and economic systems operate. This combination of technologies is seen as leading to a flattening out of social hierarchies as every user becomes a producer as well as a consumer of media, able to circulate individual opinions, products, and artistic abilities (Trippi 2005). Other arguments suggest that these technologies will obliterate time and space as we communicate across the globe, regardless of distance or time zone, and that this will have an "inevitable" impact on our sense of place, identity, nationalism, and so forth (Shirky 2008).

In a similar, although much less optimistic vein, social critics have long argued that television and other, later electronic media led to all kinds of negative social consequences, from the fall in literacy (cultural and political literacy as well as reading and writing), to a decline in civic life, to the coarsening of popular and political culture, to the breakdown of established social boundaries and gender roles (Meyrowitz 1985; Postman 1985; Putnam 2000). However, in focusing on the supposed natural and unavoidable characteristics of communications technologies, such analyses often minimize the social, political, and economic contexts in which such technologies are used.

In the case of television, for example, what difference does it make if there is a state-owned broadcasting system with a strong public service obligation, like the British or Canadian systems, as opposed to a privately owned, commercial system run for profit with a relatively weak public service obligation, as in the United States? Do these two different models of ownership and control lead to different content and consequences despite both employing the same communications technology? Similarly, will the Internet have the same consequences for political and cultural life if it is accessible primarily through private service providers, as opposed to being freely accessible via publicly owned and operated wifi systems? Will it have the same impacts if the rules for treating all information packets equally – known as "net neutrality" – are changed to allow different tiers of service? In short, can we separate the specific technologies deployed in a media system from the system of ownership and control of that media environment?

Media studies scholars indicate that the answer to this last question is no. Understanding the development of any particular communications technology requires analyzing the political (in the broadest sense of the word) decisions that shape that development. This is a vital question at all times, but especially now, as we grapple with the implications of new communications technology and the appropriate role for government and the private sector in shaping the media environment in the next few decades.

Harvard Law Professor Lawrence Lessig illustrates this point when he examines the expectations that surrounded many communications innovations of the past. He notes that when the printing press, telegraph, and radio were first introduced, they were expected by many to have a dramatic impact on the structure of society by increasing the ability of ordinary people to both produce and consume media; this is also the case today with the Internet (Lessig 2005; see also Standage 1998). So, for example, in the very early days of radio, many believed that this new medium would connect citizens to each other and most individuals would have equipment that could both broadcast and receive content (like ham radio). They did not foresee that virtually all radios would ultimately be built to only receive content broadcasts and that this content would be crafted by a few major networks given control of the airwaves by the government. In each case Lessig cites, the democratic potentials of new media technologies were never realized because of the political and economic structures in which they were used. In each case, although the technology did indeed dramatically expand the audience for mediated information, it did so while dramatically centralizing control over the production of this information.[5] In short, even though new technologies may have built-in potentials for affecting social relations in one way or another, which potentials are actually realized is a function of the specific political and economic systems in which they are actually deployed.

With this in mind, it is vital to consider the specific public policies that govern media in any given setting. For Americans, this means that most of the mass media in the United States are privately owned and operated for profit. Further, much of the mass media is financed through advertising and thus governed by the demand to provide advertisers with access to those who might wish to buy their products. For better or worse, when new media technologies arrive on the scene, this pattern of private owner-ship and control is assumed to be the best and most natural arrangement, often leading us to overlook alternative systems with very different costs and benefits.[6]

In the rest of this chapter, we will be asking two related questions about the specific political and economic systems in which media operate. First, who owns and controls the media? There is little disagreement about the answer to this question: whether we look at the United States or the globe, most of the media is owned by a very small number of very large corporations. Second, what are the consequences of this pattern of increas-ingly concentrated ownership and control? Here we shall see there is a good deal of disagreement over the answer. We will highlight the assump-tions behind competing answers to this vital question.

Alternative models of media ownership

While many Americans take it for granted that media will be owned by private corporations and financed mainly through advertising, this is not the only model for ownership and control of media in democratic societies. While the phrase "government owned" is often associated with repressive regimes using state-run media for propaganda purposes, the outcome is very different in democratic systems. In the United Kingdom, Canada, Japan, and a host of other democratic societies, most of the mass media is publicly owned, financed by the government, and dedicated to the public interest rather than the profit of private corporations.

In the United Kingdom, for example, the British Broadcasting Corporation (BBC) is publicly owned and financed through a licensing fee paid by everyone who buys a television set. The BBC is overseen by a board of governors who are accountable to the public and give a guar-antee of independence from the government. Indeed, reporting on the BBC has been critical of and criticized by both Labour and Conservative governments. So, not only do we have to keep in mind the various models of media ownership adopted around the world, but we also must evaluate their advantages and disadvantages in light of the specific political system in which they operate. For example, the presence of a strong and vibrant public service broadcasting system in the United Kingdom provides a very different context for responding to the implications of new media for democratic politics. Significantly, public trust in the BBC and its continued status as the most relied-on source of political information set the standards for newer commercial stations and might provide a forum for a less fragmented and polarized public discourse than would be possible in the United States.[7]

New models of ownership and control have emerged with the Internet, a medium that is owned collectively, controlled by no one actor, and guided by the basic principle that all packets of information must be treated alike, independent of who sends them. However, it is important to note that this model of collective ownership and network neutrality with respect to information packets is not built into the medium of the Internet. Rather, it emerged out of the specific context in which the Internet was developed, largely through government funding of the attempt by scientists to construct a network of computers. Therefore, the Internet is subject to the same political pressures to change as any other medium (Zittrain 2009).[8]

Although this is a new and unique model for ownership and control, there is a tension between it and the "default" American assumption of private ownership and commercial exploitation that surfaces in political struggles over government policy toward the Internet. Indeed, as we write this chapter, there are serious efforts to alter, through public policy decisions, the basic idea of network neutrality by allowing ISPs to charge extra fees to websites that want their sites to be given priority treatment and hence load faster. Likewise, questions of privacy – who is allowed to collect information on your browsing habits, and rules about selling such information – and other issues are all part of the policy-making process that will shape the Internet in the future. There is nothing, in short, inevitable about the type of medium the Internet will be in the future; rather, that will be decided through the political struggles over its regulation.

Given the significance of the structures of media ownership and control, it is worth asking why the United States has a privately owned and commercially operated system. As Robert McChesney (1999b) has argued, answering this question for radio and television shows that there was *nothing* inevitable about the adoption of this particular pattern: the outcome was not determined by the character of the telecommunications technologies involved. Instead, the emergence of radio in the 1930s was marked by bitter political struggles over the balance to be struck amongst commercial, educational, and democratic values. The resolution of these struggles played a major role in shaping the American media environment throughout the rest of the twentieth century.

Central were battles over whether the emerging American broadcasting system would be publicly owned and oriented toward educational and cultural goals (like the BBC) or, as was the ultimate outcome, be a privately owned, for-profit system imposing only limited public interest obligations on media companies. In the 1930s a powerful reform movement emerged that opposed advertising on the radio and supported a dominant focus on the public values that the new medium might foster. As one of these reform groups, the National Committee on Education by Radio, argued, "To allow private interests to monopolize the most powerful means of reaching the human mind is to destroy democracy. Without freedom of speech, without the honest presentation of facts by people whose primary interest is *not* profits, there can be no intelligent basis for the determination of public policy" (cited in McChesney 1999b: 153). Yet, despite the emergence of reform groups demanding serious consideration of a public service model (like the BBC or the Canadian Broadcasting System [CBC], just then being developed) and the overwhelming public opposition to advertiser-driven radio, in the end the issue was decided by Congress (without public hearings), which created the privately owned system we have today. McChesney concludes, "The media system exists as it does because powerful interests have constructed it so that citizens will not be involved in the key policy decisions that have shaped it" (1999b, p. 15).

Who owns the media?

In the many editions of his pathbreaking book *The Media Monopoly*, which first appeared in 1983 and after 2000 was renamed *The New Media Monopoly*, Ben Bagdikian, former journalist and dean emeritus of the Journalism School at the University of California, Berkeley, has chronicled the shrinking number of corporations that own and control most (i.e., over 50%) of the media in the United States. Between the first and latest editions of his book (which appeared in 2004), the number of controlling corporations had shrunk from 50 to five (Time Warner, Disney, News Corporation [News Corp], Viacom, and Bertelsmann). Reflecting the changing nature of the media environment, by 2006, there were eight media corporations that dominated the American media scene:

General Electric (owner of NBC; market value: $390.6 billion)
Microsoft (market value: $306.8 billion)

Google (market value: $154.6 billion)
Time Warner (market value: $90.7 billion)
Disney (market value: $72.8 billion)
News Corp (market value: $56.7 billion)
Viacom (market value: $53.9 billion)
Yahoo (market value: $40.1 billion)

Should we be concerned about the concentration of media ownership? If we simply look at media outlets – the number of television stations, radio stations, newspapers, magazines, publishing houses, movie studios, and so forth – there seems to be an enormous amount of diversity. There are 37,000 separate media outlets– 54,000 if you count all weeklies, semiweeklies, advertising weeklies, and any "periodicals," no matter how small or local. If we include the World Wide Web, the numbers increase exponentially. Since, as we noted above, the Internet is collectively owned with no single actor in charge, there is no definitive way of knowing how many websites and Web pages there actually are. However, estimates are that there were over 100 million distinct websites and over 20 billion Web pages as of early 2007 (Boutell.com 2007).

Some analysts essentially stop right here, arguing that the sheer number of media outlets and the even larger number of content providers are evidence that there is more diversity than ever and concentration of ownership simply is not a problem. Media economist Benjamin Compaine (2001), for example, applies the specific measures used by the federal government to determine antitrust violations. He concludes that media are actually one of the more diversified industries in the United States. C. Edwin Baker (2007) disagrees, however, noting that this argument depends on seeing the entire media environment as a single market. Baker states that this perspective makes no distinctions, for example, between producers of media content – like television stations and newspapers – and the conduits through which content is delivered to citizens, such as cable companies, ISPs, and telephone companies. He further criticizes Compaine's approach by noting that it assumes that if consumers are unhappy with the limited choices in one medium (e.g., the local newspaper),[9] they can easily substitute another medium (e.g., cable news stations). However, when it comes to some forms of information, this may be an inaccurate approach to the problems consumers face when moving from one source of information to another. In the case of local news, for example, as national chains have bought up many local newspapers and radio stations, they have cut back on the resources devoted to covering local affairs across media. Consequently, there are no real alternatives for consumers.

Baker's criticism points to a deeper problem with treating media as a single diverse market: diffusion of a new medium – the Internet, for example – does not mean that citizens stop relying on older forms of media like television or newspapers. The emphasis on the transformative properties of the Internet is a form of technological determinism. This is because it overlooks the extent to which citizens rely on specific forms of media for specific kinds of information, which may be unavailable (at least in the form many people need) in newer or different media. In this book, we argue for a focus on "media in use" (how media are actually used) as opposed to focusing on any specific new communication technology.

In our own research studying media use during the 2004 presidential election, we found that although many citizens did use the Internet for a wide variety of information, when it came to following politics they still relied heavily on traditional journalistic sources, even when they found those sources online (Press, Williams, Johnson, and Moore 2005). So, criticisms of the current state of professional journalism (to which we return in chapter 3) are not addressed by new media when we simply find the same content, produced by the same news divisions online as opposed to on the air.

Consequently, we agree with Baker that the media environment needs to be analyzed as a series of different markets with limited substitutability between them. When we take this view, the picture of "virtually limitless diversity" changes dramatically since the rapid increase in, for instance, the number of websites and cable and satellite television channels obscures the decline over time in the diversity of content *providers*. This has significant implications for the provision of information in a democratic society.

Consider newspapers. Throughout the twentieth century, the number of newspapers declined: while the US population doubled between 1900 and 1950, the number of newspapers declined from 2,226 to 1,900 (Bagdikian 1992). Even more telling, in 1923 503 American cities had more than one separately owned daily newspaper; now only 49 have more than one paper (and in 20 of these cities, competing papers have joint business and printing arrangements). Consequently, 98 percent of all cities have only one daily newspaper. There has also been increasing concentration of ownership among the declining number of papers. At the end of World War II, 80 percent of daily newspapers were independently owned; by 1986, 72 percent were owned by an outside corporation. In 1989, 80 percent were owned by outside corporations and over half of all newspapers were owned by 14 corporations.[10]

This pattern of increasingly concentrated ownership is repeated across many types of media. In 1981, 20 corporations owned 50 percent of the nation's 11,000 magazines; in 2004, three companies (Time Warner, Advance, and Hearst) owned 50 percent (Bagdikian 1992; Project for Excellence in Journalism 2006).[11] Four out of five television stations in the 100 most densely populated markets, serving almost 90 percent of US households, belong to multiple-owner groups. The advent of satellite and cable television has dramatically increased the number of stations received by the average viewer. However, when it comes to cable service providers, six firms own 80 percent of all cable systems and, when it comes to content providers, seven firms control 75 percent of the cable channels and programming.

Since the 1930s, film production has been dominated by 6–7 studios. In 1997, the six largest firms accounted for over 90 percent of US theater revenues. All but 16 of the 148 widely distributed films in 1997 were produced by these six (and even of the 16, many were produced by companies with distribution deals with these six).[12] In 1985, the 12 largest theater chains owned 25 percent of the screens; in 1998, they owned 61 percent.

Book and music publishing is also increasing its already concentrated structure. In 1998 seven firms controlled over half the publishing market. Eighty percent of all books are sold by a small number of giants like Barnes and Noble and the online giant Amazon (which controls over 50 percent of the online book market). It is no surprise, then, that the market share of independent book sellers fell from 42 percent in 1992 to 9 percent in 2008. Similarly, the five largest firms control 87 percent of the music business. In the case of popular music, four companies (Vivendi Universal, Sony/BMG, Time Warner, and EMI) produce 75 percent of recorded popular music (Longhurst 1995).

And as Robert McChesney points out, if anything, this sector-by-sector review *underestimates* the degree of media concentration because it does not capture the media firms with major holdings in two or more sectors. "Conglomeration," which refers to the ownership of different kinds of media by the same corporation, is even more troubling than concentration in any single market. So, for example, each of the six Hollywood studios also owns some combination of television networks, television stations, music companies, cable channels, cable TV systems, magazines, newspapers, book-publishing firms, and so on. Viacom chief Sumner Redstone summarized the incentive for corporations to acquire holdings in a wide variety of media outlets: "When you can make a movie for an average cost of $10 million and then cross-promote and sell it off of magazines, books, products, television shows out of your own company, the profit potential is enormous" (quoted in McChesney 1999a). To see what this means in more specific terms, the holdings of the largest media firm – Time Warner – are listed in Table 2.2.

What difference does the Internet make to this picture? On the one hand, we might argue that the 100 million separate websites and the increasing reliance of more and more people on this medium for information alter fundamentally the problem of concentration and conglomeration. This is an argument made by many scholars, commentators, and policy makers. On the other hand, despite the unimaginably large number of websites, if we look at the sites that are accessed most often, we find that, as with the case of our Google search for information about our visit to China, the most popular sites are owned by a small number of corporations. Table 2.3 shows the most popular websites when it comes to seeking information about the news. CNN and *People* magazine are owned by Time Warner. MSNBC is owned by General Electric. Fox News is part of Rupert Murdoch's News Corp. Yahoo and Google are, of course, two of the largest Internet corporations.

While there may well be an almost infinite number of sites on the Internet, it turns out that virtually all of those who seek out information use a very small number of sites, most of which are owned by very large media corporations. Many of these corporations have significant holdings in other forms of media as well. Indeed, when it comes to even searching for information, the portals one uses are also exceptionally concentrated: in July 2006, Google accounted for 60.2 percent of US searches; and Google, plus Yahoo and AOL, together accounted for 94.5 percent of searches (MarketingVOX 2006). Before moving on, however, it is important to note that establishing the reach, within the media realm, of a small number of large corporations says nothing about the actual impact such concentration has on society, a subject about which there is much debate.[13]

What is clear is that concern over the shrinking number of companies controlling the majority of media is both recognized by and troubling to the American public. A 2000 survey sponsored by the Ford Foundation

Table 2.2. Holdings of Time Warner

Time Warner Book Group	
Warner Books	Little, Brown Books for Young
The Mysterious Press	Readers
Warner Vision	Back Bay
Warner Business Books	Bulfinch Press
Aspect	Time Warner Book Group UK
Warner Faith	Time Warner Audio Books
Warner Treasures	Time Inc.
TW Kids	Southern Progress Corporation
Little, Brown and Company	Sunset Books
Little, Brown Adult Trade	Oxmoor House
	Leisure Arts

Time Warner: Cable	
HBO	CNN Radio
CNN	CNN Interactive
CNN International	Court TV (with Liberty Media)
CNN en Español	Time Warner Cable
CNN Headline News	Road Runner
CNN Airport Network	New York 1 News (24 hour news
CNN fn	channel devoted only to NYC)
	Kablevision (53.75% – cable television
	in Hungary)

In Demand
Metro Sports (Kansas City)

Time Warner Inc.: Film and TV Production/Distribution	
Warner Bros.	Castle Rock Entertainment
Warner Bros. Studios	Warner Home Video
Warner Bros. Television	Warner Bros. Domestic Pay – TV
(production)	Warner Bros. Domestic Television
The WB Television Network	Distribution
Warner Bros. Television Animation	Warner Bros. International Television
Hanna – Barbera Cartoons	Distribution
Telepictures Production	The Warner Channel (Latin America,
Witt – Thomas Productions	Asia – Pacific, Australia, Germ.)

Table 2.2. *Continued*

Time Warner Inc.: Film and TV Production/Distribution Continued

| | Warner Bros. International Theaters (owns/operates multiplex theaters in over 12 countries) |

Time Warner Inc.: Magazines

Time	Coastal Living
Time Asia	Weight Watchers
Time Atlantic	Real Simple
Time Canada	Asiaweek (Asian news weekly)
Time Latin America	President (Japanese business
Time South Pacific	monthly)
Time Money	Dancyu (Japanese cooking)
Time For Kids	Wallpaper (U.K.)
Fortune	Field & Stream
All You	Freeze
Business 2.0	Golf Magazine
Life	Outdoor Life
Sports Illustrated	Popular Science
Sports Illustrated International	Salt Water Sportsman
SI for Kids	Ski
Inside Stuff	Skiing Magazine
Money	Skiing Trade News
Your Company	SNAP
Your Future	Snowboard Life
People	Ride BMX
Who Weekly (Australian edition)	Today's Homeowner
People en Español	TransWorld Skateboarding
Teen People	TransWorld Snowboarding
Entertainment Weekly	Verge
EW Metro	Yachting Magazine
The Ticket	Warp
In Style	American Express Publishing
Southern Living	Corporation (partial ownership/
Progressive Farmer	management)
Southern Accents	Travel & Leisure
Cooking Light	Food & Wine

Table 2.2. *Continued*

Time Warner Inc.: Magazines Continued	
The Parent Group	Your Company
Parenting	Departures
Baby Talk	SkyGuide
Baby on the Way	Magazines listed under Warner Brothers
This Old House	label
Sunset	DC Comics
Sunset Garden Guide	Vertigo
The Health Publishing Group	Paradox
Health	Milestone
Hippocrates	Mad Magazine

Online Services	
CompuServe Interactive Services	WinbladFunds (18%)
AOL Instant Messenger	MapQuest.com – pending regulatory
AOL.com portal	approval
Digital City	Spinner.com
AOL Europe	Winamp
ICQ	DrKoop.com (10%)
The Knot, Inc. – wedding content	Legend (49% – Internet service in China)
(8 % with QVC 36% and	
Hummer	

Time Warner: Online/Other Publishing	
Road Runner	American Family Publishers (50%)
Warner Publisher Services	Pathfinder
Time Distribution Services	Africana.com

Time Warner: Merchandise/Retail
Warner Bros. Consumer Products

Theme Parks
Warner Brothers Recreation Enterprises (owns/operates international theme parks)

Table 2.2. *Continued*

Time Warner Inc.: Turner Entertainment	
Entertainment Networks	
TBS Superstation	Turner Classic Movies
Turner Network Television (TNT)	Cartoon Network in Europe
Turner South	Cartoon Network in Latin America
Cartoon Network	TNT & Cartoon Network in Asia/ Pacific

Film Production	
New Line Cinema	Turner Original Productions
Fine Line Features	

Sports	
Atlanta Braves	

Other Operations	
Turner Learning	Turner Home Satellite
CNN Newsroom (daily news program for classrooms)	Turner Network Sales
	Turner Adventure Learning (electronic field trips for schools)

Other	
Netscape Communications	Amazon.com (partial)
Netscape Netcenter portal	Quack.com
AOL MovieFone	Streetmail (partial)
iAmaze	Switchboard (6%)

Source: "Who Owns What"? (2009).

found that 50 percent of Americans were "highly concerned about media mergers," and another 26 percent were at least "somewhat concerned." The same study found that 70 percent of Americans thought media companies were getting too big and that 60 percent of Americans did not believe that media mergers led to "better content and services." In a less scientific survey, when the CNN business program *Moneyline with Lou Dobbs* ran an on-air poll in May 2003 asking whether "too few

Table 2.3. Top Websites for News

Rank	Website	Domain	Market Share (%)
1	Yahoo! News	news.yahoo.com	8.05
2	CNN.com	www.cnn.com	3.80
3	MSNBC	www.msnbc.msn.com	3.71
4	The Weather Channel – US	www.weather.com	3.66
5	Google News	news.google.com	1.92
6	*Drudge Report*	www.drudgereport.com	1.58
7	*New York Times*	www.nytimes.com	1.57
8	Fox News	www.foxnews.com	1.56
9	Yahoo! Weather	weather.yahoo.com	1.48
10	*People* Magazine	www.people.com	1.39

Source: Hitwise (2007).

corporations own too many media outlets," 98 percent of respondents said yes (CNN.com 2003).

Ownership and control in a global context

Conglomeration and concentration of media characterize not only the United States, but the global media system as well. For example,

> America's first broadcast network, NBC, owns and operates more than 14 stations, along with CNBC, a business-news network, and Telemundo, the nation's second-largest Spanish-language broadcaster. Viacom owns theatres in Canada (Famous Players) ... [and] CNN International can be seen in 212 countries, with a daily audience of 1 billion globally. (Gutierrez 2004)

Such facts have been used to demonstrate that the conglomeration and concentration characteristic of American media corporations extend throughout the world. While such arguments have merit, as media studies scholars would suggest, it is also important to consider the historical context in which media develop and the way media are actually used.

First, there is nothing new or surprising about the globalization of media; at least since the early twentieth century, media have been global. To take one example, Lisa Gitelman notes that the medium of recorded sound was part of a global system of production and consumption from its earliest days at the beginning of the twentieth century (2006). Raw materials for producing the records themselves came from Germany and India. By 1910, the British Gramophone Company had subsidiaries in India, Russia, and Iran, while the Edison National Phonograph Company had subsidiaries in Europe, Australia, and Latin America. By this same date, "mass-produced musical records were available to consumers in Budapest and Sydney, Santiago and Beijing, Johannesburg and Jersey City." Record labels sprung up around the globe and by the eve of World War I, there were local recordings made in Beirut, pressed in Berlin, and distributed throughout the Middle East. Similarly, Argentine tango recordings were mass marketed in South America and Europe (Gitelman 2006: 16–17).

More generally, it was changes in communication technologies themselves which allowed both governments and corporations to extend their operations and authority around the globe. In the early twentieth century, the control of the United Kingdom over its far-flung empire greatly increased, due to ownership of trans-oceanic cables, with important benefits to British industry. Later in the century, the telephone and the computer allowed corporations to manage day-to-day operations throughout the world, no matter where the actual customer, supplier, factory, or cooperate headquarters was actually located. The current use of call centers located around the globe are just the latest development in the extension of the "global reach" of multinational corporations (Barnet and Müller 1974).

Also, a focus on the global impact of American and western media risks overestimating the impact of new media on the lived experience of much of the world's population. Although we focus on the impact of the Internet on our lives, up to one third of the world's population has never made or received a phone call.[14] In many urban areas in sub-Saharan Africa, it is easier to e-mail someone in the western world than it is to contact someone living in a rural village miles away (Wresch 1996). Understanding the so-called digital divide between rich and poor (both across and within nations) is vital if we are to fully understand the potentials and pitfalls of the changing media environment.

Following from the digital divide, it is important not to overestimate the cultural impact of western media in nonwestern societies where the mix and influence of media in use may be quite different. As Susan Sontag notes (2003), there is a fashionable assumption of many western intellectuals in the media-saturated western world that mediated spectacles have become more important than the actual events they represent; this assumption ignores most of the world, where media penetration and influence are nothing like they are in the wealthy nations.[15]

With these important considerations in mind, we turn to a discussion about the debate over the consequences of concentrated media ownership and control.

Does It Matter? The Consequences of Concentration and Conglomeration

With a few exceptions, there is little debate that a shrinking number of corporations control more and more of the firms producing media content and the firms that own the conduits through which that content flows. Much more contentious are the questions about the difference this makes. Should we, as citizens and as producers and consumers of media, be concerned about it? And, even more significantly, should government do something to limit concentration and conglomeration? To a great extent, this debate is not about proof or empirical evidence (although evidence can certainly bear on the debate). Rather, it is about how one understands the relationships between media systems, markets, and democratic politics.

The argument for market-driven media

There are those who argue that, especially given the explosion in sources of information provided by new media like the Internet, there is little reason to be concerned about concentration or conglomeration. So, for example, James Gattuso of the conservative-leaning Heritage Foundation argues,

> [D]uring the recent Iraq war, Americans following that conflict could choose from a half dozen or so news networks – including three 24-hour news channels on cable.
>
> In addition, nearly limitless news was available on the Internet – from which Americans could follow reports from everything from Matt Drudge to Al-Jazeera TV. And they were doing so in large numbers: according to Pew Research, a majority of Americans with Internet access got information about the Iraq war online. Almost one out of every six said the Internet was their primary source of news.

Compare this to the situation a generation ago – when Vietnam War coverage meant catching one of the half-hour network news reports, supplementing newspaper or magazine coverage. Or the 1991 Gulf War, in which only one network – CNN – provided 24-hour coverage, and the Internet was virtually unknown. (2003)[16]

Noted political communication scholar Doris Graber develops this argument further, arguing that even given media concentration of ownership, the sheer diversity of sources and the desire of their owners to make money mean that media must still be responsive to the demands of consumers: "American journalists in large organizations, like their colleagues in small, independently owned enterprises[,] are interested in appealing to their audiences, and therefore, their stories usually reflect the values of mainstream American society, regardless of the journalists' personal political orientation (1994: 102)."

Both Graber and Gattuso argue that the desire of corporations to make a profit, consumer demand, and diverse sources of media content will all guarantee the responsiveness of media providers to the demands of consumers. In short, they assume that there is enough competition, despite concentrated media ownership, to ensure that the "invisible hand" of the market will provide the media content that consumers demand.[17] If there are unmet demands, then some provider, either a division of a large media conglomerate or a new firm (which may ultimately become part of a large conglomerate), will take care of it.

So, for example, if one were to peruse the television schedule for almost any cable or satellite system, when it comes to sitcoms, drama series, or reality shows there are a bewildering variety of offerings that would seem to meet almost anyone's preferences. Cable and satellite make possible niche markets for history buffs, golf fans, or video game enthusiasts. Similarly, if one were to glance at the magazine racks at any Barnes and Noble, it seems that there are magazines aimed at virtually any hobby or interest. And all this occurs in sectors where there is much concentration of ownership – television production, cable and satellite ownership, bookstores, and magazine publishing.

The argument against market-driven media

Scholars who argue that media concentration exists, is growing, and matters very much reject this line of argument on two basic grounds. First, no matter how diverse the number of media outlets, concentrated owner-ship means that we cannot assume that content will reflect anything like a market outcome.[18] Second, and more basically, markets themselves, even if functioning well, are poor mechanisms for insuring that adequate medi-ated information is provided to people in their role as citizens, as opposed to their role as consumers, in a democratic society (McChesney 2008).

The first line of criticism follows from the argument we noted above that we cannot treat the entire media system as if it were a single market. It may be the case that even with concentrated ownership, a larger number of outlets creates intense competition to meet certain kinds of consumer demand in certain types of media. Recording labels, even when owned by the same media giant, compete with each other to satisfy the demands of fans for popular music. However, the presence of competition to meet consumer demands in one sector – popular music or prime-time television, for example – does not mean competition in other sectors. So, there is little if any competition when it comes to cable, satellite, or Internet service providers. As well, even in the realm of content, there may be little compe-tition to provide less popular forms of entertainment (jazz or classical), or high-quality and sophisticated political coverage. Even more significantly, competition in some sectors of the media market may hide collusion, col-laboration, and control – in short, market failure – when it comes to other sorts of mediated information, especially political information.

Duke University Professor James T. Hamilton (2004) studied the impact of increasing market competition on the content of television news programs. Whatever positive effects the explosion of cable and satellite channels, despite concentration of ownership, has had on the options available to viewers for entertainment programming, he found that increasing competition from cable television, increasing concentration of ownership (resulting in more pressures for news divisions to show a profit), and the decline of public service pressures resulting from govern-ment deregulation led to an overall decline in "hard news" and an increase in stories about entertainment and celebrities.

Another example of the threat of concentrated ownership is captured in what C. Edward Baker calls the "Berlusconi" effect (2007: 18). Silvio Berlusconi, a media tycoon and one of the wealthiest men in Italy, used his extensive media holdings to create his own political party, which he led as prime minister of the longest lasting government in postwar Italy. His company, Mediaset, controls 45 percent of Italian television and many important newspapers. While this concentrated holding may not have led to any distortions of the market when it came to providing certain sorts of programming and print content to consumers, the story was quite different in the political realm. According to Alexander Stille, writing in the *Columbia Journalism Review*,

> Once Berlusconi came to power, journalists on state television were required to adhere strictly to a news formula known as "the sandwich," in which virtually every political story began by stating the government's (or Berlusconi's) point of view, followed by a sound bite or two from the opposition and concluded with a rebuttal from the government. Berlusconi himself occupied an incredible 50 percent of airtime on the state-owned newscasts, while the opposition accounted for barely 20 percent.
>
> When Berlusconi addressed a nearly empty hall at the United Nations, Italian state TV cut and pasted into the scene the audience for the speech of Secretary General Kofi Annan, to create the impression for Italian viewers that their leader had been enthusiastically applauded by a full audience. When the Italian economy struggled through three straight years of recession and near-zero growth, Rai [the state broadcasting company] showed a world of happy prosperity.
>
> … In fact, when Berlusconi won in 1994 and then again in 2001 … social scientists found to their surprise that the strongest predictors of a voter's orientation were no longer class or church affiliation but what television stations a person watched and for how long. People who watched the Mediaset channels were much more inclined to vote for Berlusconi; those who watched the state-owned network Rai were more likely to vote for some other party. The more hours a day people watched television, the more likely they were to vote for Berlusconi. (2006)

At a minimum, then, even though the concentration of media control in a few hands (despite the dramatic increase in the number of media outlets) might not pose a significant problem in certain areas of media, in other areas – especially politics and journalism – the danger may be quite severe. Even more disturbing, as Stille notes, is the broader impact that the Berlusconi effect has on the ways in which viewers see the very possibility of getting adequate and disinterested information about politics:

> One of the things that Berlusconi did by entering politics and militarizing his own media empire was to polarize the entire Italian press corps and eliminate any idea that the press might serve as an independent forum where the claims of the political world could be evaluated with an element of detachment. (2006)[19]

Such deleterious effects on the way in which citizens reflect on and seek out political information are not easily addressed in a framework that evaluates media strictly according to market principles.

It is worth noting that, despite allegations of corruption that surrounded Berlusconi's term as prime minister, in 2008 he was chosen to be Italian prime minister once again (and again faced numerous scandals). Although the example of the connection between media power and political power is not directly relevant to American politics – we have no political figure with comparable media control – it is a cautionary note about how much media can influence politics when it is unified in its political perspectives and goals.

In the United States, Fox News has been accused, often justifiably, of tailoring their news coverage to support the "talking points" of the Republican Party. Recently, for example, they ran misleading footage that greatly overestimated the size of crowds gathered at anti-health care reform rallies and a Sarah Palin book signing. Similarly, they have misinterpreted polling results to overestimate skepticism about the reality of global warming. Yet, unlike in Italy, in the United States the impact of this sort of distortion is balanced somewhat by the greater diversity of political viewpoints expressed in the media. Jon Stewart, on *The Daily Show*, for example, has exposed and lampooned these errors, arguing that Fox News "alters reality to fit a predetermined narrative" (*Daily Show*, 2009).

Focusing on the impact of media concentration on political information leads to a second, more fundamental line of criticism: evaluating a media system solely from an economic perspective misses much of what should most concern us when it comes to concentrated media ownership. That is, market logic takes the pricing of telecommunications texts and products and whether they satisfy consumers' demands for media as the central criteria for evaluation. Yet, the consequences of the power that flows to large media conglomerates may be largely outside the realm of market economics. Concentrated media ownership concerns us in our role as citizens of a democratic society and as makers of culture, not simply as producers and consumers of goods and services in the marketplace.

Baker (2007) argues persuasively that we very much miss the boat when we try to understand media entirely in terms of markets and market metaphors (like the "marketplace of ideas"). He argues, instead, that when considering the impact of concentrated media ownership, we need to recognize that the maximum dispersal of control over media outlets is a positive good that increases democratic processes and cultural creativity. All of this is quite independent of marketplace concerns. As the Berlusconi effect illustrates, a media system can provide a wide variety of attractive media options at a rock-bottom price while still falling far short of how a media system should function in a democracy. As Bagdikian argues, the increasing number of outlets combined with a declining number of owners mean that "each owner controls even more formidable communications power" (2000: 222).

Baker makes the further point that what is required is the maximum diversity of ownership and access to media production, not necessarily diversity of content or viewpoints. Often, democracy can lead to a consensus viewpoint, which emerges from open public debate. Distinguishing between conflict and consensus is vital to democratic politics, but it must be based on open debate. It makes all the difference in the world, from the perspective of democratic politics, whether public support for a war, for instance, is the result of free and open debate as opposed to tightly controlled media that only treat the war as being justified. On the other hand, sometimes market pressures can lead to the media overemphasizing conflict when, in fact, there is a good deal of consensus among citizens. In other words, market pressures can sometimes lead to a false focus on disagreement for the sake of ratings rather than deeply held political convictions.

The *Jon Stewart Show*, a Comedy Network show that predated the comedian becoming host of *The Daily Show*, once did a spoof of such "conflict" shows like *Hannity and Colmes* or *Hardball*. In a feature called "Even Steven," since both hosts are named Steven, two comedians ape the Hannity–Colmes confrontational style. After several back and forths, the right-wing Steven turns to his left-wing counterpart and says, "You know, I never thought of that. I think you're right." At this point, there is dead silence and whispers from the shocked left-wing Steven asking the other Steven, "What do you think you're doing? We're being paid to argue." Yet, the right-winger continues to carefully weigh the arguments of his opponent and often concedes the point. The left-wing Steven is distraught and finally breaks down crying, saying the show is his main source of income and if this goes on he will lose his house and car. He is only mollified when the right-wing Steven finally relents and calls him an asshole. In a media environment where cable news networks shape their coverage to partisans (e.g., conservatives for Fox News and liberals for MSNBC) and increasing numbers of Americans seek out information on the Internet that agrees with their political leanings, we can see that the media may, indeed, play a key role in the polarization of political discourse.[20]

It is important to note that the very idea that we should evaluate media systems in terms of their conformity to the economic logic of markets is itself an idea whose popularity has been dramatically increased through its circulation in the media. This is an illustration of the impact of the control of media systems by private corporations. Thomas Frank insightfully and critically chronicles the rise of what he calls "market populism," which equates private markets with freedom and democracy. In this formulation, markets are not just media of exchange but also media of consent (2000: xiv). As Frank notes, however, market populism is best thought of as an ideological tool rather than a statement of fact, because it is based on a simplified and inaccurate interpretation of history. Markets are hardly populist mechanisms of equality. Left to their own devices they inevitably lead to vast inequalities, as even classical economist Adam Smith recognized. Nor have they ever existed (in modern societies, at least) without government support; for example, consider the important role played by the government in the development of the post office, telegraph, radio, and Internet. Finally, markets and their proper role are contested terrain that is constantly subject to political debate and struggle, whether by labor unions, environmentalists, or capitalists seeking to protect themselves from competition (Polanyi 1944).

Indeed, one of the triumphs of neoliberalism as an ideological tool is that its supporters have managed to make the spread of markets – in terms of both the types of goods and services they allocate as well as their increasingly global reach – seem natural and, therefore, inevitable. (It is important to note that "neoliberalism" means economic liberalism, that is, belief in a free market with as few regulations as possible. It should not be confused with political liberalism.) The widespread acceptance of the market perspective has meant that there are fewer calls from mainstream voices for policies that seek to further democratic values by limiting or regulating markets.

In the realm of the media in general and broadcast media in particular, the triumph of market populism undercut the notion that the provision of information should be guided by anything other than supply and demand. This is because the logic of markets reduces media texts to simple products, stripped of their broader public implications (Leys 2001: ch. 5). From this perspective, media corporations' "responsibility" is simply to produce the programming that audiences demanded, and any criticism of such market-governed mass media is labeled as elitist and antidemocratic. Lost in this market populism version of democracy is any sense of the collective good other than that emerging from individual consumer behavior. Yet, as legal scholar Cass Sunstein (2001) argues, because communications systems *inevitably* serve a collective purpose in democratic societies, it is never adequate to evaluate them simply on the basis of whether they give individual consumers what they want.

An example of the clash between what the private market provides and the collective purposes of a democratic society is the current American "crisis in journalism": a precipitous decline in the number of jobs and funding for professional journalists on newspapers, magazines, and network news divisions, and the corresponding decline in the availability of reliable information about the world. As early as the founding of the Republic, Thomas Jefferson argued that the availability of accurate information was a prerequisite for a well-functioning democratic society. That is, the kind of information produced by journalists is a collective good which serves democracy. Yet, the current crisis is rooted in a failure of the private market: the precipitous decline in the advertising revenue and profitability of newspapers and television networks. As long as our thinking is limited to the logic of markets, we will never fulfill many of the collective needs of a just and democratic society (Nichols and McChesney 2009; Downie and Schudson 2009).

What this means today

That such concerns are being raised as we struggle to formulate public policies to govern today's rapidly changing media environment is unsurprising, given the long history of such struggles. Arguments over net neutrality and the limits on commercial exploitation of new media echo those of reformers of the 1930s National Committee on Education by Radio, which we discussed above.

While struggles over the degree to which we can evaluate media by market logic, the implications of commercial exploitation, and so forth have been fought before, it is also important to not lose sight of what is, indeed, new and innovative about the new media we encounter today. There is a convergence between the cultural and political potential of new media. In both culture and politics it is now possible to imagine a dramatic change in the number of individuals who can produce their own music, art, criticism, and political commentary, thus altering the public sphere in which culture and politics circulate (Jenkins 2006). However, it is the outcome of policy struggles that will determine how well the emerging media system realizes these potentials for enriching our cultural and political life. At stake in these policy debates are the answers to such questions as: what difference do interactivity and the Internet's expanded possibilities make? How can we exploit the Internet's incredible potential for providing easy access to information and giving voice to a revolutionary number of people? Will these potentials be reached if we evaluate media solely from the standpoint of market efficiency? Are there values we wish to honor that are not captured by such logics – for example, the possibilities for dramatically diversifying the number of voices and perspectives that can now be involved in public debate? What avenues for cultural creativity are opened up by the new media – pod casting, Web page design, sampling of music, and so forth? Will we sufficiently consider these values if we only view media from the perspective of market efficiency?

Conclusion

In this chapter, we have provided an overview of the structure of media ownership and control. This overview provides clear evidence of increasing concentration and conglomeration. We have also gone over the various arguments about how worried we, as citizens, should be about this trend. Understanding these dynamics is especially vital in the early twenty-first century as political decisions are currently being made that will shape the new media environment over the coming decades.

Whatever one's position on these issues, the work of media studies scholars clarifies the central questions underlying current debates. For example, do the media, in their current configuration, provide the diverse and high-quality content – in terms of both information and cultural products – that we deserve in our simultaneous roles as citizens and as consumers of culture and material products? We also need to be explicit about the criteria we use in answering this question: for example, what are the limits of using the market and the logic of economics?

The attention of media studies to both media history and cross-national comparisons is especially relevant in understanding the patterns of ownership and control we now observe. As we saw in chapter 1, changes in the media environment have a dramatic impact on virtually every aspect of our lives. However, there is nothing inevitable about how the media environment is structured. We can certainly identify the wonderful potentials or dangerous pitfalls of innovations in communications technology, whether the telegraph, the radio, or the Internet. However, whether these potentials are cashed in or not depends on the social, political, and economic structures in which they are used. Indeed, there are many alternative models of media ownership and control that have emerged both over time and across nations – from private ownership as in the United States, to the public broadcasting systems of many democratic countries, to the collective ownership of the Internet. If we are to maximize the potential of a changing media environment, it is vital for debate to be informed by the full range of alternatives and their likely consequences.

Notes

1. Somewhat ironically, Cass Sunstein in *republic.com* (2007) argues that new media, by allowing us to specifically tailor our preferences on home pages and other information outlets, leads to a potentially significant reduction in this sort of serendipity. Yet, our example shows the potential for increasing such encounters with unsought information at least in the context of Internet searches. As Sunstein argues, however, the degree to which new media technologies actually produce serendipitous outcomes depends on the rules used by Web page creators and Internet search engines.
2. This site is no longer active and simply links to a site called "June 4" – the date of the 1989 massacre – which now provides links to a set of unrelated sponsored websites, including tourism in China and help in buying a car.
3. For instance, in October 2007, the leftist website Truthout.org complained that a number of e-mail services, including Microsoft, AOL, and Yahoo, refused to pass on its e-mail alerts to those on its mailing list.
4. Twitter is "a social networking and micro-blogging service that allows its users to send and read other users' updates (known as *tweets*), which are text-based posts of up to 140 characters in length." See Wikipedia (n.d.-b).
5. Another example is provided by the invention of the phonograph. Thomas Edison originally thought this device would be used (primarily by businesspeople) to both record and play recordings, thus leading to a dramatic decentralization of access to producing as well as consuming recordings. That this was not the way things worked out was a result of marketing decisions having little to do with any inherent tendencies in the technology (Gitelman 2006).

6. This dynamic is not limited to media. In the debate over health care, for example, many opponents of reform assumed (without much consideration of alternative government-run systems, like in Canada or the United Kingdom) that a privately owned and controlled for-profit system was the best model.

7. Recent surveys of the British public reveal that 70 percent of BBC viewers say they trust it, in general, and 79 percent say they trust its news broadcasts. About three-fifths say they trust commercial news broadcasts. In contrast, recent Pew surveys find that 32 percent of Americans surveyed trust CNN and 25 percent trust Fox News. Newer research comparing a number of public service systems with commercial systems (like the United States) suggests that citizens in the former systems are more active seekers of news and better informed than those in the latter (Curran et al. 2009).

8. The first network to use packets of information was called ARPANET (Advanced Research Projects Agency Network) and was funded by the US Department of Defense.

9. And, as we discuss below, almost all Americans are now served by a single daily paper.

10. What this might mean for where Americans actually get their information is less clear. The decline in readership of print newspapers shows no sign of abating. Circulation of all American newspapers fell by almost 5 percent between 2007 and 2008, bringing the overall decline since 2001 to 13.5 percent for daily papers and 17.3 percent for Sunday papers. We note, however, that consistent with Compaine's argument about substitutability, while print circulation was down, the number of visitors to newspaper websites increased by 8.4 percent in 2009, making up for most of that year's decline in print circulation (Project for Excellence in Journalism 2009).

11. Even this understates concentration, as Time Warner has revenues larger than Hearst and Advance combined.

12. Note the shift in independent movie production as major studios create their own "boutique" production companies.

13. In this context, it is worth noting that even the largest media corporation, Time Warner, ranks "only" 51st in size amongst global corporations (Walmart, Citigroup, and Forbes are the top three); see Baker (2007: 18 n. 28).

14. It is quite difficult, perhaps impossible, to get an accurate figure on the penetration of telephones (land lines and mobile). Since the late 1990s, the claim has been repeated that one half of the people in the world have never made or received a phone call; the claim has been made by figures as diverse as Kofi Annan, Al Gore, Michael Moore, Bill Gates, and Newt Gingrich. However, given the rapid expansion of both land lines and cellular service, especially in the developing world, more conservative estimates place the figure at around one third (see Shirky 2002).

15. Such overly theorized arguments about the degree to which we live in a media-saturated or even virtual world can be interpreted as implying

("perversely" and "unseriously," as Sontag [2003] notes) that real suffering does not occur.

16. Gattuso goes even further, taking the approach of Compaine and the Federal Communications Commission (FCC), which we discussed and rejected above, to deny that media concentration is even occurring:

> Critics, however, point out that the existence of many outlets doesn't necessarily mean more owners. NBC, MSNBC, and msnbc.com are clearly not independent from each other. Media firms today tend to own many outlets – putting broadcast, cable, print and even Internet outlets under the same roof. But despite this expansion of media holdings, ownership concentration has not increased. A study released by the Federal Communications Commission last fall found the number of separately owned media outlets (including broadcast, cable and newspaper outlets) skyrocketed in most cities between 1960 and 2000 – growing more than 90 percent in New York, for instance. (2003)

However, his argument about the diversity in outlets, along with the assumption of responsiveness to consumer demand that is noted by Graber below, makes this (unwarranted, in our view) assertion unnecessary to his basic argument.

17. Classical economist Adam Smith's "invisible hand theory" states that

> if each consumer is allowed to choose freely what to buy and each producer is allowed to choose freely what to sell and how to produce it, the market will settle on a product distribution and prices that are beneficial to all the individual members of a community, and hence to the community as a whole. (Wikipedia n.d.-a)

18. By "market outcome," we mean that media content will actually be determined by the preferences of the audience, as would be the case if there were a large number of independent providers of content.

19. And, even though the Berlusconi case may be extreme, Stille notes that "what Berlusconi has done ... bears a striking resemblance to the American right's attack on mainstream media: both undermine the idea of objective facts" (2006).

20. A survey after the 2008 election by the Pew Foundation found, "One-third (33%) of online news consumers say they typically seek out online political information from sites that share their political point of view, up from the 26% who said that at a similar point in 2004" (Rainie and Smith 2008).

References

Bagdikian, Ben H. 1992. *The media monopoly*. Boston: Beacon Press.

Bagdikian, Ben H. 2000. *The media monopoly*, 6th ed. Boston: Beacon Press.

Baker, C. Edwin. 2007. *Media concentration and democracy: Why ownership matters.* Cambridge: Cambridge University Press.

Barnet, Richard J., and Ronald E. Müller. 1974. *Global reach: The power of the multinational corporations.* New York: Simon & Schuster.

Boutell.com. 2007. "WWW FAQs: How many websites are there?" February 15. www.boutell.com/newfaq/misc/sizeofweb.html.

CNN.com. 2003. "Transcripts: CNN *Lou Dobbs Moneyline.*" May 12. http://transcripts.cnn.com/TRANSCRIPTS/0305/12/mlld.00.html.

Compaine, Benjamin M. 2001. *Communications policy in transition: The Internet and beyond.* Cambridge, M.A.: MIT Press.

Curran, J., S. Iyengar, A. Brink Lund, and I. Salovaara-Moring. 2009 "Media system, public knowledge and democracy: A comparative study." *European Journal of Communication* 24:5–26.

Daily Show. 2009. [Jon Stewart commentary]. Aired November 12.

Downie, Leonard Jr., and Michael Schudson. 2009. "The reconstruction of American journalism." *Columbia Journalism Review* (October): www.cjr.org/reconstruction/the_reconstruction_of_american.php.

Frank, Thomas. 2000. *One market under God: Extreme capitalism, market populism, and the end of economic democracy.* New York: Doubleday.

Gattuso, James. 2003. *The myth of media concentration: Why the FCC's media ownership rules are unnecessary.* Heritage Foundation WebMemo no. 284, May 29. www.heritage.org/Research/InternetandTechnology/wm284.cfm.

Gitelman, Lisa. 2006. *Always already new: Media, history and the data of culture.* Cambridge, M.A.: MIT Press.

Google. 2009. "Corporate information: Company overview." www.google.com/corporate/index.html.

Graber, Doris. 1994. *Processing the news: How people tame the information tide.* New York: University Press of America.

Gutierrez, Miren. 2004. "MEDIA: Fewer Players, Less Freedom." International Press Service (Rome), March 20. www.ipsnews.net/interna.asp?idnews=22950.

Hamilton, James. 2004. *All the news that's fit to sell: How the market transforms information into news.* Princeton, N.J.: Princeton University Press.

Hitwise. 2007. "Weekly ratings for the week ending September 22, 2007." News and Media Category. www.hitwise.com.

Jenkins, Henry. 2006. *Convergence culture: Where old and new media collide.* New York: New York University Press.

Keen, Andrew. 2007. *The cult of the amateur: How today's Internet is killing our culture.* New York: Doubleday/Currency.

Lessig, Lawrence. 2005. *Free culture: The nature and future of creativity.* New York: Penguin.

Leys, Colin. 2001. *Market-driven politics: Neoliberal democracy and the public interest.* London: Verso.

Longhurst, Brian. 1995. *Popular music and society*. Cambridge: Polity Press.

MarketingVOX. 2006. "Google's share of U.S. searches passes 60 percent mark." www.marketingvox.com/archives/2006/08/07/googles_share_of_us_searches_passes_60_percent_mark/.

McChesney, Robert Waterman. 1999a. "Oligopoly: The big media game has fewer and fewer players." www.lehigh.edu/~jl0d/J246-02/oligopoly.html.

McChesney, Robert Waterman. 1999b. *Rich media poor democracy: Communication politics in dubious time*. Urbana: University of Illinois Press.

McChesney, Robert Waterman. 2008. *The communication revolution*. New York: New Press.

McHugh, Josh. 2003. "Google vs. Evil," Wired online, January. www.wired.com/wired/archive/11.01/google_pr.html.

Meyrowitz, Joshua. 1985. *No sense of place: The impact of electronic media on social behavior*. New York: Oxford University Press.

Nichols, John, and Robert Waterman McChesney. 2009. "The death and life of great American newspapers." *The Nation*, March 18.

Polanyi, Karl. 1944. *The great transformation*. New York: Rinehart.

Postman, Neil. 1985. *Amusing ourselves to death: Public discourse in the age of show business*. New York: Viking.

Press, Andrea L., Bruce A. Williams, Camille Johnson, and Ellen Moore. 2005. "Connecting the private to the public: Media and the future of public life." Paper presented at the American Political Science Association annual meeting, Washington, D.C., September.

Project for Excellence in Journalism. 2006. Magazine ownership: 2006 annual report. March 13. Philadelphia: Pew Charitable Trust. www.journalism.org/node/433.

Project for Excellence in Journalism. 2009. "The state of the news media." Philadelphia: Pew Charitable Trust.

Putnam, Robert D. 2000. *Bowling alone: The collapse and revival of American community*. New York: Simon & Schuster.

Rainie, Lee, and Aaron Smith. 2008. "The Internet and the 2008 Election." Pew Internet and American Life Project, June 15. www.pewinternet.org/Reports/2008/The-Internet-and-the-2008-Election.aspx.

Schiller, Dan. 2007. *How to think about information*. Urbana: University of Illinois Press.

Shirky. Clay. 2002. "Half the world." Clay Shirky's Writings About the Internet: Economics and Culture, Media and Community, Open Source, September 3, v. 1.03. www.shirky.com/writings/half_the_world.html.

Shirky, Clay. 2008. *Here comes everybody: The power of organizing without organizations*. New York: Penguin.

Sontag, Susan. 2003. *Regarding the pain of others*. New York: Farrar, Straus and Giroux.

Standage, Tom. 1998. *The Victorian Internet: The remarkable story of the telegraph and the nineteenth century's on-line pioneers*. New York: Walker.

Stille, Alexander. 2006. "Silvio's shadow." *Columbia Journalism Review*, September–October.

Sunstein, Cass R. 2001. *republic.com*. Princeton, N.J.: Princeton University Press.

Sunstein, Cass R. 2006. *Infotopia: How many minds produce knowledge*. Oxford: Oxford University Press.

Sunstein, Cass R. 2007. *republic.com 2.0*. Princeton, N.J.: Princeton University Press.

Tapscott, Don, and Anthony D. Williams. 2006. *Wikinomics: How mass collaboration changes everything*. New York: Portfolio.

Trippi, Joe. 2005. *The revolution will not be televised: Democracy, the Internet, and the overthrow of everything*. New York: Harpers.

Vaidhyanathan, Siva. Forthcoming. *The Googlization of everything*. San Francisco: University of California Press.

"Who owns what?" 2009. *Columbia Journalism Review*. www.cjr.org/resources/.

Wikipedia. N.d.-a. "Invisible hand." http://en.wikipedia.org/wiki/Invisible_hand.

Wikipedia. N.d.-b. "Twitter." http://en.wikipedia.org/wiki/Twitter.

Wresch, William. 1996. *Disconnected: Haves and have-nots in the information age*. New Brunswick, N.J.: Rutgers University Press.

Zittrain, Jonathan. 2009. *The future of the Internet – and how to stop it*. New Haven, C.T.: Yale University Press.

Zittrain, Jonathan, and Benjamin G. Edelman. 2003. "Internet Filtering in China." *IEEE Internet Computing*, March–April. http://ssrn.com/abstract= 399920.

Chapter 3

Media and Democracy

Introduction

The long US presidential campaign of 2008, culminating in the election of Barack Obama, was one of the more dramatic presidential elections in living memory. For someone interested in politics, the new media environment provides an embarrassment of riches as it transforms the way we follow elections.

While we might have, as in the past, consulted print newspapers and magazines or the nightly network news broadcast, now cable and satellite television made it possible to follow the campaign around the clock. Turning to the Internet, one could watch the latest campaign ads, see what new campaign-related videos had been posted on YouTube, visit candidate websites, read a wide variety of the online editions of news-papers, track the latest polling results, and discuss what this all means with other political aficionados on a wide range of blogs. You could even program your cell phone to receive the latest updates on the campaign from an equally wide range of sources. If you were more ambitious and creative, you might have created your own campaign messages and posted them to YouTube; and, if you were lucky and skilled enough, your video might have "gone viral" and attracted the sort of attention devoted to "Obama Girl," the young woman whose video tribute to the candidate was viewed by tens of millions of people.

At no time in the past was it easier to follow the unfolding presidential election campaign on a round-the-clock basis in a variety of media con-duits too numerous to mention. Indeed, for the first time, over half the voting age population (55 percent) went online in 2008 to get involved in the election or to simply get information (Smith 2009). Eighteen percent of Internet users went beyond simply consuming information and posted their thoughts, comments, or questions. As we might expect, younger people were the most active: "Fully 83% of those age 18–24 have a social networking profile, and two-thirds of young profile owners took part in some form of political activity on these sites in 2008" (Smith 2009).

Conversely, if you had little interest in politics, it had never been easier to ignore the campaign. Coverage of politics on television is largely sequestered into easily avoidable cable news channels, C-SPAN, and weekend political talk shows. The nightly network news broadcasts now compete with numerous alternatives and have the shrinking and aging audiences to prove it. Even if you come across an unwanted political advertisement, if you have TiVo, a quick push of the 30-second skip allows you to avoid it. The voluminous political information available on the Internet does not intrude on those who use it for purposes other than politics. Searching eBay for a long-sought-after collectable, finding out the latest about Britney Spears, or checking out MySpace is unlikely to bring you in contact with any information about politics you were not specifically searching for. Just as the new media environment makes it possible for a political junkie to immerse herself in politics 24/7, so too it makes it possible to avoid political information almost entirely.

Consider how different this situation is for Americans compared to only 20 years ago. In the 1988 presidential race between George H. W. Bush and Michael Dukakis, the political junkie would have had far fewer options. His or her main sources of news about the campaign would be either the nightly network news broadcast or a local newspaper, since the Internet and 24-hour cable news networks did not yet exist. If he or she wanted to talk to others about the campaign, the only options were face-to-face or telephone (on a land line).

The situation of those who wished to avoid politics would be considerably different as well. Since most households received only a few television stations, all of which showed the network news broadcasts at the same time, it would be almost impossible to avoid some exposure to information about the campaign if one had the television turned on during the news hour. Given that the network news broadcasts were viewed by 75 percent of those who had their sets on, the campaign coverage on these broadcasts would have been more likely than today to become the subject of conversations one might have with family, friends, and coworkers.[1] A similar situation obtained for any campaign events – candidate debates, the conventions, or Election Night – that were covered by the networks; the choice was to either watch the coverage or turn off the tube. Even if you avoided the nightly news broadcasts by doing something other than watching television, when you did turn on the set later during prime time, you would likely be exposed to campaign ads. If you sub-scribed to a local newspaper (and one was much more likely to do so in 1988 than 2008), even if you were simply looking for the latest grocery ads or favorite comic strip, you would likely glean some information about the campaign simply by looking at the front page. In a nutshell, as com-pared to 2008, in 1988 political information was *both* scarcer *and* more difficult to avoid.

The impact of the new media environment on the way we follow the political world also alters the ideological character of the political informa-tion we routinely receive. In 1988, most of the information citizens encountered about the elections would have been provided by profes-sional journalists, committed to norms of nonpartisanship. Aside from clearly identified editorials, both the nightly news broadcasts and news-papers attempted to cover the campaigns evenhandedly and so, whether a Republican, Democrat, or Independent, the average citizen would have encountered campaign coverage that took seriously perspectives different than his or her own.

The situation is quite different today. If I am a passionate liberal, I can gather all my information about the campaign from sources that agree with my perspective and cover politics accordingly. I might check the latest campaign news from the Democratic candidates or left-leaning sites like the Daily Kos or Moveon.org, where I can also chat with like-minded partisans. When I turn to television, I can avoid the network news or conservative stations like Fox News and watch Keith Olbermann on MSNBC. When it comes to relaxation and laughs, I can turn to *The Daily Show* and *The Colbert Report*.

Conversely, if I were a fierce conservative, I could get my campaign news from the Republican candidates or conservative Web pages like The Drudge Report, and talk to the like-minded on RedState. I could watch *Fox News* on the tube or listen to Rush Limbaugh on the radio, and then get my laughs from Dennis Miller or Fox's take-off on the *Daily Show*, the ½ *Hour News Report*. In short, whether conservative or liberal, I can now gather voluminous amounts of political information and even create my own political media without ever encountering opinions or informa-tion filtered through ideological lenses that differ significantly from my own. Indeed, surveys indicate that individuals increasingly seek out sources of information that agree with their own political beliefs.

What are the effects of this changing pattern of acquiring and using political information on democratic politics? In this chapter, we provide ways of thinking about how to answer this question by drawing on the work of media scholars. At the outset, we want to emphasize two very general insights that flow from employing the methods of media studies analysis. First, although we mainly focus in this chapter on media that are generally assumed to be sources of political information – cable and network news broadcasts, print and online newspapers and magazines, political websites and blogs, the information provided by candidates, and so forth – this does not come close to exhausting the influence of media on political life.

Other media, less often thought of as conduits for political information, also have significant influence on the way Americans think about and behave in the political world. So, episodes of *The Simpsons, CSI,* or *The Wire* often deal with issues that have significant political content, whether it is a humorous take on elections, an analysis of the way the criminal justice system works, or the relationship between inner-city poverty, drug dealing, and city government. Indeed, the new media environment often blurs the lines between types of media (i.e., television, the Internet, and mobile phones) and the genres through which information is passed to citizens (i.e., blogs, comedy shows, or cable news shows hosted by well-known media figures), making it more important than ever to keep in mind the broad range of media through which political information flows.

In 1992, when Bill Clinton played the saxophone on the *Arsenio Hall* program to help generate positive publicity for his flagging campaign, it was seen as both unusual and vaguely undignified. By 2008, however, when Senator Hillary Clinton appeared on both *Saturday Night Live* and *The Daily Show* in the week before the crucial Texas and Ohio primaries, the fact of her appearance on such shows was seen as quite unremarkable and just part of the normal campaign strategy for serious candidates – Senators Mike Huckabee, Barack Obama, and John McCain had all made appearances on the same shows. Such nontraditional shows provided more than an opportunity for candidates to present themselves to the public in a humorous setting; the jokes and skits of comedy shows can actually shape the campaigns themselves. So, Clinton's campaign used a skit on *SNL* poking fun at the press's infatuation with Obama to reinforce her claim that she was being treated unfairly in the press. And, the strategy paid off as the press began to take a more critical look at Obama.[2] One of the most dramatic stories of the election, the rise and fall of Republican vice presidential nominee Sarah Palin, turned on Tina Fey's biting impersonation of the Alaskan governor on *SNL*.

We miss much of the relationship between media and politics if we focus too narrowly on traditional sources of political information. Although the new media environment makes it easier to see that political information is circulated through a bewildering number of genres and media conduits, it has actually always been the case that a wide variety of media have political implications: for example, consider the treatment of abortion in Hollywood movies, which we discuss in chapter 4, or the influence of rock-and-roll on the political tumult of the 1960s (see also Williams and Delli Carpini forthcoming).

Second, approaching the political world through the lens of media studies means that we focus on the structure of the media system as a primary explanation for changes in the political world. What does this mean in practice? Consider some of the most common critiques of American politics in the early twenty-first century. Many decry Americans for being uninterested in or ignorant about the political world. One explanation is itself another critique – the political system has become so partisan, politicians so cynical and deceitful, and the whole system so beholden to campaign contributions, it is no wonder most American pay little attention. Implicit in such critiques is the notion that somehow today's voters and politicians are less publicly minded and responsible than in the past. These arguments mesh nicely with the criticisms leveled at young people for not being more engaged in politics. Such explanations rely on what we might label "individual-level explanations" – the causes are ascribed to changes in the ways individual citizens and politicians behave (Prior 2007).

Media studies offers a different explanation by focusing our attention on changes in the structure of the media system itself as explanations for the changes we discern in American politics. In this chapter we first discuss the development of scholarly thought about the relationship between changes in the media, especially the emergence of what we now call the "mass media." The mass media's appearance, in the first decades of the twentieth century, led to questions about the media's influence on democratic politics in the United States – questions we still wrestle with today.

We then trace declining participation and interest, increasing partisanship and rancor in the political world, and the vast increase in the role of campaign contributions. We examine these not as individual changes, but rather as the changes in the media system that have occurred over the last 20 years – what Markus Prior (2007) calls "post-broadcast democracy."

Changing Media Environments and Changing Democratic Politics

Changing media systems have had a profound impact on the development of American democracy from the founding of the Republic in the eighteenth century to our own time. With an extraordinarily high level of literacy amongst the general population and subsidies for the mail distribution of political information, newspapers, pamphlets, letters, and other print forms, mediated political communication played a significant role in the political debates of the eighteenth and nineteenth centuries (Postman 1985; Wilentz 2007). Yet, we would be mistaken if we thought that the time of George Washington, Thomas Jefferson, John Adams, and Benjamin Franklin was a period of elevated and thoughtful political debate. Indeed, the late eighteenth- and early nineteenth-century Age of Print had more than a passing resemblance to the rough-and-tumble media world of today.

A refreshing window on the partisan press of the early Republic is provided in Richard N. Rosenfeld's *American Aurora: A Democratic-Republican Returns* (Rosenfeld and Duane 1997). The book recounts the day-to-day issues covered (between 1798 and 1801) in the *Aurora*, a newspaper founded by Benjamin Franklin and edited by his nephew Benjamin Franklin Bache. The *Aurora* was highly critical of the emerging Federalist political elite; indeed, Bache actually died in prison after being jailed by President John Adams under the Alien and Sedition Acts.

Rosenfeld tells the story of the newspaper and its Federalist antagonists, especially the *Gazette of the United States*, almost entirely through reprinting actual newspaper articles. While the debates taking place in the press were intensely political in their substance – elections, events abroad, and so forth – the newspapers of the time were very far from the thoughtful, enlightened texts we might assume. Over its history, the *Aurora* claimed

> that Washington and Adams opposed the French Revolution because they were enemies to democracy, and had been even during the American Revolution; that Washington was not the father of his country, but an inept

general who would have lost the American Revolution had Benjamin
Franklin not gotten France to intervene; that Washington, Adams, Hamilton,
and other founding fathers had denied Franklin his credit (partly by under
stating France's), had mythologized Washington's, and had adopted a
British-style constitution to avoid Franklin's design (and many Americans[']
hopes) for a democracy; and that Adams, Hamilton, and other Federalists
really wanted an American king. (Rosenfeld and Duane 1997: x)

The claims and counterclaims, turning on accusations about the sex lives
of the founders (especially Thomas Jefferson and Alexander Hamilton),
conflicts of interest, financial improprieties, secret plans, ad hominem
attacks, and so forth, seem to the modern reader much closer to *The
National Enquirer* than *The New York Times*. Indeed, the era had its own
Matt Drudge (the notorious Internet political gossip who played a central
role in the Clinton–Lewinsky scandal) in the person of James Callender,
who, while working at the behest of the anti-Federalists led by Jefferson,
leveled accusations about the sexual and financial misdeeds of George
Washington's favorite, Alexander Hamilton. Later, disillusioned at being
abandoned by the patrician Jefferson, he unearthed accusations about the
patriarch of Monticello's illegitimate children with one of his slaves, Sally
Hemings.[3] One cannot escape the conclusion that current figures like Bill
O'Reilly, Rush Limbaugh, Michael Moore, Jon Stewart, and Stephen
Colbert would have felt right at home during the late eighteenth and early
nineteenth centuries.

Although an understanding of the relationship between media and
politics during the eighteenth and nineteenth centuries provides perspective on current debates, developing a sophisticated analysis of today's
mediated politics needs to be rooted in the specifics of the emergence of
electronic media during the twentieth century. It was during this turbu-
lent century that the issues with which we still struggle came into clear
focus: the power of the electronic mass media, especially radio and television, and the influence of mediated messages to unduly influence ordinary
citizens.

A good place to start is with the work of Walter Lippmann (1889–
1974), one of the most important print journalists of the twentieth
century and a well-respected media scholar whose work on the relationship between media and democracy still influences scholars and students
today (Steel 1980). As a young man fresh out of Harvard University,
Lippmann did wartime propaganda work for the US government during

World War I and learned just how easily facts could be distorted and suppressed in order to influence public opinion. He drew on these experiences to argue that in a modern society, most citizens' political actions are based not on firsthand knowledge, but rather on the ephemeral "pictures in their heads" that are largely created by media.

This led him to a far-ranging critique of what he saw as the naïve beliefs Americans made about democratic politics and citizenship in a complex modern society. He argued that the ideas of the founders were based on a society of yeomen farmers (excluding women and slaves, he tartly noted) in which citizens had both direct knowledge of the local issues that structured politics and ample opportunity to converse with their neighbors about these issues. This set of circumstances led to a centerpiece of democratic theory: the assumption that the average citizen could make intelligent and rational judgments on public issues if presented with the facts.[4]

Yet, these preconditions of democratic theory were under assault by the time Lippmann wrote his seminal work, *Public Opinion*, in 1922. When it came to the knowledge on which citizens based their political beliefs and actions, the public was dependent on the press (he had in mind newspapers, but his argument applies even more forcefully to radio and television). Yet, the press cannot provide the truth because truth and news are not the same thing: the function of news is to point out the significance of events, but the function of truth is to bring hidden facts to light. In a much used metaphor, he said that the news was like the beam of a search light that moves restlessly about, bringing one episode and then another out of the darkness into vision.

In this formulation, Lippmann presciently identified the central concern of media studies: the implications of the displacement of direct experience and face-to-face interactions by a mass media system as the fundamental source of political information and site of debate. Although prior to World War I, discussions of public opinion glossed over the role of newspapers, public relations, and advertising, by the middle of the twentieth century, it would be impossible to think about public opinion without a consideration of the impact of the mass media.

Lippmann went beyond the role of media to discuss a second, related dimension of modern democracy that still confronts us today: the basic capacity and interest of ordinary citizens when it comes to politics. Even if the press could provide an accurate picture of the world, Lippmann argued, the average person had neither the time nor the ability to deal with this information, since most people have little interest in political life and are unmotivated to learn enough to develop informed opinions about the vital issues of the day. In *The Phantom Public* in 1925, Lippmann argued that what he called the public's "civic retardation" was not all bad, since "when public opinion attempts to govern directly it is either a failure or a tyranny." This ruthless analysis left Lippmann with the conclusion that democracy could work only if people escaped from the "intolerable and unworkable fiction that each of us must acquire a competent opinion about public affairs" (Steel 1980: 182). The solution, for Lippmann, was a form of elite democracy that strictly limited the participation of the public to elections where easily understood choices could be offered between incumbents and challengers.

Although we may reject his solution, Lippmann's statement of the problem of democracy still resonates today. Whenever we despair at the ability of voters to understand the great issues of the day (usually this means we want others to see things the way we do), to reject the ranting of ideologues of the left and right, or to even participate in political life, we are restating the problem of the capacity of ordinary citizens articulated by Lippmann so long ago.

Worries about the implications of a modern electronic media combined with the limited capacities of ordinary citizens were stoked by the propaganda campaigns waged by the major belligerent countries in both world wars. Of special concern was the extensive use of radio and film, especially in totalitarian Germany and the Soviet Union, but also in the democracies. These fears created what Archibald MacLeish called "nervous liberals," an anxiety about how to balance, on the one hand, civil liberties and a commitment to democratic discourse with, on the other hand, a fear of the limitations of the public's abilities and the power and effectiveness of mediated messages (Gary 1999).

Why nervous liberals are still with us: The enduring problem of propaganda

What do concerns with propaganda campaigns waged in the early decades of the twentieth century have to do with the concerns about media politics of the twenty-first century?[5] In 1927 Harold D. Lasswell (1902–78), another "nervous liberal" who would go on to be one of the most influential political scientists of the twentieth century, published his doctoral dissertation as a book entitled *Propaganda Technique in World War I*

(1971). A close study of the propaganda campaigns waged by both Central and Allied powers during World War I, the book is especially relevant today since it demonstrates that although we may consider ourselves sophisticated when it comes to how the government uses the media to manipulate public opinion, the techniques chronicled by Lasswell, developed in the early decades of the twentieth century, are still used at the dawn of the twenty-first. The methods used to mobilize populations from 1914 to 1918, to support a war that was fought for obscure reasons and that left tens of millions dead, are quite familiar to anyone who lived through the 2003 buildup to the invasion of Iraq. The issue is less whether there is some truth to the propaganda claims made by government – even the worst atrocity stories of World War I had a core of truth – than the continuing implications for democracy when these techniques are used by governments to mobilize populations for war or other policies.

Lasswell argued that justification for war had to be widely understandable and capable of fostering total popular commitment to the conflict. Echoing Lippmann, he noted that since Americans have long been poorly informed about international affairs, it is difficult to communicate to a mass audience the inevitably complex and usually debatable reasons for one nation's use of force against another. Therefore, the leader of the enemy state must be turned into a symbol for the entire enemy nation, and then demonized. Lasswell meant the term quite literally: the enemy leader must be portrayed as the incarnation of evil, the devil himself. Sound familiar? Just as Saddam Hussein became the personification of both Iraq and evil, so too was Kaiser Wilhelm II used by Allied propagandists in World War I. Although the strategy of demonization is familiar to us, so too are the problems it creates once the war ends. If the cause of war is an evil leader, then his elimination should be the solution. Once that leader is dead or captured, problems faced by the victors as they attempt to reconstruct a shattered society are no easier to explain to Americans today than they were to the Allied populations in the wake of World War I.

Lasswell also argued that, no matter the facts, popular support for a war requires that it be portrayed as defensive. Claims about the threat posed by weapons of mass destruction (WMDs) or about connections between Saddam Hussein and Osama bin Laden became the linchpins of our Iraq mobilization because they were central to portraying the US invasion, without UN backing, not as an unprovoked attack but as a defensive action necessitated by an evil enemy preparing to strike us. Just as it was impossible for Allied governments to resist exaggerating claims of atrocities by German troops in neutral Belgium, a driving force behind false claims of Iraqi WMDs or connections to the terrorists of September 11, 2001, was their power to drum up public support. If we focus too closely on the accuracy of prewar intelligence estimates, we miss the more disturbing point that governments are simply unable to resist "cherry-picking" those estimates for use in propaganda.

Lasswell's analysis is even more prescient when it comes to the need for developing different propaganda appeals to different segments of the populace. We call this "segmenting," or "slicing and dicing," and wrongly assume it is a new technique. Portrayal of an evil leader, who is guilty of unspeakable atrocities and possesses aggressive intent against one's country, works with the more jingoistic and aggressive segments of the population, Lasswell wrote. These are people who, he concluded, find "peace in war" and are labeled today as "NASCAR dads" living in the "red" states.

Yet, he argued, there need to be as many different justifications for war as there are interests in the population. So, for example, more "sophisticated" middle-class intellectuals need appeals based on international law. In a discussion that anticipates the uses of the United Nations by the Bush administration, Lasswell argued that even if an international body (he had the League of Nations in mind) opposed your country's plans for war, that could be overcome by an argument that war was required by a "higher and truer" vision of international law, which international organizations failed to uphold.

But what of the long-run consequences when a government, once the war is over, is found to have manipulated the truth? Lasswell did not think that was a problem as long as your country won, since "victory required no explanation." Americans are now grappling with what happens when "victory" does not occur and the justifications for a controversial and long-lasting conflict are called into question.

Reflecting the ambivalence of "nervous liberals," in other writing Lasswell believed that "propaganda is surely here to stay; the modern world is peculiarly dependent upon it for the coordination of atomized components in times of crisis. ... Propaganda as a tool is no more or less immoral than a pump handle," and "the only effective weapon against propaganda on behalf of one policy seems to be propaganda on behalf of an alternative" (1944). In short, Lasswell, like Lippmann and many critics who came after them, doubted the basic intelligence, responsibility, and rationality of the American people. This skepticism has been supported by decades of social science research demonstrating that Americans have very low levels of basic knowledge about the world around them and, despite easy access to information through the media and increasing levels of educational attainment, these levels have not increased over the last 50 years (Delli Carpini and Keeter 1997). Lasswell, in a memorable phrase, concluded that management of a complex society, even in a democracy, meant that "[i]f the masses will be free of chains of iron, it must accept chains of silver" (1944).

Despite the dramatic changes in the media environment between the early twentieth century and the early twenty-first century, these questions are still with us as we see the propaganda techniques identified by Lasswell being used again, to great effect, in the mobilization for war with Iraq. What should we conclude? Are people capable of critical analysis of information? Is the media able to provide a disinterested and sophisticated perspective on the central issues of the day? Must we fall back on cynicism?

John Dewey and the reconstruction of media and democratic politics

A very different response than that of Lippmann and Lasswell to the success of propaganda and the apparent limited political capacities of the American public was offered by John Dewey (1859–1952), often labeled the most influential American philosopher of the twentieth century. Dewey accepted the conclusions of Lippmann as accurate descriptions of American politics; however, he argued that shortcomings of democracy as it exists cannot be accepted as if they were natural or inevitable outcomes, but rather must be recognized as the result of imperfect institutions and so worked on and improved: "The important consideration is that opportunity be given ideas to speak and to become the possession of the multitude. The essential need is the improvement of the methods and constitution of debate, discussion, and persuasion. That is *the* problem of the public" (Dewey 1927).

Dewey believed that there was nothing inevitable about the abilities or inabilities of citizens, but rather that they flow from the ways in which education, community, family, and (for our purposes) the media work in any particular society. Do these institutions instill a sense of civic obligation, offer abundant opportunities for people to participate and make the decisions that affect their everyday lives, or discourage such interests and offer abundant distractions to direct attention away from public concerns?

Dewey believed that the emergence of a modern mass media had the potential to improve the conditions and operations of American democracy, if structured with those ends in mind, but he worried that the particular shape of the American media system, governed primarily by commercial interests, would have a much more negative influence.[6] Given his faith in democracy and public engagement, he saw the rise of public relations and advertising, especially as it informs propaganda work, as a threat to democracy. While Lippmann and Lasswell saw the manipulation of public opinion by public relations professionals as a potentially good thing, necessitated by the limitations of the public, Dewey saw it as a social pathology working against improving the abilities and interests of citizens.

When we despair about the bias of journalists and their ability to provide disinterested and critical perspectives on the actions of the government and the wisdom of political elites; when we worry about the impact of the media on what people think; when we decry the lack of knowledge that ordinary Americans have about the political world and doubt that many people are even capable of making an intelligent choice at the polling place (assuming they vote at all); when we criticize young people, especially for being overly concerned with celebrities, consuming the latest fashions or video game, and not taking interest in the serious issues of the day; and when we argue about whether the Internet and other new communications technologies will improve or further damage democratic politics, we are returning to the unresolved issues raised and debated by Lippmann, Lasswell, and Dewey at the very birth of the modern electronic media in the early part of the twentieth century.

Empirical research: How do media actually affect citizens?

While many intellectuals grappled with the broad implications of the relationship between media and democracy, a second tradition of media research is also relevant to our current concerns: empirical analysis of the impact of media exposure on political attitudes and opinions. While scholars and citizens alike have worried about how much propaganda in a modern media system would alter American democracy, Paul Lazarsfeld and his colleagues at Columbia University's Radio Research Bureau were pioneering techniques for precisely studying the actual impact of this new media system on Americans. In doing so, they laid the groundwork for much of the random sample polling that has, for better or worse, become an everyday feature of American political life. As well, Lazarsfeld pioneered the distinction in media studies between the analysis of media texts and the study of how these texts actually influence people, a distinction we return to in chapters 4 and 5 when we discuss the difference between textual analysis and audience reception studies.

How do we actually measure the impact of the mass media? This remains a difficult problem, given that the ubiquity of media makes isolating its impact a bit like studying the effect of water on fish. Even conceptualizing the questions that needed asking was difficult at the dawn of the modern mass media (the term "mass media" was coined by John Marshall of the Rockefeller Foundation in the 1930s).[7] The basic questions that Lazarsfeld and his colleagues formulated were as follows: what exactly was the persuasive power of the media when it came to influencing the voting decisions of Americans? Did the political perspective of the media translate into changing or influencing the attitudes of Americans about the candidates?

Reflecting the assumptions of a rational citizenry, a belief that was attacked by Lippmann but is still shared by many of us today (including most journalists who cover elections), Lazarsfeld assumed that most voters would make up their minds during the course of the campaign and be influenced by news media and political propaganda (i.e., what we now call "political advertisements"). In one of the earliest systematic surveys of American public opinion, conducted in the 1940 presidential election between Franklin Delano Roosevelt and Wendell Willkie, Lazarsfeld and his team interviewed 600 residents of Erie, Ohio, several times throughout the campaign (Lazarsfeld, Berelson, and Gaudet 1948). What he found was that less than 10 percent of his subjects ever shifted from one candidate to the other, and even fewer did so as a result of exposure to the media. Anticipating a half century of political science research, Lazarsfeld and his colleagues observed,

> For while people hesitate and meditate and imagine that they decide rationally on the better road to take, it would often have been possible to predict at the outset what they would decide to do in the end. Knowing a few of their personal characteristics, we can tell with fair certainty how they will finally vote: they join the fold to which they belong. (1948: 73)

Rather than changing minds, campaigns served to activate the usually dormant interest of citizens in politics and then reinforce their preexisting political values and preferences. "Those who are open-minded and weigh the alternatives exist mainly in deferential campaign propaganda and textbooks, but are few indeed" (Lazarsfeld et al. 1948: 95). Like Lippmann, Lazarsfeld's research undermined the exalted model of citizens as omnicompetent folks who reflected on the issues of the campaign and then carefully weighed both sides to reach a decision about whom they would cast their vote. Rather, voting preferences are a function of existing patterns of political socialization that depend on family, friends, coworkers, and other conduits of personal influence that lie outside the mass media.

Why was the impact of the mass media so limited? One answer is a point of emphasis for us in this book. Just because new forms of media emerge does not mean that people stop using older forms of communication. So, in the 1940s and 1950s when Lazarsfeld and his colleagues were doing their research, although television and radio were emerging, people still relied heavily on the face-to-face interactions with coworkers, friends, and so forth that they always had used when it came to politics.

This led to another of the enduring insights of this line of research, the two-step flow. As Lippmann argued, most citizens are not what we would today call "political junkies" – people who find intrinsic satisfaction from closely following the political world. Yet it is precisely those most interested in and knowledgeable about politics who paid the most attention to the media's campaign coverage. Given their high level of knowledge and preexisting political predispositions, these folks were also the surest of their initial vote choice and least likely to have their minds changed by the media. On the other hand, those who were less interested in and informed about politics, and so less likely to pay attention to media coverage of the campaigns, tended to rely on their friends who were knowledgeable about politics to inform them about campaigns. It was through these interpersonal relationships that the less informed obtained information about and perspectives on politics; this is the "two-step flow."

> In the last analysis, more than anything else, people can move other people. From an ethical point of view this is a hopeful aspect in the serious social problem of propaganda. The side which has the more enthusiastic supporters and which can mobilize grass-roots support in an expert way has great chances for success. (Lazarsfeld et al. 1948: 158)

The two-step flow is emblematic of much that we emphasize in this book; indeed, we will return to the elaboration of this idea by Lazarsfeld and Elihu Katz in chapter 4. Despite the attention paid to innovations in media technology – television in the late 1940s and early 1950s, and the Internet in the 1990s – new modes of communication are always diffused within a well-established social, political, and economic system of existing patterns. Any sophisticated understanding of media and politics requires a careful analysis of the ways in which citizens come to use new technologies in conjunction with the patterns of political communication they have already established.

Despite the impact of the electronic media (radio and then television), people still used older forms of communication – face-to-face conversations with coworkers, friends, and relatives. Many of the almost utopian claims about the Internet, for example, fall apart when compared to this finding from media researchers. Just because we now use the Internet does not mean we cease watching television, reading newspapers, listening to the radio, or talking to our friends, relatives, and coworkers. Indeed, much of the political information we receive from the Internet is actually drawn directly from older sources (e.g., the common practice of linking to or copying stories from newspapers and magazines). Below, we describe some current research that focuses on the ways in which citizens use both new and old forms of media in their political deliberations.

Yet, we can take this observation too far, as did many scholars, by ignoring the changes wrought by new media. As we noted in chapter 1, old media, even when they survive, are often changed by the emergence of new forms of communication technologies. We must be open to this in the case of the Internet.

We emphasize this half-century-old research, obtained at the dawn of the Age of Electronic Media, to draw attention to how often the findings of media scholars provide insights that are often obscured by media coverage of politics. For example, political scientists have long known that very few citizens actually change their opinions – Republicans do not very often vote for Democrats, and vice versa. So, media coverage of the 2008 election, which seemed to say that voters (1) are or should be open-minded in their consideration of the candidates and (2) pick a candidate only after weighing the information presented in the campaign, assumed a model of voting that has been discarded by social scientists for over 60 years.

Instead, campaigns turn, as they have for over half a century, on the degree to which campaigns can mobilize supporters to come to the polls and discourage supporters of the opposing candidate enough so they stay at home.

So, if media have only limited impact on the outcome of elections and, as Lazarsfeld demonstrated in other work, many other walks of life (fashion, moviegoing, etc.) (Katz and Lazarsfeld 1964), were the fears of people like Lippmann, Lazarsfeld, and Dewey about the potential for propaganda in the United States overblown? That depends on the specific issue we are examining. Lazarsfeld and his colleagues were careful to say that what lets political junkies maintain their own opinions and attitudes is the availability of a diverse media. That is, even political junkies can be swayed if they only encounter media that oppose their viewpoint. So, even though campaign coverage is usually diverse and/or nonpartisan, in times of war when media simply tend to copy the statements of the government, as for example during the run-up to the Iraq invasion in 2003, the effect of propaganda can be as profound as it was in Lasswell's examination of propaganda in World War I. It remains important to study the propagandistic function of the media (see, for example, Bennett, Lawrence, and Livingston 2008).

Television and the "Age of Broadcast News"

While political socialization and the two-step flow continued to play important roles in shaping political attitudes and behaviors and so limiting the independent impact of media messages, the emergence of television as the dominant medium and "electronic hearth" of American society for the second half of the twentieth century dramatically altered the media environment in which American politics operated. By the 1970s, over two thirds of Americans relied primarily on television for their political information. It was the most trusted source for news, and the late Walter Cronkite, venerable anchor of the *CBS Evening News*, was the most trusted man in America, according to surveys.

From the perspective of media studies, such a dramatic shift in the nature of the media environment would inevitably affect the dynamics of democratic politics, and so it did. For example, one of the key findings of Lazarsfeld and the political scientists who followed in his footsteps was that media impact was limited by the robustness of political socialization, especially early childhood socialization, which occurred outside the realm of media, in families, churches and synagogues, schools, and so forth.

Yet, the underlying assumption here that there is a clear divide between the realm of mass media and other walks of life was undermined by the ways in which television came to be used in society. As television programs aimed at children proliferated, as commercial "carpet-bombing" of the Saturday morning television hours increased, as children were taught to read and write by shows like *Sesame Street*, and as the tube became used as a kind of electronic babysitter for harried parents, media became central to the socialization of Americans and other societies adopting the American media model (McChesney 1999).

As well, television became the gathering place for citizens to spend half an hour each night finding about what elite journalists thought were the most important events of the day. At its height of dominance, what might be called the Age of Broadcast News, nightly television news broadcasts attracted 75 percent of all the television sets turned on. Of course, these impressive ratings were the result of the allocation of the 6:00–7:00 PM hour to local and national news broadcasts on virtually all available stations on the air, rather than some form of more committed citizenship on the part of the masses (Prior 2007).

Also, although it seems impressive from the vantage point of today's lower network news viewership and newspaper readership, several limitations of the Age of Broadcast News need to be noted. First, the very idea that citizenship obligations could be met by watching a half-hour television news broadcast and, for the truly interested, reading a daily newspaper is a considerable decline from the expectations of social studies texts and the debates between Lippmann and Dewey. It is unlikely either of them would have seen watching the evening news as the hallmark of enlightened citizenry.

Second, public opinion polling reveals that the Age of Broadcast News did little to improve the levels of knowledge about the political world possessed by most Americans. Between the 1950s and 1980s, there was virtually no change in the levels of basic knowledge about politics, despite greatly increased levels of education and exposure to the electronic media (Entman 1989; Delli Carpini and Keeter 1997).

As profound changes occurred in the media environment, wrought by the increasing dominance of television as the central carrier of our society's culture and politics, so too were there major changes in the relationship between media and politics. Although the findings of Lazarsfeld and those who followed him emphasized the "minimal" effects of media on politics due to the richness of other forms of associational life and the diversity of viewpoints in the American media, the Age of Broadcast News led to a reexamination of these findings. Especially significant to the relationship between media and politics was the emergence of television journalists – especially the nightly anchors – as the primary gatekeepers between the booming, buzzing, blooming confusion of politics and the assumed limited attention and interest of most Americans for politics.

As significantly, the two-step flow depends on the general apathy of most Americans for politics – and hence their lack of interest in following issues in the media and their reliance on trusted coworkers, friends, and so forth. With the large audiences watching the evening news each night, television itself had become the interpreter of politics for even those with minimal interest.

Researchers began to see that while television might not change people's attitudes and behaviors, it might still have powerful effects. In particular, two important effects of media were identified by a wide range of researchers using a variety of methods and theoretical perspectives. First, one of the strongest effects of the electronic media, especially the evening network news broadcasts, was their ability to set the agenda ("agenda setting"). Contrary to the worries of critics on both the left and the right who accused them of bias, the news broadcasts could not tell viewers what to think, but could shape what they thought about. So, if the nightly news broadcasts led with stories about the environment, for example, while this would not change what viewers' opinions were, it would determine that they thought the environment was a particularly important issue that day (McCombs and Shaw 1972; Iyengar and Kinder 1988).

Researchers have also identified "priming" as another significant impact of the network news. How journalists tell a particular story – whether they emphasize personal stories, macro statistics, the role of government, and so forth – has a significant impact on how viewers evaluate that particular issue and who they hold accountable. So, for example, if journalists show pictures of the Capitol Building or the White House in stories about economic troubles, viewers are more likely to want to hold political actors responsible for creating the problem and developing solutions. On the other hand, telling the same story about economic distress by citing national statistics and focusing on the plight of individuals and businesses primes viewers to see the trouble as part of the inevitable economic cycle, and to move away from holding government officials responsible (Iyengar 1994).

This line of investigation illuminated other significant implications of the rise of television as the dominant medium in twentieth-century America. With television comes, of course, the rise of political advertising as an important aspect of modern campaigns. The effects of campaign advertising need to be considered through the lens of the original insights of Lazarsfeld and his colleagues. The news (when viewed) is understood as part of a citizen's public obligation and is viewed as a kind of political communication. This is far from the case, however, with campaign advertising (Jamieson 1993). In this case, the viewer is watching his or her regular fare of entertainment programming, not thinking about politics at all, when he or she is exposed to campaign advertising. As survey research indicates, it is inattentive viewers, like the person we just described, who are the most susceptible to persuasion.

Political advertising, although endlessly dissected by political pundits and other political junkies, is actually aimed primarily at this inattentive audience whose critical perspective is not engaged when exposed to these ads. In addition, consistent with the conclusion that elections are not about changing people's minds (something that almost never occurs), the point of negative advertising is not to convince a passionate Democrat to vote Republican, but rather to increase the suspicion one might have about one's own party's nominee and so to cause a voter to be less likely to vote on Election Day (Ansolabehere and Iyengar 1995).

In short, the research conducted by media scholars during the last half of the twentieth century concludes that elections, and by inference much of democratic political life, are not about thoughtfully weighing ideas and making reasoned choices. At the same time, this newer research grappled with the growing role of television in all aspects of life. This new media environment undermined the basic assumption of researchers like Lazarsfeld that there is a clear distinction between mediated political information, such as on television, and real life. Significantly, what this means is that many of the effects on politics that were played by non-mediated (direct) forms of communication – interpersonal relationships, education, the church, and so forth – have been taken over by different portions of the media landscape itself.

An echo of Lippmann's warnings about the limitations of journalists and the news is found in *Out of Order* by Thomas Patterson (1993). The book provides an analysis of the role of journalists in covering today's political campaigns. Like Lippmann, Patterson questions whether the news can really serve the needs of the electorate. He argues that the dominant frames, or perspectives, used by journalists in covering elections emphasize which candidate is ahead, who is behind, and what strategies the campaigns are using to attract voters – what is often called the "horse race" aspect of elections. In contrast, what voters need is information and insight into what candidates will do if elected, what Patterson calls a "governance frame."[8]

If we look deeper, there are other, more subtle, but even more profound impacts of the Television Age on politics. For example, as Neil Postman (1985) pointed out, the evolution of a commercial media system, financed by advertising, has had important impacts on the way we communicate about politics. To the extent that television is a medium of brief episodes showing problems being solved by simple solutions, this has influenced understandings of the political world by encouraging and requiring politicians to offer easily digestible, but oversimplified problem definitions and solutions, as well as encouraging public impatience for extended discussions of problems and recognition of the difficulty of solving them.

As we noted in chapter 2, it is not simply television as a technology that leads to this outcome, but also the specific ownership regime enacted by Congress in the 1930s. This is the decision that allowed the exploitation of the airwaves by private media corporations that relied primarily on advertising to turn a profit. Indeed, while we may decry politicians for their subservience to those who contribute money to their campaigns, it is worth noting that the major reason why campaigns require so much money is the need to produce and purchase the time for airing campaign advertisement.

In turn, the purchase of campaign advertising is a major source of revenue for the television and radio stations that air them. This may explain why so little media attention is devoted to this connection or the seemingly obvious remedy, adopted in many other western democracies, of providing free and equal access to the airwaves for all candidates. At the very least, it emphasizes the media studies perspective that attributes the behavior of politicians not to any increase in venality or personal greed, but rather to the political and economic structure of the media.

Finally, at an even deeper level, some scholars, like Robert Putnam (2000), have argued that the sheer amount of time that Americans spend watching television in their own homes has adversely affected the time and willingness of most people to participate in the civic life of their communities.

Politics in the New Media Environment

The insights of 60 years of media research are especially valuable as citizens try to develop a sophisticated understanding of the connection between media and politics in the twenty-first century. Concepts like the "two step flow," "agenda setting," and "attentive versus inattentive audiences" are still useful. But as in the past (e.g., the changes wrought by the dominance of television in the mid-twentieth century), these insights must be rethought in light of the dramatic changes in the media environment over the last two decades. An approach rooted in media studies reminds us to be cautious of explanations for current political problems that rely on assumed changes in the moral qualities or intellectual abilities of either citizens or politicians. Instead, we highlight changes in the media environment that might better explain current problems.

One very general example is provided by debates over the increasing conflict and partisanship of political debate in the United States. Many public figures decry the degree to which many Americans identify themselves as "hyphenated-Americans," rather than simply Americans. Others call for us to move beyond harsh political conflict to create a postpartisan political world that would allow elites and ordinary citizens to work together for the greater public good. Yet, such arguments seldom acknowledge the profound changes in the media system that have played a significant role in such political developments. While our political leaders continue to search for unifying principles for the American public, as we saw in chapter 2, the structure of the media system has fragmented the media audience and so too the polity.[9]

The explosion of media conduits through which political information passes, which we have discussed in previous chapters, has had a more specific impact on the conclusions drawn by media scholars about the role of television in American democracy. As the audience for the nightly news broadcasts ages and shrinks, the ability of the networks to set the agenda also declines. If fewer Americans are going to these three sources for their political information, then their ability to determine what people think about also declines.

Numerous examples highlight the ways in which the Internet challenges the underlying tenets of the Age of Broadcast News. In several high-profile cases, bloggers managed to maintain public attention on issues that had been dropped by professional journalists, eventually forcing mainstream news sources to revive them and thereby encroaching on one of the most significant roles of professional journalists: the ability to set the agenda.

The first example was when Joshua Marshall's blog, "Talking Point Memo," played a significant role in keeping then-Republican Senator Trent Lott from becoming the Senate Majority Leader in 2003.[10] At Strom Thurmond's 100th birthday party, Lott had expressed (jokingly, he insisted) his support for the aged South Carolinian's 1948 segregationist third-party run for the presidency. While covered briefly by mainstream journalists, the story had begun to disappear from the news. As Marshall himself noted, "This was a story that the [established] press in DC was very well suited to miss…. [T]he way daily journalism works, a story has a 24-hour audition to see if it has legs, and if it doesn't get picked up, that's it" (quoted in Burkeman 2002). However, reflecting the breakdown of the ability of professional journalists and political elites to set the agenda in the new media environment, Marshall and his audience of liberal political activists were able to keep the Lott affair alive, forcing it back onto the news and political agendas.

In the 2004 election, right-wing bloggers played a major role in focusing public attention on the questionable practices of *CBS News* in checking whether documents they used to show that President George W. Bush had ducked Air Force Reserve duty during the Vietnam War were genuine. Here, blogs managed to intrude on the priming role formally thought to be played by professional journalists: they successfully shifted the criteria used to judge the issue from the validity of the claims themselves, to the narrower question of whether specific documents were real or forged. In more recent debates over health care reform or even President Obama's citizenship, bloggers have become part of the basic fabric of mainstream news coverage. Even when journalists simply repudiate demonstrably false claims made by bloggers (e.g., false claims about government-run "death panels" in health care legislation, or that the president was born in Kenya), this coverage can result in increasing public awareness of the claims.

Chat groups and online discussions provide new venues for citizens to directly discuss public issues. Nonmainstream and/or international websites serve as alternative sources of information and opinion, challenging the agenda-setting and gatekeeping functions of the traditional news media. Networks of political and social activists use the Web to mount virtual and real-world opposition to traditional political elites or create alternative spaces for discussing issues ignored by mainstream media and elites.[11] Fringe candidates and spokespersons are able to enter and even help shape public debate to an extent that would have been impossible in an earlier era. And citizens are able to access information about political, social, and economic life directly, bypassing many of the traditional media gatekeepers.

At the same time that the day-to-day power of the networks to set the agenda declines, the significance of moments when disparate media focus on a specific issue, creating a media event and consequently setting the agenda, becomes even greater. "Media events" such as that surrounding 9/11 or Hurricane Katrina serve as powerful examples of the media's continuing agenda-setting power, focusing public attention on a single issue in ways it no longer can on a day-to-day basis. As noted by Daniel Dayan and Elihu Katz (1992), media events can also serve a more basic human function, acting as public rituals of grief, mourning, and reconciliation. Examples of past media events that have played this role are the John F. Kennedy assassination, the death of Princess Diana, and the loss of the two space shuttles. Such mediated public experiences tap into shared foundational beliefs that can unify seemingly disparate segments of society. Although various media may cover these events in somewhat different ways, underlying assumptions about the public agenda are *shared* across both outlets and audiences.

Clearly, much of the coverage of 9/11 – and public reaction to it – was consistent with Dayan and Katz's (1992) notion of media events as public rituals. But the terrorist attacks also set off a political crisis that raised profound and much-debated questions about the role of the United States in the world and the most appropriate response to the attacks. As such, the coverage also had many elements of a different definition of "media event" offered by media scholar John Fiske (1994).

Rather than rituals of reconciliation, Fiske argues that some media events can provide opportunities for marginalized "publics" to enter mainstream discourse, challenging the hegemonic or uniform interpretations that normally dominate considerations of political and social issues. As examples of such media events, Fiske points to the way in which the

O. J. Simpson trial or the Clarence Thomas–Anita Hill hearings raised broader issues of race and gender. We saw in chapter 1 that Hurricane Katrina sparked a very unusual public dialogue over the plight of poor African Americans.

Overall, media studies helps us to understand that what has changed over time are not the qualities of citizens or politicians, but rather the fundamentals of the media environment through which we find out about politics (Prior 2007). This perspective makes clear how significant it is to evaluate of the potentials and pitfalls of the new media environment when addressing the enduring questions of media and democracy. Remember that these questions go back to the dawn of the twentieth century and the emergence of the mass media.

- What are the implications for democratic politics of the interactivity of new media and the resulting increase in the ability of citizens to produce (and not just receive) political texts?
- What will the fragmentation and targeting of media mean for the ability of citizens to ignore politics?
- Will the new media environment sustain interest only around elections – as Lippmann would have wanted?
- What does it do for actual participation in the political process?

Conclusion

Ultimately understanding the ways in which a changing media environment does or does not enhance democracy requires an expanded definition of "citizenship." The distinctions between political, cultural, and economic elites; between information producers and consumers; and even between elites and "the masses" are becoming more fluid. Consequently, notions of press responsibility that underlie traditional models of media and politics must be expanded to other individuals and institutions that influence politically relevant media texts. Similarly, notions of civic responsibility that are applied to the general public must be expanded to also apply to traditional political, cultural, and economic elites – to any individual or organization that is given access to the media soapbox in our expanded public square.

In the end, the issues raised by the changing media environment are like those underlying the debate between John Dewey and Walter Lippmann of nearly a century ago. At its core remains the issue of the limitations of the public – "the public and its problems," as Dewey (1927) called it. As the position of journalists as authoritative gatekeepers declines, citizens are left more on their own to sort through competing perspectives and multiple sources of political information. So, the critical capacities and interests of the public – media literacy – again become a central problem for democratic life. Indeed, a primary goal of media studies is to provide a framework for defining media literacy, which is now at least as important as literacy in reading and writing.

Notes

1. We shall return to this important impact of television news coverage on public opinion, (i.e., the ability to set the agenda) later in the chapter.
2. Howard Kurtz, the media critic for *The Washington Post*, attributed the intensified scrutiny of the press to the *SNL* skit in his appearance on *The Colbert Report*.
3. For a wonderful treatment of Callender, see *New York Times* columnist William Safire's historical novel *Scandalmonger* (2000).
4. For an excellent overview of the assumptions of this approach and their limited current application, see Schudson (1998).
5. This section draws heavily from Williams (2004).
6. Dewey actually worked, early in his career, on a newspaper devoted to providing its readers with the most important findings of academic social scientists (see Ryan 1997).
7. For example, compared with print media where one knows how many issues of a newspaper or magazine are sold, it was initially difficult to even conceptualize, let alone measure, the radio audience. Once you send the signal over the air, how do you figure out who is listening or why? In the early days of radio in the 1920s, radio executives thought that the main reason folks listened to one show rather than another was simply signal strength and not interest in a particular type of programming. It was only after much study of actual radio listeners that the industry discovered that people searched for shows they were interested in.
8. Interestingly enough, Patterson (1993) argues that what leads to the dominance of the horse race frame is the long length of campaigns and the boredom of journalists at covering the same stump speech day after day. Given carefully limited and controlled access to the candidate him or herself, journalists rely on campaign advisors as sources, who not surprisingly also obsess about the strategies of the campaigns. Given the seemingly endless 2008 campaign, what Patterson proposes is that the press might better serve the public interest if campaigns were dramatically shortened.

9. This is not to claim that media changes are the *only* explanation for this fragmentation. For an explanation that emphasizes changes in the media in the
context of broader political, social, and cultural changes like the end of
the Cold War and the rise of multiculturalism, see Williams and Delli Carpini
(forthcoming).
10. Marshall himself was a little-known freelance journalist.
11. These networks span the political spectrum from Moveon.com on the left to
FreeRepublic.com on the right.

References

Ansolabehere, Stephen, and Shanto Iyengar. 1995. *Going negative: How attack
ads shrink and polarize the electorate.* New York: Free Press.
Bennett, W. Lance, Regina Lawrence, and Steven Livingston. 2008. *When the
press fails: Political power and the news media from Iraq to Katrina.* Chicago:
University of Chicago Press.
Burkeman, Oliver. 2002. "Bloggers catch what *Washington Post* missed." *Guardian*
(London), December 21, p. 13.
Dayan, Daniel, and Elihu Katz. 1992. *Media events: The live broadcasting of history.*
Cambridge, M.A.: Harvard University Press.
Delli Carpini, Michael X., and Scott Keeter. 1997. *What Americans know about
politics and why it matters.* London: Yale University Press.
Dewey, John. 1927. *The public and its problems.* New York: H. Holt.
Entman, Robert M. 1989. *Democracy without citizens: Media and the decay of
American politics.* New York: Oxford University Press.
Fiske, John. 1994. *Media matters: Everyday culture and political change.*
Minneapolis: University of Minnesota Press.
Gary, Brett. 1999. *The nervous liberals: Propaganda anxieties from World War I
to the Cold War.* New York: Columbia University Press.
Iyengar, Shanto. 1994. *Is anyone responsible? How television frames political issues.*
Chicago: University of Chicago Press.
Iyengar, Shanto, and Donald R. Kinder. 1988. *News that matters: Television and
American opinion.* Chicago: University of Chicago Press.
Jamieson, Kathleen Hall. 1993. *Dirty politics: Deception, distraction, and democ-
racy.* New York: Oxford University Press.
Katz, Elihu, and Paul Felix Lazarsfeld. 1964. *Personal influence: The part played
by people in the flow of mass communications.* New York: Free Press.
Lasswell, Harold D. 1944. "Propaganda." In *Encyclopedia of the social sciences,* ed.
Edwin R. A. Seligman. New York: Macmillan.
Lasswell, Harold D. 1971. *Propaganda technique in World War I.* Cambridge,
M.A.: MIT Press.

Lazarsfeld, Paul Felix, Bernard Berelson, and Hazel Gaudet. 1948. *The people's choice: How the voter makes up his mind in a presidential campaign.* New York: Columbia University Press.

Lippman, Walter. 1922. *Public opinion.* New York: Harcourt, Brace.

Lippman, Walter. 1925. *The phantom public.* New York: Harcourt, Brace.

McCombs, M. E., and D. L. Shaw. 1972. "The agenda-setting function of mass media." *Public Opinion Quarterly* 36:176–87.

McChesney, Robert Waterman. 1999. *Rich media poor democracy: Communication politics in dubious time.* Urbana: University of Illinois Press.

Patterson, Thomas E. 1993. *Out of order.* New York: Knopf.

Postman, Neil. 1985. *Amusing ourselves to death: Public discourse in the age of show business.* New York: Viking.

Prior, Markus. 2005. *Post-broadcast democracy: How media choice increases inequality in political involvement and polarizes elections.* New York: Cambridge University Press.

Prior, Markus. 2007. *Post-broadcast democracy.* New York: Cambridge University Press.

Putnam, Robert D. 2000. *Bowling alone: The collapse and revival of American community.* New York: Simon & Schuster.

Rosenfeld, Richard N., and William Duane. 1997. *American Aurora: A Democratic-Republican returns: The suppressed history of our nation's beginnings and the heroic newspaper that tried to report it.* New York: St. Martin's.

Ryan, Alan. 1997. *John Dewey and the high tide of American liberalism.* New York: Norton.

Safire, William. 2000. *Scandalmonger.* New York: Simon & Schuster.

Schudson, Michael. 1998. *The good citizen: A history of American civic life.* New York: Martin Kessler.

Smith, Aaron. 2009. "The Internet's role in campaign 2008," Pew Internet and American Life Project, April 15. www.pewinternet.org/topics/News.aspx.

Steel, Ronald. 1980. *Walter Lippmann and the American century.* Boston: Little, Brown.

Wilentz, Sean. 2007. *The rise of American democracy.* New York: Norton.

Williams, Bruce 2004. "War rhetoric's threat to democracy." *The Chronicle of Higher Education*, April 4.

Williams, Bruce A., and Michael X. Delli Carpini. Forthcoming. *After the news: Media regimes and American democracy in the new information environment.* New York: Cambridge University Press.

Chapter 4

Studying Popular Culture
Texts, Reception, and Cultural Studies

Introduction: Hollywood and Representations of Reality

If in 2007 you could tear yourself away from your online pursuits long enough to search for a good movie to see – and especially if you were on a date, looking for a film that appealed to both men and women – you might have ended up in the theater seeing *Knocked Up*, a film written and directed by Judd Apatow. In this film you would see the story of Alison Scott (Katherine Heigl) and Ben Stone (Seth Rogan), two young single adults who meet on a one-night stand that results in Alison's pregnancy. The ensuing comedy-drama details their journey from casual sexual partners to marriage and parenthood. Presented as an old-time boy-meets-girl romance, the film is extremely well written, funny, and well acted, and works successfully as an entertaining Hollywood movie. Though not a blockbuster, it did well at the box office, making a great deal of money for all concerned. Recent trips to the video store indicate its continuing popularity for home viewing.

On the surface, *Knocked Up* is light entertainment, a simple romantic comedy that, if it tackles any serious issue at all, addresses a young man's journey from a prolonged adolescence to a position of adult responsibility as a husband and father. Yet the sophisticated student of media studies sees a great deal more in this deceptively simple tale. All of the interest that *Knocked Up* has generated in the theaters, amongst critics, on the Web, and in daily conversation indicates that media are not merely innocuous entertainment, but are reflective of, and constitutive of, cultural conversations about our most intimate values, beliefs, ideas, and confusions.

That is what this chapter, and much of media studies, is about. Media studies gives us the conceptual tools we need to make the journey from the perception of a simple story, from just watching a movie, to understanding the movie and its influence in our society – that is, from simply enjoying a text to understanding the way that enjoyable stories have multiple meanings (the study of texts) and selectively influence our beliefs and worldviews (the study of media effects). Media studies helps us become media literate by enabling us to see that media stories reinforce certain fundamental beliefs, create others, and ensure that some become entirely impossible for most people in our society to embrace, as we saw with our discussion of Lasswell's propaganda studies in chapter 3. How? An analysis of this case will help us to break down the process of media analysis.

The text of *Knocked Up* well illustrates the ideological work that a simple film can perform. What do we mean by the term "ideology"? In this sense of the term, we are not talking about an explicit political belief that members of a particular party or group openly promote. Here, the term "ideology" refers to its hidden dimensions, as an integral part of most of the stories we tell, or hear, in our popular culture. When applied to the analysis of a media text, "ideology" simply refers to the assumptions that remain consciously hidden, yet are often unconsciously understood, when most people merely watch a movie or read a text. A film's, or a text's, "ideological work" means that viewers of that film or text are subtly encouraged to adopt these assumptions, and understand these messages, rather than others. Although a story may seem simple, the hidden assumptions that it makes mask the complexity of the "work" that it does in the realm of ideas.

So in the case of *Knocked Up*, Alison's decision to have her baby, clearly an explicit decision in an age when women have the medical and legal capabilities of deciding whether to give birth or not, is masked. It is masked by being presented as a "nondecision" – indeed, as the "natural" course of things – rather than a conscious decision she had to make. Social science statistics indicate that women in Alison's position (single women becoming pregnant) often choose not to give birth by obtaining safe, legal elective abortions, yet this common pattern is simply ignored by the film. When characters in the film do bring up the possibility of this choice, they are silenced.

For example, Alison's mother, presented unattractively as a hard-bitten, "feminist" career woman, commands her – in a discussion about her pregnancy – simply to "take care of it," "it" meaning her pregnancy. By this, it is clear to the audience that she means Alison should have an abortion. Yet this way of thinking is presented as a retro, evilly "feminist" viewpoint – and is so delegitimized by the film that the choice seems implausible, out of the question to Alison.

Also, a cursory reading of much literature about women beginning with the novels of Jane Austen, as much of the women's studies literature of the past three decades indicates (Kaplan 1992; Walters 1992), shows that mothers are often portrayed critically. Their opinions are considered irrelevant in much popular Western literature, as they are in this story. It is noteworthy that Alison's mother is represented in this instance, and presented *as a feminist*, in such an unsympathetic manner. (See Goodman [2008] and Pollitt [2008] for an explicitly feminist critique of *Knocked Up* that touches on this and other issues as well.)[1]

Similarly Ben's friends, when discussing his situation, eschew the option of abortion. Indeed, they are reluctant to use even the word itself, and find it necessary to make up a word – "shmashmortion" – to stand for the real thing, presumably because we all know such an option is literally unspeakable in a Hollywood film, at least at this moment in time. Yet in direct contrast to the rhetorical rules of Hollywood, 47 percent of the US population believe that abortion should in most cases be legal, versus 45 percent who believe abortion should in most cases be illegal.[2]

Knocked Up, a popular text, assumes a particular value stance on the issue of abortion as a legitimate choice. It presents abortion as unspeakable; identifies it with hard-bitten, marginalized "feminist" characters in the film; and generally presents the lead characters as sympathetic in part because they are unable to think about abortion as a choice. In this sense, the film takes an "ideological" stance on feminists, and on reproductive choice, presenting both as unsympathetic. Viewers are encouraged to similarly adopt this position on the issue of abortion.

Though most probably will be influenced by the text to see abortion this way, some will not. Only audience analysis, performed by scholars in media studies, can tell us the way actual viewers have read this text. Yet the textual analyst aids the audience researcher by pointing out the ways in which the text itself privileges, or promotes, certain readings over others. Audiences, who are often diverse and subjected to other influences besides the text alone, certainly might read the film in the way its writer intended; but other readings are possible as well. For example, feminists in the audience who are sensitized to the way abortion is presented in popular cultural texts might see the film as biased against the option of abortion, for the reasons we have discussed above.

The ideological work of *Knocked Up* does not stop with the issue of abortion. It extends to other issues as well, making the film an explicitly political text on several levels, even though it is simultaneously a work of Hollywood entertainment. Not only is *Knocked Up* a tale of the lack of reproductive choice for women in the United States in 2007, particularly at a symbolic level; but also it is a tale of the desirability of the resurgence of the traditional family.

Like couples in Hollywood films of the 1950s and 1960s, an era when abortion was illegal and when safe abortions were almost impossible to obtain in the United States, the male protagonist Ben in *Knocked Up* feels compelled to propose marriage to Alison in the most traditional way. He also feels he must enter into family life with her and their unborn child, despite the fact that he barely knows her. Alison takes some convincing in an age in which the stigma of single parenthood is much reduced, and women are often able to support themselves and their children.

When Alison decides to marry Ben, this choice is narratively unconvincing, underlining its ideological component. Why would a successful and beautiful young career woman choose to marry an uneducated, unemployed, not particularly attractive drifter – let's face it, a loser – like Ben? The only reason, in the logic of *Knocked Up*, is that the value of having a traditional family – dad, mom, and baby – far overwhelms the drawbacks for Alison of this choice. This is despite the fact that, statistically speaking, the chances of her marriage to someone as different from her as Ben succeeding are relatively small.

In addition, *Knocked Up* downplays the impact that pregnancy and motherhood will have on Alison's career as an on-air news announcer by creating the unlikely plotline that Alison's pregnancy massively increases her ratings, leading the network to promote her rather than fire her upon hearing the news! Such a storyline is a clear distortion of the statistical reality that for most women, pregnancy and motherhood lead to a very clear loss in revenue and do indeed damage most careers, given the family-unfriendly attitudes of most US employers (Douglas and Michaels 2005). In the real-life case of Meredith Vieira, the *60 Minutes* co-host who was thrown off the show when she became pregnant a second time and asked for a continuation of her reduced time schedule, or of Elizabeth Vargas, who lost her position as news anchor for ABC following her maternity leave for her second pregnancy (Kurtz 2007), we see that pregnancy and the rigors of child-rearing do not normally benefit the careers of on-camera broadcasters.[3] Given the high risk of failure inherent in Alison's marriage to Ben, these career risks could be dangerous both for Alison's future, and for the future of her child.

In *Knocked Up*, pregnant women have increased career success, men transform themselves from adolescents into responsible adults, and women and children are indeed cared for and not constrained. Such systematic distortions in the interests of portraying the nuclear family as an institution with no downsides, despite the historical record present in academic and popular analyses, are the heart of ideology. And if these are the measure of an ideological text, *Knocked Up* fits the bill in the extreme. Far from the simple romantic comedy it is presented to be, *Knocked Up* is a piece of conservative political ideology, part of the backlash against feminism and women's rights that Susan Faludi so eloquently described (1991).

Since these ideological assumptions about the traditional family and working women are so pronounced in the text of *Knocked Up*, yet at the same time are woven seamlessly into an enjoyably told tale, they remain both invisible and powerful. As a result, many viewers might be influenced by the film's narrative – along with the many other similarly biased cultural products which form the cultural context for this particular narrative – to take a similar stance in support of the traditional family as the solution to unplanned pregnancies, and similarly to minimize the impact of unplanned motherhood on women's career success. Yet again, other viewers, influenced perhaps by their feminist convictions or sociological education, will identify these perspectives in the film, and may or may not agree with them. It remains for the audience researcher to tell us the extent, and limits, of the influence of this and other popular cultural texts.

Contrast the presentation of abortion in *Knocked Up* with the presentation of this issue in an earlier, pre-backlash film made by avowedly feminist director Amy Heckerling, 1984's *Fast Times at Ridgemont High*. This film, about the sexual behavior of teen girls in a Los Angeles high school, depicts the sexual adventures of Stacey, who loses her virginity in a one-night stand, and becomes pregnant in another. Upon learning of her pregnancy, Stacey immediately makes plans to have an abortion, without considering any alternatives and without discussing the choice with her family, her friends, or the baby's father, another high school student named Mike Damone. Abortion in this case is presented matter-of-factly, as the only reasonable solution to Stacey's predicament, and a rather unproblematic one.

Displaying a high degree of gender egalitarianism, Stacey merely asks Mike to help her in obtaining the abortion by giving her a ride to the clinic and paying half the cost (she does not ask to be compensated for bearing the physical burden of pregnancy in any way). Though he tries to call in some loans, Mike cannot come up with his half of the money, and out of shame does not show up to drive Stacey to her appointment at the clinic. Stacey goes on her own (her brother drops her off for "bowling" with her girlfriend), pays for it herself, and afterward catches a ride with her brother to a restaurant for lunch. That is the last we hear of the abortion except for her best friend Linda's attempt to punish Mike Damone for failing to show up (by writing "Little Prick" in large red letters on his car and locker).

Using this film in our courses on gender and film over the years, we have been able to chart students' ever-changing reactions to the depiction of Stacey's abortion. While we noted no particularly strong reactions to Stacey's story when we began using the film in the late 1980s, by the mid-1990s there began to be a strong negative response amongst student viewers to what they viewed as the film's "casual" treatment of abortion. This progression amongst student viewers vis-à-vis the abortion issue raises the question of whether ideological slants in film reflect general shifts in our popular attitudes and beliefs, influence these attitudes and beliefs precipitating shifts, or both. The scholarship in media studies indicates that both are equally true.

Therefore, media studies begins from the assumption that the representations of reality that people consume influence the way people in our increasingly media-saturated society think about the world. It also assumes that media content is a good barometer of these thoughts and ideas. Since its beginnings, the heart of media studies has always been a critique of the *way* the media represent reality, or in fact define reality, shaping our choices, identities, and beliefs. In this chapter, we will discuss the tools of the analytic critique of representation practices by media studies scholars, and the analytic critique of media influence as practiced by media studies audience researchers.

Of course, we begin from the premise that no representation is a simple reflection of reality: this is impossible given the complexity of the issues, objects, people, and situations the media represent, and the limited nature of representation. As noted media scholar James Carey argued, taking a cultural perspective on media analysis dictates the notion that reality as we imagine it is itself *shaped* by representations of it. In actuality, what does this theory mean? Imagine a camera simply running, capturing every aspect of every event in an attempt to reflect its reality. This would be impossible to accomplish. Even in a documentary or newspaper story, authors, filmmakers, writers, directors, camerapeople, and so on all make selections that influence the kind of depiction of reality that appears in their media product.

There has been considerable theorizing and research done by scholars analyzing the media in many different fields that support and illustrate this conclusion. No one expects representations to be transparently "realistic," because this is not the nature of representation and its meanings. Meanings are created through interpretation, and are open to interpretation on many levels and from many perspectives. Therefore, representations operate on many levels as well. This makes some scholars believe that it is fruitless to attempt to uncover the "perspective" or bias of a given media product; instead, such scholars urge us to examine only the specific interpretations made by particular members of particular social groups.[4] Yet an exercise like our close reading of *Knocked Up* illustrates that certain media products do incorporate specific ideological slants that are simply too apparent to deny.

So, we (and many others)[5] argue that despite the complex nature of representations and meanings, it is possible for scholars and sophisticated media consumers to comment on what is sometimes called the "dominant meaning" of a representation or a text. The "dominant meaning" simply refers to the most probable interpretation that will be made by the majority of people occupying a particular social position. So, for example, although religious, unmarried women might read the film *Knocked Up* as a cautionary tale about the dangers of premarital sex, secular, less religious unmarried men and women might read the same film as merely a light comedy. Still others, more feminist in their views, might criticize the film by viewing it as a misrepresentation of the choices available to unmarried women who find themselves facing an unplanned pregnancy.

One important contribution of media studies has been to show that many representations – in particular, the most popular representations, those that are most plentiful and are products of the dominant media system – produce meanings that are systematically slanted in particular ways to elicit the same set of readings from members of several different social groups. This notion of an identifiable and systematic slant is also at the heart of the term "ideology."

We defined "ideology" above to refer to the assumptions that remain hidden when one watches or receives a media text. Here we would like to push this definition further, and assert that ideology in media consists of images that are represented with systematic slants that can be related to the economic, social, and political power structures that characterize a society, and the inequality that results from these structures. These images are slanted to support certain views about the way reality is, but not other views, often supporting the viewpoints and perspectives of those occupying positions of economic, social, or political power. The relationship between ideological perspectives in the media, and those that predominate at any given time in a particular society, is not simple, however. The study of these relationships involves the work of "unpacking" which perspectives are held by whom, and which perspectives are interpretable in various media products.

For instance, in the example of the film *Knocked Up*, described above, the ideological aspect of the images that the film contains dictate that most readers will read the film either as a light comedy about young people getting married, *or* as a cautionary tale about the need to avoid premarital sex. The reading that is *not* privileged by the film and its images would be a feminist interpretation, which would criticize the film for not presenting abortion as a viable choice to Alison's dilemma. The feminist critique would focus on the following issues:

The way abortion remains unspoken throughout the film
The way abortion is referred to indirectly as an unacceptable action, by the film's discrediting of Alison's mother, who recommends it without using the word; by Ben's friend's attempt to discuss abortion coupled with his reluctance to use the word; and by Alison's own refusal to consider the option
The way the cost to Alison's career is entirely discounted by the improbably presentation of her pregnancy as a career boost
The way the traditional nuclear family is offered as the perfect solution to Alison's dilemma

Media studies scholars spend a lot of their time and energy figuring out which views are privileged both in society and in its representations, and the explanations for these choices by those who create these texts. Often, image analysts find themselves dependent upon "reception studies" to illustrate that, although analysts may find one particular interpretation of a text to be "dominant," readers, viewers, or users sometimes interpret that same text differently. There are several classic examples in our literature that illustrate the openness of various texts to a series of competing interpretations.

One such study is the pathbreaking work *Reading the Romance* by American media scholar Janice Radway (1984). Radway found that although scholars had interpreted romance novels to tell the stories of weak and subservient women, fans of these works found the heroines in them uplifting, strong, and independent instead, and liked particular romances that stressed these qualities. Radway's reception study of actual fans opened up an entirely new line of textual analysis, revealing that romance novels were open to an entirely different perspective than scholars had previously thought. As feminist ideas had become more predominant in our culture, so romance readers had begun to read romances from a feminist perspective, looking for strong, independent heroines, rather than weak women ravaged by strong men. What were seen as the dominant meanings encoded in romance novels (e.g., messages against women's strength and independence) were actually found to be at odds with the types of meanings readers and fans identified in many of these novels, which often were entirely opposite readings.

New feminist perspectives have been termed by some as feminism's "third wave," or even "postfeminism." They have entirely rethought the relationship between romantic literature and other forms of popular culture, on one hand, and feminist ideas and meanings, on the other, in light of the findings of this and other reception studies, which have established the open nature of such texts.[6] Now, some scholars speak of the new "chick lit," which is an integral part of third-wave feminist culture.[7] According to these perspectives, the accoutrements of traditional femininity such as romance, or extremely feminine or highly sexualized clothing such as high heels or low-cut dresses – once rejected by second-wave feminists – can be reinterpreted by women and given feminist meanings. Romance novels or films can be seen as part of "women's culture," rather than products of the patriarchy manufactured to oppress women, as feminists had interpreted them before. Feminine and highly sexualized clothing can be seen as an active and feminist expression of women's sexuality, long suppressed in our culture.

Another classic case of multiple interpretations of a media text was found in the reception study of the popular 1970s television situation comedy *All in the Family*, developed by Norman Lear. Lear's apparently

liberal perspective seemed obvious to many media scholars, who interpreted the character of Archie Bunker, Lear's avowedly racist and sexist
leading character, critically. Contrary to critics' judgment that the show
was avowedly liberal, even radical, in its mocking perspective on Archie
Bunker's racism, sexism, homophobia, and general political conservatism,
audience studies of the show's actual reception revealed that many viewers
liked Archie and felt him worthy of emulation. These findings seemed to
fly in the face of Lear's intentions and of what seemed to scholars the
"obvious" intent of the creators of the show to expose racist and sexist
attitudes and beliefs in a critical light (Vidmar and Rokeach 1974).

A more recent example of the multiple meanings of various texts is the
2006 film *Borat*. Filmmaker Sacha Baron Cohen seemingly (according to
critics, and to Cohen himself in interviews) intended the film to be a
critique of the kinds of ignorant and unschooled attitudes and prejudices
that leading character Borat both elicits and exhibits. Borat often exposes,
in the course of the film, the ignorance of most Americans regarding the
world map and the social and political realities of other peoples. The film
features Cohen adopting the persona of a Kazakhstani television reporter
sent to the United States to make a documentary about American society
and culture. The film incorrectly portrays Kazakhstan as a prejudiced and
backward country and creates an entirely fictional persona for the character of the TV reporter Borat.

Borat is filmed in real-life settings with Americans who do not know
that Borat is actually Cohen, the actor, making an American film in which
they are characters. Their reactions to his fictional persona constitute the
humor of the film, and many of their prejudices, and their ignorance of
Kazakhstan, are depicted in the footage that results. While Cohen seemed
to be making the film in an attempt to uncover American prejudices and
ignorance of those from other parts of the world, there is evidence in the
critical literature and media attention inspired by the film's success that
the character Borat was often received as a likeable and indeed loveable
character by many actual viewers of the film, who might have shared
the character's prejudices (Klawans 2006).

These examples begin to illustrate how complex the issue of media
reception is. Therefore, a brief history of the findings of media reception
researchers is instructive for the purposes of this chapter. The impact of
popular media has been assessed in many different ways, and some brief discussion of the way researchers have approached this topic will be useful for
distilling exactly what the field of media studies has to offer on this issue.

Media Studies and the Study of Reception: A Brief History of Its Methods and Findings

Much has been written on the topic of media reception, certainly enough to merit an entire book of its own. In fact, many books have been written with precisely this focus.[8] Scholarly thought has moved from a simplistic theory of media reception – a stimulus–response model sometimes called the "magic bullet theory," or the "hypodermic needs theory" – predominating in the early years of media studies (Klapper 1960), to much more complex notions of how media convey meaning to viewers and users (Allor 1988; Livingstone 2003b). A brief survey of this journey will set the stage for a more in-depth discussion of reception study in the new media environment.

Early thinking about media reception imagined that the media presented information that then strongly influenced its viewers and users. This simple stimulus–response model, borrowed from psychology, placed the individual receiver between the stimulus of the media message, and the reaction to it. The "magic bullet theory" had an extremely simple view both of the kind of information communicated in the mass media, and of the way individuals, and social groups, derived meanings from this information. Rather than focusing on the multiple ways any type of information could be interpreted, and therefore the multiple meanings it might carry, the magic bullet theory imagined a simple type of information that then could be (figuratively, of course) "injected" into those who read, viewed, or used the media in question. Media influence was therefore a simple affair. Those who listened, read, or viewed were influenced by their exposure in clear, measureable ways.

The magic bullet theory, therefore, would deem the influence of *Knocked Up* as a simple assessment process: once the meaning of the text was determined (as per our discussion earlier in this chapter, which finds this, from a scholarly perspective, to be an overtly anti-abortion text), exposure should lead to opinion change (e.g., more Americans would turn against abortion rights, proportional to the number of viewers exposed to this text). The impact of television advertisements, for example, would also be easy to measure according to this perspective. A specific advertisement's influence could simply be measured by assessing how people's consumer behavior actually changed following exposure. If an ad for Comet cleanser was viewed by 4 million consumers, and sales of Comet increased measurably in the week following its airing, such a change in behavior would, according to this theory, be directly attributed to consumers viewing this ad. From this perspective, campaign ads during a presidential or other election could be similarly evaluated in terms of their impact on a candidate's poll standing.

Early on in reception research, the simplistic nature of a hypodermic theory of media influence was challenged. As we discussed in chapter 3, Lazarsfeld, Berelson, and Gaudet, in their influential book *The Peoples' Choice* (1948), studied the effects of political campaigning and discovered that campaign ads reinforced what voters already believed, and were highly affected by influential people who voters knew. Later, Lazarsfeld and Katz in their book *Personal Influence: The Part Played by People in the Flow of Mass Communications* (Katz and Lazarsfeld 1955) further elaborated and refined Lazarsfeld's earlier findings that the impact of media is tempered by the influence of important people and contacts. In their study, Katz and Lazarsfeld identified the influence of what they termed "opinion leaders," people who were influential amongst their peers and others in various communities. Katz and Lazarsfeld found that opinion leaders were important to the process of *how* the media influence people: media influence was not simply direct, but was tempered through their social influence.

These works offered some of the first empirical evidence that media influence was not the simple affair that early media studies scholars had thought. From the day in 1938 when Orson Welles read H. G. Wells' popular nineteenth-century novel *The War of the Worlds* (Wells 1898) over the radio, and millions had fled their homes as they heard what they thought was news of a Martian invasion, the public had adopted the idea that media influence was a straightforward affair. In this case, media reported, and the public believed. Katz and Lazarsfeld's findings challenged this simplistic view with their two-step flow theory. According to this theory, an opinion leader filters and tempers the influence of the media. So, for example, the teenaged girl who sees an ad for pre-torn jeans may be influenced either to buy them, or to ignore them, by the conversations she has in school with other friends, particularly with friends who sport fashions that most of the girls admire. Or the husband who views a political television commercial during a presidential campaign may be more influenced by the discussion he has with his wife afterward than by the commercial itself. Groups of teens viewing *Knocked Up* might influence each other greatly in their postfilm conversations, exceeding the film's influence on any individual teen viewer.

The study of media reception has gone through several stages. The introduction of television as a mass medium in the 1950s sparked a series of intensive studies of its influence on children, in particular by Hilde Himmelweit and her team (Himmelweit 1958). Social science studies of influence in the 1950s and 1960s often focused on the issues of television's influence on children (Hodge and Tripp 1986; MacBeth 1996; Pecora, Murray, and Wartella 2007), or on the media's influence on politics – in particular, on voting behavior (Klapper 1960). Such studies, again, often took the position that media influence could be extensive. Few had emphasized the abilities of audiences to critically process the information they received.

A body of work called the "uses and gratifications" tradition did set the stage for a different type of theory of the media audience, one which emphasized audiences as active rather than simply passively being affected by media. In particular, uses and gratifications research emphasized that audiences used media to satisfy various psychological needs (Rosengren 1974). It was a functionalist, systems-oriented method that detailed the many useful functions that media served for users. Uses and gratifications research used primarily survey methods to investigate the types of uses that audience members made of the media, or the gratifications they received from the media they used. One study, for example, found watching was a "habit," because it was a good way to pass the time (Greenberg 1974, quoted in Schroder 1999: 41). These findings were contradicted by another study (Rubin 1986), which found that people's main reasons for watching television related to program content (quoted in Schroder 1999: 41) and their appreciation of particular shows. While their findings differed, the focus in all of these studies was on the uses that individuals made of television watching, or of other types of media.

Over the next few decades the tradition that came to be known as "active audience" research grew, shaping the field of reception in media studies in new ways. Researchers in the active audience tradition built on the findings of uses and gratifications researchers to stress the abilities of audiences to consciously and deliberately appropriate, interpret, and use media products. But active audience researchers focused more on the social meanings of media, and on whether and how audiences accepted, appropriated, or resisted those meanings. The notion that audiences "resist" the meanings they encountered in the media became central to this tradition, because in part this tradition rested on a critical interpretation of media content as reflecting dominant social values, particularly with regard to identity issues such as gender, social class, race, sexuality, and ethnicity, as we further discuss in chapter 5.

Many date the inception of active audience research to the publication in 1984 of Janice Radway's influential book *Reading the Romance* (1984), which we have discussed. As we described, Radway investigated the way women fans of mass-marketed romance paperbacks interpreted the books they loved. One of her findings, counter to then-current feminist interpretations of romance novels as sexist and harmful to women, was that the fans she interviewed found strong, feminist heroines in their romance novels, and interpreted many of the stories as feminist. Another was that fans used their reading time to actively claim space for themselves, away from the multiple demands of workdays that for many included round-the-clock housework and child care. And, indeed, both these findings supported the key tenets of the active audience tradition. Romance readers were not cultural dupes, influenced by the books to lose themselves in futile romantic fantasies. Instead, they were consciously constructing role models from the strong women heroines who populated the books most appealing to them.

Following Radway, a spate of media studies scholars found that audiences actively appropriated many types of media otherwise thought of as harmful or strongly influential. Ang (1985), Brown (1990, 1994), Press (1991), and Liebes and Livingstone (1994; see also Livingstone and Liebes 1998) studied the way women appropriated television soap operas in ways similar to those Radway discussed for romance readers.

Fiske (1991, 1994; see also Fiske and Hartley 1978) became one of the most widely read of the active audience theorists. The most famous statement of the active audience position is probably Fiske's description of the way young women fans of the pop artist Madonna spoke about her image and message. While Madonna was generally felt to offer a rather nonfeminist image of overt sexual display, Fiske hypothesized that many of her fans actually read her as a feminist image of a powerful woman who took ownership of her sexuality (Fiske 1991). Seeing fans' feminist interpretations of Madonna involved a major revisioning of her as spectacle and media image, transforming her from a very traditional, mainstream, sexualized, and objectified female image to one that challenged these very values in mainstream media representations.

Liebes and Katz (1993) extended active audience theory into the global comparative realm, finding that the American soap opera *Dallas* was read and evaluated differently by viewers of different ethnic backgrounds in different national contexts (they studied Arab and Jewish viewers in Israel, Japanese viewers in Japan, and other groups as well, all viewing the same televisual texts). For example, although the prime-time soap opera was extremely popular in the United States and Israel, in Japan the show did not succeed. Their study revealed that this was true in part because the cultural attitudes of the Japanese made it incomprehensible that women could treat senior family members with as little respect as that depicted in the show.

Scholars like Jenkins (1992, 2006), Bacon-Smith (1992), and Lewis (1992) looked at fan groups and their active appropriation of various media texts, and fan cultures became a large subtopic amongst active audience researchers. Both Jenkins and Camille Bacon-Smith's work investigated in depth the way fans of the long-running television series *Star Trek* actively and imaginatively appropriated, rewrote, and reimagined the show's characters and plots. Imagining gay sex between Kirk and Spock was a major theme in fans' rewritten texts, and marked a significant extension and departure from the overt meanings of the stories as presented on the popular television shows.

In some important respects, the active audience tradition supported Katz and Lazarsfeld's model. Certainly the sense that media effects are not all-encompassing, and do not reduce viewers or media users to passive "dupes," is the same in each tradition. Those who focused on the social harms of various types of mass media were at times disturbed by these arguments, since they seem to downplay some of the potentially harmful social impacts of the proliferation of mass media.

Others have taken issue with what they see as too pronounced a focus on audience resistance to media influence. Responding in part to Lazarsfeld and Katz, and in part to some of the evidence political scientists have discovered regarding the limited impact of political advertisements on voting behavior and choices, sociologist Todd Gitlin argued against theories of limited media influence, asserting that they did "not see the forest for the trees" (1978). He stressed that – and this is even more relevant in the new media environment – the fact that media are so ubiquitous in our culture indicates that any attempt to isolate their influence is bound to be incomplete. The impossibility of controlled studies comparing our media-saturated society to one less saturated precluded the possibility of accurate academic information about the actual reach of media influence. Media studies scholars were left to simply, and abstractly, "theorize" media influence in general, rather than to conduct controlled research studies of its specific, actual influence on particular aspects of our beliefs and behaviors. This made the social science community at times reluctant to take the findings of the field of media studies seriously. Yet many prominent media studies scholars have argued that theorizing about media influence ought to be taken seriously in the case of a media-saturated society that could hardly turn back (Gitlin 2007). The media studies field, as a result, remains poised between the humanities and the social sciences, with one foot planted firmly in each camp.

Press' own previously published work (1991; Press and Cole 1999) shows the influence of Gitlin's theoretical perspective in her tempered use of the active audience tradition. In studying prime-time television, she found that it both influences and is appropriated by women of different social classes and ages (1991), and women with different perspectives on the abortion issue (Press and Cole 1999). For example, Press found that working-class women were influenced by the fact that most families pictured on prime-time television were middle class or upper class. This influence led them to believe that they would ultimately achieve this level of prosperity, unrealistic as this was given the educational level and occupational skills of many of the women she interviewed. Yet on another level, they took issue with the representations of working-class life that they did see on the medium. So, for example, one woman found the working-class waitress Alice, featured on the show of that name, to be an unrealistic image in many ways, living in a house that was inconveniently arranged and speaking rudely of her boss to her customers. Yet the same woman did not find the Cosby family unrealistic, although they mirrored the situation of few African-American families of the time. Middle-class women, in contrast, attended more to the gender-specific images they viewed. So if the women pictured on television were thin, white, and blonde, and displayed typical "feminine" behaviors such as passivity or excessive "niceness," it was these aspects of television's images most discussed by this group.

This tendency to acknowledge that media can still influence, though audiences are often active, is the direction of much of the more current reception work in media studies, which tends to combine the insights of active audience theory with other theories of media influence. Recently, for example, Skeggs, Thumim, and Wood (2008) found that reality television actually reinforces and helps reproduce inequalities between working-class and middle-class women. The shows they looked at included *Wife Swap*, a show in which wives trade families for a period of time, living in another woman's family and dealing with her husband, children, family traditions, and housework. This and other shows focused on women's construction of an explicitly middle-class type of self as part of the story that the show told. Working-class women were uncomfortable with the values these shows often supported, values that included a high-achieving working mother, a disciplined household, and quiet, high-achieving children. They took issue with the perspective endorsed by the shows on these activities, which were pictured as desirable for women but were in fact ultracritical of many of the values that working-class women held, and expressed these views actively in discussions with researchers and each other.

Conclusion

Reception study and image analysis in media studies offer us the tools to go beyond our commonsense readings and apply historical, sociological, economic, literary, and other analytical frames that help us to contextualize and critically analyze the media images we see. Media studies scholars have been particularly interested in looking at the different forms of inequality that have informed media representations over the decades. Borrowing from scholarship in the humanities and the social sciences, which have for several decades now identified gender, race, class, and sexuality as the four fault lines, or cleavages, around which inequality coalesces, media studies scholars examine the way media contribute to how these various types of inequalities are maintained and reproduced. In chapter 5, we will consider a series of key works and traditions in the field, each of which contributes to our developing perspective on inequalities in society, and on how the media contribute to maintaining, and overturning, these inequalities.

Notes

1. On the issue of mothers in literature, see Walters (1992). On mothers in film, see Kaplan (1992).
2. A recent poll by the Pew Research Center for the Internet and the Press (2009) indicates that more Americans support legalized abortion than oppose it.
3. See Daley (1991). Later, following the birth of her third child, Vieira returned to broadcasting and resumed an extremely successful career culminating in her

current position as anchor of the morning news program *The Today Show*. However, for years she was plagued with comments questioning her dedication to her work, sparked by her pregnancies. See Kurtz (2007) for an in-depth discussion of decisions at ABC that led to Elizabeth Vargas being let go after only a few months as evening news anchor, coincident with her second pregnancy and the birth of her second child.

4. See for example Morley's discussion of media reception study, and other discussions of the nature of media reception: Livingstone (2003b) and Morley (1992).
5. See especially here Williams (1977) and Hall (1980).
6. On third-wave feminism, see McRobbie (2004) and Hogeland (2001).
7. See Gill and Herdieckerhoff (2006).
8. See, for example, Silverstone (1994), Ang (1996), Alasuutari (1999), Lotz (2000), Bird (2003), Schroder (1999), and many others.

References

Alasuutari, P., ed. 1999. *Rethinking the media audience: The new agenda*. London: Sage.

Allor, Martin. 1988. "Relocating the site of audience." *Critical Studies in Media Communication* 5:217–33.

Ang, Ian. 1996. *Living room wars: Rethinking media audiences for a postmodern world*. London: Routledge.

Bacon-Smith, Camille. 1992. *Enterprising women: Television fandom and the creation of popular myth*. Philadelphia: University of Pennsylvania Press.

Bird, Elizabeth. 2003. *The audience in everyday life: Living in a media world*. New York: Routledge.

Brown, Mary Ellen. 1990. *Television and women's culture: The politics of the popular*. London: Sage.

Brown, Mary Ellen. 1994. *Soap opera and women's talk: The pleasure of resistance*. Thousand Oaks, C.A.: Sage.

Daley, Suzanne, 1991. "Networks, motherhood and careers." *New York Times*, March 4.

Douglas, Susan J., and Meredith W. Michaels. 2005. *The mommy myth: The idealization of motherhood and how it has undermined all women*. New York: Free Press.

Faludi, Susan. 1991. *Backlash: The undeclared war against American women*. New York: Crown.

Fiske, John. 1991. *Television culture*. London: Routledge.

Fiske, John. 1994. *Media matters: Everyday culture and political change*. Minneapolis: University of Minnesota Press.

Fiske, John, and John Hartley. 1978. *Reading television*. London: Methuen.

Gill, R., and E. Herdieckerhoff. 2006. "Rewriting the romance: New femininities in chick lit?" *Feminist Media Studies* 6(4):487–504.

Gitlin, Todd. 1978. "Media sociology: The dominant paradigm." *Theory and Society* 6:205–53.

Gitlin, Todd. 2007. *Media unlimited: How the torrent of images and sounds overwhelms our lives.* New York: Henry Holt.

Goodman, Ellen. 2008. "In the movies, she keeps the baby." *Alternet*, January 3. www.alternet.org/reproductivejustice/72405/in_the_movies,_she_keeps_the_baby/.

Greenberg, Bradley S. 1974. "British children and televised violence." *Public Opinion Quarterly* 38:531–47.

Hall, Stuart. 1980. *Culture, media, language: Working papers in cultural studies, 1972–79.* London: Hutchinson.

Himmelweit, Hilde T. 1958. *Television and the child: An empirical study of the effect of television on the young.* London: Published for the Nuffield Foundation by the Oxford University Press.

Hodge, Bob, and David Tripp. 1986. *Children and television: A semiotic approach.* Cambridge and Oxford: Polity Press in association with Basil Blackwell.

Hogeland, L. M. 2001. "Against generational thinking, or, some things that 'third wave' feminism isn't." *Women's Studies in Communication* 24:107–21.

Jenkins, Henry. 1992. *Textual poachers: Television fans & participatory culture.* New York: Routledge.

Kaplan, E. Ann. 1992. *Motherhood and representation: The mother in popular culture and melodrama.* London: Routledge.

Katz, Elihu, and Paul Felix Lazarsfeld. 1955. *Personal influence: The part played by people in the flow of mass communications.* New York: Free Press.

Klapper, Joseph T. 1960. *The effects of mass communication.* Glencoe, I.L.: Free Press.

Klawans, Stuart. 2006. "Coming to America!" *Nation* 283:32–36.

Kurtz, Howard. 2007. *Reality show: Inside the last great television news war.* New York: Free Press.

Lazarsfeld, Paul Felix, Bernard Berelson, and Hazel Gaudet. 1948. *The people's choice: How the voter makes up his mind in a presidential campaign.* New York: Columbia University Press.

Lewis, Lisa A. 1992. *The adoring audience: Fan culture and popular media.* London: Routledge.

Liebes, Tamar, and Elihu Katz. 1993. *The export of meaning: Cross-cultural readings of Dallas.* Cambridge: Polity Press.

Liebes, Tamar, and Sonia Livingstone. 1994. "The structure of family and romantic ties in the soap opera: An ethnographic approach." *Communication Research* 21:717–41.

Livingstone, Sonia. 2003a. "Children's use of the Internet: Reflections on the emerging research agenda." *New Media Society* 5:147–66.

Livingstone, Sonia M. 2003b. "The changing nature of audiences." In *The Blackwell companion to media research*, edited by A. N. Valdivia, pp. 337–59. Oxford: Blackwell.

Livingstone, Sonia M., and Moira Bovill. 2001. *Children and their changing media environment: A European comparative study.* Mahwah, N.J.: Lawrence Erlbaum.

Livingstone, Sonia, and Tamar Liebes. 1998. "European soap operas: The diversification of a genre." *European Journal of Communication* 13:147–80.

Lotz, Amanda. 2006. *Redesigning women: Television after the network era.* Urbana: University of Illinois Press.

MacBeth, Tannis M. 1996. *Tuning in to young viewers: Social perspectives on television.* Thousand Oaks, C.A.: Sage.

McRobbie, Angela. 2004. "Post-feminism and popular culture." *Feminist Media Studies* 4:255–64.

Morley, David. 1992. *Television, audiences, and cultural studies.* London: Routledge.

Pecora, Norma Odom, John P. Murray, and Ellen Wartella. 2007. *Children and television: Fifty years of research.* Mahwah, N.J.: Lawrence Erlbaum.

Pew Research Center for the Internet and the Press. 2009. "Support for abortion slips: Issue ranks lower on the agenda." October 1. http://people-press.org/report/549/support-for-abortion-slips.

Pollitt, Katha. 2008. "Maternity fashions, junior style." *The Nation*, January 3.

Press, Andrea Lee. 1991. *Women watching television: Gender, class, and generation in the American television experience.* Philadelphia: University of Pennsylvania Press.

Press, Andrea Lee, and Elizabeth R. Cole. 1999. *Speaking of abortion: Television and authority in the lives of women.* Chicago: University of Chicago Press.

Radway, Janice A. 1984. *Reading the romance: Women, patriarchy, and popular literature.* Chapel Hill: University of North Carolina Press.

Rosengren, Karl Eric. 1974. "Uses and gratifications: A paradigm outlined." In *The uses of mass communications*, edited by J. G. Blumler and E. Katz, pp. 269–86. Beverly Hills, C.A.: Sage.

Rubin, Alan. 1986. "Uses, gratifications, and media effects research." In *Perspectives on media effects*, edited by B. Jennings and D. Zillmann. Hillsdale, N.J.: Lawrence Erlbaum.

Schroder, Kim. 1999. "The best of both worlds? Media audience research between rival paradigms." In *Rethinking the media audience: The new agenda*, edited by P. Alasuutari. London: Sage.

Silverstone, Roger. 1994. *Television and everyday life.* London: Routledge.

Skeggs, Bev, Nancy Thumim, and Helen Wood. 2008. " 'Oh goodness, I am watching reality TV': How methods make class in audience research." *European Journal of Cultural Studies* 11:5–24.

Vidmar, Neil, and Milton Rokeach. 1974. "Archie Bunker's bigotry: A study in selective perception and exposure." *The Journal of Communication* 24: 36–47.

Walters, Suzanna Danuta. 1992. *Lives together/worlds apart: Mothers and daughters in popular culture.* Berkeley: University of California Press.

Wells, H. G. 1898. *The war of the worlds.* London: Heinemann.

Williams, Raymond. 1973. *Marxism and literature.* Oxford: Oxford University Press.

Chapter 5

Studying Inequalities
Class, Gender, Race, and Sexuality in Media Studies

The critical study of representations of gender, race, class, sexuality, and the media has a long history in the field of media studies. Scholars in the field have devoted much effort toward describing the history of biases in the representation of these issues in film, television, and radio, and now in analyzing such biases in the use of the new technologies, such as the Internet and cell phone, which define the new media environment. These findings are generally important for everyone in our society to know, and remain relevant to understanding our continually evolving media environment. Though dominant media forms have changed and are still changing, many argue that the stereotypes that media have helped to create persist in an alarmingly reliable fashion.

In this chapter we consider scholarly findings about the way media represent various social inequalities and forms of social oppression – in particular social class, gender, race, and sexuality – in order to form the basis for our concluding discussion of how we are beginning to transport the study of inequalities into scholarly understandings of the new media environment.

A Critical Perspective on Inequality in Media Studies

The case of *The Wire*, an HBO television series that began in 2002 and continued through 2008, serves as an excellent example of television

**Official HBO summary of episode 1, season 1 of
The Wire, "The Target"**

Directed by: Clark Johnson
Story by: David Simon and Ed Burns
Teleplay by: David Simon

Baltimore Homicide Detective Jimmy McNulty drops in on the murder trial of young drug dealer D'Angelo Barksdale, who is acquitted because witnesses are reluctant to testify against him.

Across town, Narcotics Detective Shakima "Kima" Greggs searches a car stopped in a drug bust more thoroughly than her male colleagues and finds two additional guns hidden in the back seat.

McNulty had been checking out Barksdale's trial because his uncle, Avon Barksdale, is a major terror in the drug life of the high-rises, and tells the judge in the courtroom that the force has been too busy to follow them. McNulty's boss reprimands him for speaking to the judge as now he is under pressure to produce a report on Barksdale. Now a new unit is organized to pursue Barksdale, and many are pissed off at McNulty for starting all this trouble. McNulty claims they must use surveillance and wiretaps to capture Barksdale but then visits FBI Agent Fitzhugh, who shows him sophisticated TV technology the FBI has used to film drug deals, not yet available to the police.

McNulty complains over drinks to partner Moreland that his ex-wife prevents him from seeing his two kids enough. D'Angelo drinks at a stripper bar. Greggs arrives home, where she is kissed by her girlfriend.

Another dead body turns up in the middle of the projects. The victim had identified Barksdale as the shooter in his murder trial. D'Angelo sees the body, recognizes who it is and why he was shot, and suffers pangs of conscience.

Source: Adapted from HBO (2009).

programming in the current media environment. Set in Baltimore and loosely based on two nonfiction books depicting the real situation of police and drug dealers in the inner city, the show courts verisimilitude

Figure 5.1. Sonja Sohn as Detective Shakima "Kima" Greggs, Dominic West as Detective James "Jimmy" McNulty, and Clarke Peters as Detective Lester Freamon in HBO's *The Wire*.

by shooting on location in Baltimore and casting nonactors for many of its roles, including former prisoners and drug dealers. As a result, the look of the show, and the people on it, departs dramatically from the conventions of popular television. (See Figure 5.1.)

Certainly the show is unrecognizable when compared with television shows characterizing the network era (Taylor 1989; Coontz 1992; Spigel 1995). Television's "network era" normally refers to the decades of the 1960s, 1970s, and 1980s, when the most viewed television shows in the US were aired on the three major television networks, ABC, CBS, and NBC. It arose out of an early phase in the 1950s during which television programming was characterized by considerable ethnic and socioeconomic diversity (Lipsitz 2001) in such shows as *The Goldbergs* or *I Remember Mama*, discussed in more detail below. The network era that succeeded early-1950s television depicted, through most of its decades, overwhelmingly white, middle-class, often intact families, "happy people with happy problems" as scholars are fond of saying (Spigel 1995). Sponsor pressure was a big part of this – they wanted their products associated with affluent, middle-class American homes, rather than the downscale sets of *The Honeymooners* or *The Goldbergs*, which were no way to sell products and promote consumerism.

Yet the rise of cable television, and the concomitant proliferation of television channels (many of which are available only to homes who subscribe to them by paying a fee – fees that replace the advertising revenue that supports network television), has given rise to a different sort of programming than characterized the network era. Now we witness more targeted, niche programming, and more overall diversity of representations on prime-time television. Producers of television for the paying cable audience are not limited by the responsibilities inherent in producing for the public airwaves; they are not forced to censor potentially offensive images to the same degree as those airing on the free networks.

In the HBO show *The Wire*, and in many other cable shows, we see a departure from the "happy people with happy problems" norm. On *The Wire*, multiple members of what some sociologists term "the underclass" are represented; many of the main characters are nonwhite, as well as non-middle class; two of the main characters are a lesbian couple; and many of the women are represented in non-stereotypical-looking ways. For these reasons we have chosen to use *The Wire*, in its different dimensions, to introduce the different segments of this chapter.

The Wire has often been lauded for its nontraditional, realistic, and detailed depiction of poor African-American inner-city characters, many of whom are connected to, or are themselves, drug dealers. In the episode just summarized, we meet a drug lord, D'Angelo Barksdale, and several of the police who attempt to shut down his business. In many other episodes we meet African-American children living in Barksdale's neighborhood who are employed by him, and sometimes imprisoned, or even killed, as a result of the work they do in his drug-dealing business. We meet their families, enter their apartments, and generally become acquainted with their way of life, a life with which few middle-class whites (who form the majority of HBO's subscribers) are familiar.

Are these images a departure from the way poor blacks, and whites, have traditionally appeared on television and in other media? If so, how?

How does exposure to these images affect the white, middle-class audience that constitutes the majority of its viewers? These are some of the questions addressed in the discussion that follows, which recounts the way various inequalities and identities have been depicted in mainstream media, and how researchers in media studies have assessed these images and their influence on our society.

A concern with the relationship between media and inequality can be traced to two separate theoretical traditions in media studies, influenced by the writings of both Karl Marx in the nineteenth century and his subsequent twentieth-century interpreters. The first is the Frankfurt School, and the second is cultural studies.

The Frankfurt School

The Frankfurt School was a group of German Jewish émigrés who traveled to the United States to escape the Nazis during the 1930s. Specifically, in a work of Max Horkheimer and Theodor Adorno entitled "The Culture Industry: Enlightenment as Mass Deception" (1944), but in other essays as well, the Frankfurt School turned their attention to the impact of Hollywood films on society. They argued that popular Hollywood products were actually mass-produced mass entertainment, which served the purpose of dulling the critical consciousness of the vast majority of people who constituted their audience, in particular the working classes. (See especially Adorno 1954a; Benjamin 1977.)

The Frankfurt School, in their writings, singled out various movies and television programs for particular mention. In one essay Adorno (1954b) discusses the early television show *Our Miss Brooks*. The show pictured the single schoolteacher Miss Brooks. One show made fun of how little money she made and, consequently, how little she had to eat. Adorno criticized the show in this essay for belittling the problems of low-paid workers under the capitalist system, who often did not earn enough wages to eat, or to live well. The show, he argued, encouraged viewers to receive this plight comically, rather than to seriously consider political action that might help to increase the wages that workers earned.

Cultural studies

In 1950s Britain, a different sort of attention – but again inspired by the works of Karl Marx – began to be turned toward popular culture. With the works of Raymond Williams and Richard Hoggart (Williams 1958, 1961, 1966, 1976; Hoggart 1998), conventionally accepted views about the elite nature of great literature – and, in fact, the nature of high culture itself – began to be challenged. These scholars argued that culture was not the province merely of the elite, but was "ordinary," and that important cultural works were made and consumed by the lower classes as well as the higher classes. This set the stage for serious, indeed politicized, attention to popular culture that went beyond the dismissive attitudes of the Frankfurt School, who had argued that popular culture contrasted sharply with high culture, and was by definition "mass produced" from above for the purposes of pacifying the great mass of people who received it. Out of Williams' and Hoggart's work, the field of cultural studies was born in the United Kingdom. Cultural studies linked popular culture with the political concerns of those who were members of lower or marginalized class groups.

Institutionalized first at the Centre for Contemporary Cultural Studies of the University of Birmingham in 1964 under the direction of Richard Hoggart and then Stuart Hall, cultural studies focused on the intersections of culture and ideology (Kellner 2006: 141) but argued that useful and resistant forms of popular culture could potentially be created by the popular cultural audience. The emerging tradition of cultural studies in the United Kingdom spawned a number of works on media reception, media production, social movements, and what has become known as "subcultures," pockets or spaces in which culture is appropriated in ways that resist dominant cultural values and meanings. Works produced by the early cultural studies scholars included a study of crime coverage and its social impact (Hall, Critcher, Jefferson, Clarke, and Roberts 1978), the interpretation of television news shows (Morley with Brunsdon 1978), and the cultural influence of images in popular teenage girls' magazines (McRobbie 1991).

The legacy of what has become known as "Birmingham School" cultural studies has produced some of the most significant works in media studies. Their focus has tended to be on social class inequalities, race, and gender, and the way the mass media either contribute to them or help to counter them. David Morley's important works on television and its reception serve here as paradigmatic examples of this tradition. In his work, Morley draws on the earlier work of Raymond Williams, Antonio Gramsci, and Stuart Hall.

Raymond Williams' (1958, 1961, 1966, 1976, 1991) work was particularly influential in inspiring the later, media-oriented work of the

Birmingham School. Williams most famously, in an essay entitled "Base and Superstructure in Marxist Theory" (Williams 1991), developed a typology of the types of ideologies encoded in cultural and media products: "dominant," which we have already discussed; "oppositional," which referred to the ideologies that explicitly differed from, and opposed, the dominant perspectives; and "alternative," related to ideologies simply different from the dominant perspective.

So, for example, using Williams' categories, we might say that a dominant reading of the film *Knocked Up* would find it a lighthearted romantic comedy, while an oppositional reading might find it an antifeminist diatribe given its support for the traditional nuclear family and its refusal to treat the choice of abortion seriously. An alternative reading might stress the positive image of "boys' culture" that the film highlights in its treatment of the boyfriend Ben's character and his culture of friends, and Alison's brother-in-law Pete's character and his culture of friends. All readings of this text are possible, though again, it remains for the audience analyst to determine which are most prevalent, and which audience members view the film through which particular lenses.

The concept of the "hegemonic ideology," developed by the Italian cultural theorist Antonio Gramsci, became influential in Birmingham School cultural theory after initial translations of Gramsci's work were first published in English in 1971 (see Gramsci, Hoare, and Nowell-Smith 1971). This notion implied that social coercion takes place partly through the cultural or media products societies produce, in that these products are constructed so as to encourage certain beliefs and attitudes that are then internalized by those who listen to, read, view, or otherwise receive these cultural products. The film *Knocked Up* promulgates a hegemonic ideology in terms of social class as follows. Most of the characters are depicted as living a middle-class lifestyle, which is presented as normal and, indeed, almost universal in American society. Though Ben is essentially unemployed, basically a slacker – whacked out on drugs much of the time, and living a fun, undisciplined lifestyle – in the course of the film we see him following a path that will lead him to a sober, middle-class normalcy. By marrying Alison he will acquire a middle-class lifestyle by connecting himself to her salary and lifestyle. The assumption we make, as viewers of the film, is that Ben will himself soon have a job, yielding his own middle-class income.

In contrast, *The Wire*, by explicitly portraying the lower class throughout much of the show, deviates from the hegemonic portrayal of middle-class life that predominates on entertainment television in the United States. For that reason, *The Wire* may be read as an oppositional show vis-à-vis social class and its customary, hegemonic portrayal. The theory of hegemony argues that citizens are disciplined through ideas, rather than by external force. The idea of hegemony is central to Birmingham School cultural studies and to much later work in media studies (see Press in press).

Stuart Hall's seminal essay "Encoding and Decoding in the Television Discourse" (1973) is an important cultural studies text. In this essay Hall had argued that meanings in television texts can take one of several forms. First (following Williams), there is what he calls a "preferred reading" or a dominant reading, which most closely conforms to the views of the dominant culture that informs the cultural industry that produces mainstream television shows. Viewers can read the dominant meanings, or they can interpret the meanings in the text in what Hall calls a "negotiated" way, which incorporates some aspects of the dominant readings, or in an "oppositional" way that entirely opposes it.

How viewers will decode a text depends in part, according to Hall, upon their situatedness within a particular social class position, or on other aspects of their social position. While these categories are easier to apply to news programs that might have a particular point of view, they are less easy to apply to the case of cultural products like entertainment television or film, including films like *Knocked Up* as in the example above.

Media studies research findings on class, gender, race, and sexuality

Reception research David Morley's work on television reception is important in that it gives us examples of attempts to apply these earlier theoretical concepts to the context of mediated modern life. His first influential study was written up in two books, *Everyday Television: Nationwide* (with Charlotte Brunsdon; 1978), and later *The Nationwide Audience* (Morley 1980). In the first book, Morley and Brunsdon code the content and meanings of a popular British evening news television show according to its political resonance and slant. In the reception study *The Nationwide Audience*, Morley organizes group interviews with members of different types of occupations, members of different social classes, and different genders (some women's groups, some men's groups) to probe how they interpreted and received a particular episode of the news program according to Williams' schema of dominant, oppositional, and alternative ideologies.

What he found is that people's gender, and their social class and occupational positions, strongly inflected and influenced their interpretations of the meanings of the television show *Nationwide*. This set the stage for the ideas, developed further with the American cultural studies tradition (Barker 2008; Grossberg 1992; Grossberg, Nelson, and Treichler 1992; Schwichtenberg 1992),[1] that audiences receive media content actively, rather than being passively influenced by the ideological content and ideas encoded in the media. Those who were inclined to be critical of social and political policies – the homeless, for example, members of the underclass who constituted one of Morley's groups; or union workers, members of the working class who constituted another – were also able to read the news program critically or oppositionally, in Williams' terms, and to perceive cracks in the dominant or hegemonic ideologies that they saw embodied in the show. Middle-class bank managers, in contrast, did not see these oppositional elements in the show. They read it as supporting the hegemonic or dominant ideology that a capitalist system was fair and worthy of support. Morley's position, then, is that social class is certainly an important determinant of one's reading of dominant media.

Two examples of our own work (Press 1991; Press and Cole 1999) illustrate the need to look at gender and class together, as both are variables that interact to influence how women interpret popular television. These works build on Morley's research to engage the issues of social class inequality and television reception, and take seriously his emphasis on the importance of studying viewers or users of media, and not just analyzing media texts in abstraction from their reception. As discussed in chapter 4, Press' books *Women Watching Television* (1991) and *Speaking of Abortion* (Press and Cole 1999) investigate the way American women of different social classes watch American television and interpret it in particular ways, building on the work of Antonio Gramsci to look at how prime-time television helped to promote and reproduce hegemonic ideologies of gender and class in US society. For example, Press' findings in the former (1991) were that for working-class women, the middle-class biases of prime-time television were most salient, and helped them to construct a picture of American society in which the middle-class experience was dominant and overshadowed their own. This illustrated the power of the hegemonic ideology in establishing the "normal" view of society. The finding that for middle-class women, television reinforced traditional norms of appropriate gendered behavior and appearance for women, norms that were currently being called into question by the feminist movement, illustrated the continuing importance of their gender identity in the perspective of women of the middle class.

In *Speaking of Abortion*, Press and Cole reinforce Morley's finding that the meanings of television images can be highly variable, depending on an individual's social class position, and in this case adherence to particular religious, ethical, and moral viewpoints on the abortion issue. Women viewed television treatments of abortion differently depending on whether they were working class or middle class, religious or secular, and pro-life or pro-choice. This study well illustrated that no particular dominant perspectives in these television entertainment products could be assumed to receive a uniform interpretation from different types of viewers. Social class is a variable that certainly deserves further investigation in our literature. But Morley's pathbreaking work has ensured that the tradition of looking at this variable in the study of media reception continues.

Image analysis   Turning to image analysis, media studies scholars have examined the history of social class representations in our dominant media (Lipsitz 1990; Press and Strathman 1993; Foster 2005). A few examples will illustrate the importance of social class biases in these media. One notable case is the plethora of popular Hollywood films depicting the lives of the fabulously rich that were produced during the 1930s, at the same time that US society was undergoing the Great Depression, in which hunger and poverty were widespread (Muscio 1997). The tendency to bombard society with images of the fabulously rich helped to establish the tradition of escapism that came to be expected in the American media, particularly in Hollywood film and television but also in the currently popular entertainment format for news media, as we've discussed earlier in this book.

The social problem films of the 1950s and 1960s again established a tradition in American (and British) films, this time of presenting issues – often social class related – plaguing both societies. Examples of the latter include the treatment of anti-Semitism in *Gentleman's Agreement* (1947); criticism of the life of the suburban "company man" in *The Man in the Gray Flannel Suit* (1956); and criticism of restrictive attitudes toward female sexuality in relation to the desire for upward mobility in *Ruby Gentry* (1952), *A Summer Place* (1959), and the renowned *West Side Story* (1961).

The British film industry has a particular tradition of realistic portrayals of social class, particularly films of the British New Wave in the late 1950s and early 1960s.[2] Sometimes called the tradition of "kitchen sink realism," these films borrowed from the documentary movement to display working-class life, and various social problems, with gritty realism. Amongst the best-known British New Wave films were *A Taste of Honey* (1961), which portrayed working-class life, and *Leather Boys* (1964), which concerned the previously taboo subjects of homosexuality and abortion.

American television has its own history of treatment of social class (Lipsitz 2001), long displaying a middle-class bias (Press 1991). As we discussed above in this chapter, in the early years of the situation comedy, there were a series of specifically ethnic and working-class characters in popular shows like *The Honeymooners* (1952–6), about a white working-class bus driver and his wife in New York City; *The Goldbergs* (1949–4), about a Jewish family living in the Bronx; *Mama* (1949–57), about a Norwegian immigrant family; and *The Life of Riley* (1953–58), about a white working-class aircraft plant worker and his family living in California. Serious dramatic series treated the social problem of poor and minority Americans; some examples of these early series are *East Side West Side* (1963–4), about the problems of a social worker in New York City; and *Route 66* (1960–4), focusing on two adventurers who tour the United States and help the oppressed people they encounter.

However, by the mid- to late 1960s, representations of the working class and their problems had waned. Times were changing in the United States, and the flight from the cities to the new location of the suburbs was having an impact on the types of representations we saw on prime-time television (Spigel 1992; Spigel and Mann 1992). It was at this moment that most American television programming became infused with a middle-class bias. Shows like *Father Knows Best* (1960–72), *Bewitched* (1964–72), *The Brady Bunch* (1969–74), and many others replaced television's early working-class and ethnic families with a series of white, middle-class families featuring a different set of problems set in a different ambience and social context (see Figure 5.2). While in part these changes in television programming – with its increasingly suburban location and focus on the nuclear family – reflected the changing demographic of the United States, the changes in programming themselves also influenced the hopes, dreams, and visions of Americans living during this era. This complex interaction between reality and its representation is one of the key areas of interest for media studies scholars.

Figure 5.2. The all-American family of ABC's *The Brady Bunch*.

During the era of social unrest in the United States in the 1960s and 1970s, society changed rapidly, and television programming shifted as well. Urban flight continued, and the feminist and civil rights movements began to have an impact on society at this point; both were reflected in changes in prime-time television. Several shows featuring single women in the leading roles appeared on prime time: *That Girl*, about a young woman attempting to become an actress (1965–71), appeared in 1965; and *The Mary Tyler Moore Show*, featuring a rather more mature single heroine pursuing a career in journalism, appeared in 1970 and continued through the decade (1970–7).

In addition, we began to see nonwhites featured in some prime-time situation comedy shows: *Julia* (1968–71), for example, which featured the African-American actress Diahann Carroll playing a widowed single mother who worked as a nurse. Social activism itself is reflected in a slew of 1970s situation comedies by producer Norman Lear, including *All in the Family*, about a racist white working-class man and his family; *Maude*, about an older feminist woman; and *Sanford and Son*, about an African-American junk dealer and his son.

As mentioned above when introducing this section, currently we have witnessed an increase in the complexity and variety of images of social class, together with race, gender, and sexuality, on television, particularly in cable shows like *The Wire*. One result of this departure is the increased diversity of images now seen on prime-time television. On *The Wire*, for example, one sees women who do not have the upper-middle-class look of the "airbrushed," model-thin images more often seen on television. Instead, these women represent a range of ages, races, and sexual orientations wider than that in other television representations.

Featuring a plethora of characters from various racial backgrounds, *The Wire* presents race differently as well: rather than relying on racial stereotypes, representations are more nuanced. African-American characters, for example, range from drug dealers and users on the street to police commissioners and mayoral candidates. Several of the characters, including a black lesbian police officer with a steady, live-in girlfriend, stand in sharp contrast to the glamorized images characterizing cable television's show specifically about lesbians and their lifestyles, *The L Word*.

In all, the diversity of gender, racial, social class, and sexual representations offered by *The Wire* and other television, particularly subscription cable shows, has been made possible only by a new media environment in which the mass audience for television has achieved a new level of fragmentation; and although true departures from stereotypes of these categories remain rare, this show indicates that we do have some examples of real diversity of representations, examples that are proliferating in the current media moment.

Gender in Media Studies Research: Are Gender Roles Culturally Reproduced?

The *I Love Lucy* show was one of the earliest, most popular prime-time situation comedies on network television, airing from 1951 to 1957 (see Figure 5.3). Lucy, played by former film actress Lucille Ball, became a popular American heroine, an icon of the American housewife first in an urban New York apartment, and later in suburban Connecticut. Her extremely comic exploits usually involved attempts to break into show business, and to break out of her housewife role. In one episode, Lucy and her friend Ethel get jobs, switching roles with their husbands Ricky and Fred, who stay home to do the housework and cooking. The results of each pair breaking with their traditional gender roles are predictably disastrous, with Lucy and Ethel getting fired from their jobs on a candy assembly line, and Ricky and Fred almost destroying the house and kitchen in their attempts to cook and clean. The show's comic resolution

Figure 5.3. Lucy Ricardo, zany housewife of *I Love Lucy*, with husband Ricky Ricardo (played by Lucille Ball and Desi Arnaz).

of these put everyone back in their assigned places, reinforcing the traditional gender arrangements of American families in the 1950s.

While *I Love Lucy* is at one level merely enjoyable fun, once again, as we have seen above, other readings of the show are possible. One reading that is also possible, for example, is that *I Love Lucy* serves as one of the clearest, and earliest, feminist statements about women's discontent with their roles in the 1950s as housewives and mothers. Some interview data in media studies indicate that women did read precisely this message as they received the show (Press 1991). It is with questions like these that those studying gender issues in media studies are preoccupied. They consider the study of media images and their reception from the perspective of how they support, challenge, oppose, or otherwise comment on gender identities and roles in our society.

Currently, a whole new set of issues – some of them germane to the new media environment – is preoccupying scholars of gender and the

Figure 5.4. The women of HBO's *Sex and the City.*

media. Consider the popular television show *Sex and the City* (1998–2004), recently made into a Hollywood film with the same name and cast (2008). (See Figure 5.4.) The television show boasted one of the largest and most fanatical audiences in recent television history, and remains extremely popular in the form of reruns, DVD packs, and online forums (see Dempsey 2003; Appleson 2006; Elliott 2008). It is an integral part of college student culture; the majority of students in our media classes over the last 10 years are familiar with the show, and many are active fans of it.

   How might a media studies scholar understand this show? In particular, what tools might he or she use to assess its cultural importance, and its influence on ideas about gender – for gender identities and roles are one of its main topics – at a cultural, social, and psychological level? Any studies of this show must take into account the constant reruns on television, the ready availability of whole seasons of the show on DVDs for purchase or rental, the online fan sites and discussions of the show both on its official website and on unofficial ones, and the spin-off of the show into a major motion picture with the probability of one or more sequels being made over the next several years – all of these are aspects of the new media environment that affect the reception and influence of television today.

Debates about the influence, significance, and meaning of this hit television show (and now the film spin-off) embody some of the most interesting issues currently under discussion in the media studies subfield of gender and media. First, media studies scholars look toward historical changes in the culture to explain, in part, the development of the show's characters and themes. As some feminist perspectives have become partly assumed in the culture (e.g., women's freedom to be single, to have access to jobs formerly occupied almost exclusively by men, and to receive equal pay for their work), their position has shifted in the culture. Single women, and career women, are much more visible and much more accepted. This is reflected in television programming. The family orientation of the earlier situation comedies has been clearly replaced, in this and other shows of the last two decades, with a more liberal set of ideas about women's roles vis-à-vis work and family. So we have shows like *Sex and the City* that feature older, single career women with relatively free sex lives.

Scholars in media studies, studying both the meaning of this text *and* its reception from a feminist perspective, have used the show to help uncover a new feminist perspective they see as pervasive in our culture, which some have termed "third-wave feminism."[3] Feminism of the third wave retains some of the critiques of women's traditional roles that characterized the second-wave feminism of the 1960s and 1970s (e.g., emphasis on women's access to paid labor, and on equal pay for equal work); yet third-wave feminism couples these notions with the idea that women should be free to express their sexuality in both heterosexual and lesbian contexts. So the notion of the "sex kitten" image, a staple in films of the 1950s, is back with some current television and film images. The women of *Sex and the City* embody this to a degree: the show features prominently expensive "sexy" clothing, impractical high-heeled shoes (usually expensive, designer brands), and sexy lingerie, all of which were criticized by second-wave feminism. Yet in this text, such accoutrements are tied to women's right to express themselves sexually, and therefore to dress as sex objects, if they so desire.

In the section that follows, we will discuss how media studies has developed the theoretical tools for gender analysis. Some trace the inception of media and gender study to Herta Herzog's interest in women listeners of radio soap operas (Herzog 1941). Herzog found that listening to soap operas helped women cope with some of the difficulties arising from their subordinated social positions. Following Herzog, there began to be an enormous interest in the way women were depicted in popular Hollywood films. We will discuss this and the theoretical paradigm and findings it gave rise to, followed by a very brief discussion of the vast literature about gender and television.

Film and gender: Issues of reception and representation

The study of film and gender began in the early 1970s when film critics like Marjorie Rosen (1973) and Molly Haskell (1974) wrote critical histories of the types of images of women present in popular Hollywood film. Each mentioned the tendency of popular film to treat women as sexual objects, yet they noted also the presence of strong women characters in films of various genres. These books used the accessible, everyday language of film criticism to begin to levy a feminist critique of women's roles in popular film, focusing on the notion that women did not often play leading roles in a variety of genres, and that when women were depicted, their sexual characteristics were highlighted. However, the presence of strong women, such as in "women's pictures," often played by mature established female stars like Bette Davis, Katharine Hepburn, or Joan Crawford, offered some alternative roles as well, many of them featuring strong women played by these stars in leading roles.

The scholarly interest in gender and Hollywood film continued with a turn toward psychoanalytic theory to understand how films are received. Psychoanalysis and its associated body of theory provided important theoretical tools used by those interested in gendered relations in these texts, and their influence on gender identities in our society. Psychoanalytic "spectator theory" was developed to analyze in a theoretical way the way audiences watched Hollywood cinema. Originally, spectator theorists discussed the dream-like state of the movie theater, leading them to embrace a series of psychoanalytic concepts to explain what they called the "preconscious" state the viewer entered as he or she entered the darkened movie theater and prepared to understand a media text (Metz 1976).

Spectator theory became of particular importance to those interested in studying gender. Mulvey's essay "Visual Pleasure and Narrative Cinema" (1975) drew on psychoanalytic theory to establish a theory of gender in the "classical Hollywood cinema" (explained below). Mulvey's work became paradigmatic for studying the way that film texts influenced gendered identities in our culture. She set the stage for an entirely new way of looking first at film, and then at other types of media texts, through a psychoanalytic prism that foregrounded issues of gender. Until very recently, Mulvey's work was the most influential piece for those interested in examining how gender inequalities are represented in American media.

Mulvey departed from earlier psychoanalytic theorists (Baudry 1974–5, 1976; Metz 1974a, 1974b, 1982) with her assertion that gender was at the center of the meaning system of classical Hollywood cinema. According to Mulvey, women are represented according to a set of particular norms within the classical Hollywood film of the "studio era," a term referring to the years approximately from 1929 (the inception of the sound film) through the 1950s (when the studios began to break down and lost control of film distribution). These norms of representation focus attention on women's body parts and overall quality as the object of the male gaze. Mulveyan scholars of women in film have coined a term – "to-be-looked-at-ness" – to describe the qualities characteristic of many representations of women in the classical Hollywood cinema. As a result, they theorize that Hollywood played a strong role in solidifying the objectification of women in our culture. This objectification, it is argued, led to a certain stereotyping of what counts as "beautiful." Heroines of popular Hollywood films were most often white, young, slim, blonde, and conventionally beautiful, to an extreme degree that did not match the instances of such women in the general population, yet has had a major impact on the way women and girls view, judge, and experience their own bodies (Harrison and Cantor 1997; Harrison 2000). (See Figure 5.5.)

Examples of this abound. Mulvey discusses several popular films of Alfred Hitchcock in her essay, including the films *Vertigo*, in which male protagonist James Stewart makes over female lead Kim Novak according to his own ideal of beauty; and *Rear Window*, which again features male lead James Stewart, wheelchair bound, this time watching as the story of his neighbor's murder, along with female lead Grace Kelly's investigative role, unfolds from the vantage point of his apartment window. In fact, Hitchcock became famous for favoring one type of heroine: cool, blonde, and mysterious. Using a series of popular Hollywood actresses including Ingrid Bergman, Grace Kelly, Vera Miles, Kim Novak, Janet Leigh, and Tippi Hedren, Hitchcock recreated this heroine repeatedly in his films.

Figure 5.5. Jimmy Stewart and Kim Novak in Alfred Hitchcock's *Vertigo* (1958).

Certainly Mulvey's paradigm is useful for understanding the power of the *Sex and the City* text, both in its televisual and in its filmic form. The women in *Sex and the City* are constructed partly in the "spectacular" fashion Mulvey describes. As with the Hitchcock heroines Mulvey explicitly discusses, enormous and focused attention is paid to each detail of the four leading women's hair, clothing, makeup, and overall appearance. These details constitute an enormous part of the spectacle of the show, and its appeal.

The traditional modes of representing men and women that Mulvey describes characterized a large portion of classical Hollywood images. Yet there are some notable exceptions to these normative representations, and Mulvey's thesis has been widely challenged on these grounds. In particular the tradition of the woman's film has been written about extensively (Walsh 1984; Gledhill 1987). In the woman's film, which some consider a genre, and some merely a descriptive type, narratives focus on women as the central protagonists. Often these women characters, and the stars who played them, are older than the typical protagonist of classical Hollywood films, and fill strong leading roles. Rarely are they filmed in an objectified or fetishized manner. Some examples of traditional women's films include *Now, Voyager* (1942), starring Bette Davis (based on a popular women's novel of the same title); *Stella Dallas* (1937), starring Barbara Stanwyck, again based on a popular women's novel by the same author, Olive Higgins Prouty); and *Mildred Pierce* (1945), starring Joan Crawford. More current women's films include 1995's *Waiting to Exhale*, which was based on the extremely popular Terry McMillan novel (1994), as was 1998's *How Stella Got Her Groove Back* (based on McMillan 1997). *The Sisterhood of the Traveling Pants* film adaptation (2005) was based on the popular novel with the same name (Brashares 2003). While the wartime 1940s was a heyday for the woman's film, with men away in the military leaving a largely female film audience on the home front, industry experts view today's film audience as more male than female, and this leads to fewer women's films being produced.[4]

The woman's film represented an important break with the norms of classical Hollywood film. Unlike the films that predominated in the classical Hollywood cinema, these films focused on central women characters. Emotion, and domestic and romantic events, take center stage in these narratives. Scholarship on the woman's film countered Mulvey's overarching assertions about classical Hollywood cinema. And the tradition of the woman's film continues in current Hollywood, though these films are a minority of all films released. Recent films like *Bridget Jones's Diary* (2006) or, to return to our running example, *Sex and the City* (2008) are constructed using the basic tropes of the woman's film and illustrate its continued importance as a genre.

In the case of *Sex and the City* (both the film and television show), for example, the portraits of the four leading women are the centerpiece of its texts. The show follows the lives of four female friends, one married, the others single, and all in their thirties (at least when the series began). Each embodies a different attitude and moral stance toward women's sexual values and behavior. Samantha is the most radical, a woman who "sleeps around"; Charlotte, the most conservative, is married, and seeks to become a mother; Miranda is the most career oriented, a hard-working attorney; and Carrie, the narrator, stands somewhere in the center of all of these extreme attitudes, and considers them in the course of the show's many dilemmas regarding women, their sexuality, their relationships with men and with other women, and their relationship to work. All the characters are glamorous and extremely well dressed; live in nicely appointed New York City apartments, houses, or lofts; and suffer from no shortage of spending and shopping money. In short, the consumerist values of the show are clear. In fact, its ability to depict these four different women's personalities and lives over a number of years is what gives the television series version its strength. In order to interpret this dimension of the *Sex and the City* text, we would have to leave Mulvey and spectator theory behind, and turn to other types of work that are equally useful in decoding the power, influence, and importance of this text.

Recent scholars have used feminist theory to understand the particular combination of traditional, traditionally "feminist," antifeminist, and consumer culture elements we see present in a text like the *Sex and the City* film, or other recent "chick flicks" like *Bridget Jones's Diary* or even the film *Knocked Up*, which offers some pleasure to the female viewer but retains the male-centric bias of classical Hollywood cinema. To explain this, scholars have coined the terms "postfeminism" and "third-wave feminism." As discussed above, these are usually described as combining some of the insights and demands of second-wave feminism – a focus on women's economic inequality, for example – with a loosening of the second wave's culturally prescribed restrictions concerning women's ways of dressing, expressions of sexuality, and general culturally encoded forms of gendered behavior. While a second-wave feminist might criticize the high-heeled shoes predominating in the footwear of *Sex and the City*'s central female characters, a third-wave or postfeminist sensibility would describe *Sex and the City*'s fashions as helping its central women explore fashion as a means of both aesthetic and sexual expression (see Gill 2003, 2008). Current approaches to film analysis by scholars of gender and media tend to combine historical, psychoanalytic, and social theoretical perspectives to make sense of popular film texts and their reception.

Television and gender: Issues of reception and representation

Studies of gender representation in popular television have often yielded similar results to the analyses of film discussed above. Lichter and colleagues (Lichter, Rothman, and Lichter 1986; Lichter, Lichter, and Rothman 1994) found that television heroines were disproportionately white, young, slim, pictured in the home rather than at work, and pictured in subordinate positions vis-à-vis men, and generally were underrepresented in prime-time television. Yet in recent years women's roles on television have expanded. In the early years of television, roles like Wally and Beaver's mom on *Leave It to Beaver* or Donna Reed's relentless homemaker on *The Donna Reed Show* became cultural icons of feminine domesticity, which as scholars have pointed out did not in any way reflect real family patterns at the time (Coontz 1992). Over the decades, television families evolved to include single-parent families (beginning with the single-father families of *My Three Sons* and *The Courtship of Eddie's Father*, and continuing through the single-mother families of *Who's the Boss?* and *Kate and Allie*), blended families (the iconic *Brady Bunch*, 1969–74), workplace families like those on *The Mary Tyler Moore Show*, and the more diverse set of families and issues that comprise the recent *Desperate Housewives*. Images of women evolved as well. Single women's roles evolved from those of the early *Our Miss Brooks* to the career women of *That Girl* and *The Mary Tyler Moore Show* and the more recent *L.A. Law*, *Ali McBeal*, *Grey's Anatomy*, and *Sex and the City*.

Recently, television as a medium has changed so dramatically that the kind of early studies carried out by Lichter, Lichter, and Rothman (1994) are difficult if not impossible to conduct. These scholars were able, in their early studies, to code and analyze gender images in the entire universe of prime-time television, an exercise that they carried out at periodic intervals from the 1970s through the 1990s. Their studies indicated overall trends amounting to the underrepresentation of women on television as a group, and their overrepresentation in subordinate and traditionally stereotyped roles as caretakers, housewives, and mothers.

As prime-time images have proliferated with the breakdown of the network era and the concomitant proliferation of channels, however, we find much greater fragmentation in programming, and much more targeting to niche audiences. From the perspectives of gender as well as race, sexuality, and social class (as argued below), this has meant that there has been much greater variety in the images that are present on television. Shows featuring minority women, older women, and lesbians have slowly become more common on prime-time television. Some new shows – particularly those on subscription cable channels that are not beholden to advertising revenues – treat issues that are controversial in women's lives, and often treat them in a feminist, progressive manner. Lotz (2006) offers an exhaustive discussion of these changes in women's television since the decline of the network era. She finds that, overall, this level of fragmentation has meant more variety in gender representation, and at the same time less overt stereotyping, than in the network era.

Some television shows in particular have garnered critical and popular attention partly for the innovative nature of their representations of women. Much attention has focused, for example, on the television show *Buffy the Vampire Slayer* (1997–2003, FX Network). Scholars have found this show particularly interesting for its strong portrayal of a beautiful young woman who, coincidentally, has supernatural powers that enable her to kill vampires, thus keeping the world safe. They have argued that *Buffy the Vampire Slayer* marks a new era in the representation of young women, in which women are depicted not only as sex objects but also as extremely strong, powerful, and sexual in themselves (Lotz 2006). The new media environment has facilitated the excitement about Buffy, in that the many Internet fan groups that still exist (Fanpop n.d.; Fan-Sites.org n.d.; VIP Limited Partnership 2002; BuffyWorld.com n.d.) help facilitate continuing interest and involvement with this show, even as it is shown only in reruns.

Desperate Housewives (HBO, 2004–current) is another show that deserves particular note in this regard as well for its progressive depictions of older women embroiled in a series of difficult and changing work–family relationships, set in the context of women's changing contemporary roles vis-à-vis work and family. On the show, issues such as mothers' troubled relationships with their children, difficult marriages, sex and the single and/or married girl, single parenting, teenaged sex, and so on are featured from a woman's perspective. This show presents issues that women find difficult in their lives, and attempts to portray them in a fair and balanced manner that treats the women sympathetically, despite their difficulties.

For example, take the case of Lynette, formerly a high-powered career woman working in advertising who left her job to stay home, the mother of four small children – the little angelic terrors that constantly misbehave and make her life a nightmare. Admirable is the honesty with which the show portrays her ambivalence about her life as a full-time mother, her tiredness, and her ongoing frustrations. Admirable too is the investigation of her ambivalent feelings about having left her job, and how much she misses her former fast-paced life as a career woman.

In one episode (season 1, episode 25), her husband receives a promotion he has been angling for, to a job as vice president, which will require much more travel and a higher workload, thus making her life even harder and more isolated. Though Lynette begs her husband not to accept the promotion, he frankly tells her how much it means to him to become a vice president, and how much he wants the position, although he will be away more. Lynette refuses to play the supportive wife, however, and go along with her husband's ambition. Unbeknownst to her husband, she connives with his boss' wife to ensure that the boss reverses his decision and gives the promotion to someone else. She simply cannot face life as the mother of four without her husband's proximity, and she is willing to sacrifice his ambition to these feelings. Though Tom clearly is disappointed when he gets the news that he has been passed over, Lynette does not reveal that she has interfered. The new housewife and mother pictured in this show simply cannot coexist with the older models of the super-successful man and the woman who stands by him, no matter what.

Of course, despite these departures from stereotypical portrayals of women and the family, certain stereotypes do persist, even in this show. All the "housewives" on *Desperate Housewives* are beautiful in the conventional sense of having clear skin, regular features, and elfin thin bodies, although there is an attempt to make Lynette look tired and to give Susan bad hair (Wilson 2005; McCabe and Akass 2006). We simply have not reached the point in our visual media where it has become generally acceptable to portray women whose bodies approximate normal proportions, whose faces exhibit the signs of normal aging, and who accept this state of affairs as normal. Whereas we would argue that men have won the freedom to be represented in their natural body shape and appearance, for women this era is yet to come. (See Figure 5.6.)

Largely missing in the current television and film literature about gender are definitive audience studies of television's influence on gender identity and development, particularly in the new media environment

Figure 5.6. Lynette of ABC's *Desperate Housewives.*

where often television reception is coupled with participation in online groups, or where reception is supplemented with information gathered online by users (Livingstone and Bovill 2001; Livingstone 2003). Yet studies of children's exposure to television are numerous and indicate that violent and other images do influence children's development in a variety of ways, including influencing their own violent behavior, their eating behavior and body weight, and their perceptions of the social world; this has led to some regulation and reform on the part of the US government (Packard 1991; Centerwall 1992; Hendershot 1998, 2004; Livingstone and Bovill 2001; Singer and Singer 2001; Livingstone 2003; Pectora, Murray, and Wartella 2007; Tushnet 2000).

In sum, studies of the influence of television viewing on adults have sometimes shown that media have effects that are difficult to quantify. We are currently still at the stage of imagining, and beginning to study, the influence of film, television, and new media on adult gender identities. More audience studies, and reflections on the question of how to study these phenomena, are needed in our literature.

Media and Race

Race has been a crucial issue in American society since the early days of the Republic. Certainly in the bygone era of slavery, and continuing throughout the decades since slavery was abolished, race has been an organizing principle of American life. Similarly, race has been central to American electronic media since their inception and over the decades of their evolution. Take the case of Hollywood cinema. The origin of narrative cinema is often traced to D. W. Griffith's film *Birth of a Nation* (1915). *Birth of a Nation*, a famous early narrative film focused on the rise of the Ku Klux Klan in the American South, includes a side story of the alleged attempted rape of a white woman by an African-American man, and his subsequent lynching by a white mob dressed in the familiar garb of the Ku Klux Klan, set against the background of pre- and post-Civil War American society. (See Figure 5.7.)

Film scholars for decades have judged this story to be extremely racist – indeed, white supremacist – in its sentiments. Yet its historical importance in the development of American narrative film is unquestioned (Rogin 1992, 1996; Jackson 2008).[5] This fact and other qualities of the Hollywood film industry have led scholars to theorize the centrality of

Figure 5.7. The Klan "saves" white womanhood in D. W. Griffith's *Birth of a Nation* (1915).

racism to the system, whether the particular racism of white supremacy (Rogin 1996), anti-Semitism (Gabler 1988; Brodkin 1998), or other forms of racism as well (Ono 2008; Chong forthcoming).

The history of Hollywood film has been littered with evidence of racial stereotyping. First and foremost, for years American media images have been extremely segregated vis-à-vis the skin color of their protagonists. Images of African Americans, Asians, Latinos, and other minorities have historically been absent or extremely degrading and stereotyped, or confined (in the case of African Americans) to "black-only" productions in which all the characters are African American. These problems with minority representation have only just begun to be addressed by our media over the last two decades.

In a landmark work of critical media studies scholarship on race and film, Bogle (2001) offers one of the first discussions of the images of African Americans in Hollywood film. First published in 1973, this book identifies five main stereotypes governing early depictions of African Americans in film: the "tom," a depiction of the "socially acceptable 'good African-American'"; the "coon," a lackadaisical, clownish figure; the "mulatto," a fair-skinner, sympathetic African-American person; the "mammy," a large, fiercely independent, motherly black woman; and the "buck," a carnal, lustful, and violent African American. All of these stereotypes stressed blacks' inferiority to whites, and were extremely degrading depictions.

Rogin (1996) takes Bogle's argument one step further, asserting that the entire history of American film can be read as the history of struggle in our culture between whites and blacks. He traces this through a discussion of what he has identified as the four main films that set the tone for race in Hollywood film: *Uncle Tom's Cabin, Birth of a Nation, The Jazz Singer,* and *Gone with the Wind.* Each of these films engages stereotypes described by Bogle, and each depicts, quite uncritically, the racist treatment to which blacks have been subjected in American history. *Uncle Tom's Cabin* tells the story, made famous in the popular novel by Harriet Beecher Stowe, of a black slave who accepts the mistreatment to which he is continually subjected. His very name – "Uncle Tom" – has become synonymous with African Americans who supposedly comply with their mistreatment at the hands of white society.

Gone with the Wind features as one of its most prominent characters black actress Hattie McDaniel playing what came to be the most familiar role for African-American actors and actresses in classic Hollywood films, the domestic servant (see Figure 5.8). McDaniel's portrayal was so well drawn that she became the first African-American actress to win an Academy Award, despite the stereotyped nature of her role. *The Jazz Singer,* famous as the first sound film made in Hollywood, is the story of an immigrant Jewish singer who must choose between his secular success on the jazz scene and following in his father's footsteps as a cantor, the singer in traditional Jewish religious services. This film uncritically portrays whites performing with blackface makeup, which was common earlier in the twentieth century. The success of these films, and their central status in the scholarly canon of Hollywood films, underscores that Rogin's argument for the centrality of racism to the system and language of Hollywood films is a powerful one.

What is not always popularly recognized in white America is that prominent black filmmakers like Oscar Micheaux made films alongside white films in early Hollywood. Between 1919 and 1948, Micheaux made

Figure 5.8. "Now what's my little lamb goin' to wear?" Mammie, played by Hattie McDaniel, to Scarlett, played by Vivian Leigh, in the 1939 MGM classic film *Gone with the Wind*.

a series of films during the early decades of the Hollywood film industry tailored specifically to African-American audiences (but sometimes viewed by white audiences), with many featuring all-African-American casts.[6] He struck deals with southern theater managers whereby his movies were sometimes shown at matinee performances specifically for black audiences, or at midnight showings for white audiences. He cast a series of black actors and actresses, often modeling them on white movie stars of particular types. Sometimes his films were in the style of particular Hollywood genres like the gangster film (*Underworld*) or the melodrama (*The Deceit, The Dungeon*). At other times the films focused on themes particular to African Americans' issues of the time such as the ability to attend college (*Birthright*), or the problems of light-skinned blacks "passing" for white (*God's Stepchildren*).[7]

Over the past several decades, there have been a spate of films produced constituting what became known in the 1980s and 1990s as the "new black cinema" (Watkins 1998). Directors like Spike Lee and Matty Rich produced a series of films that became quite popular with both African-American and white audiences, many of which focused on themes of particular interest to African Americans. Of particular importance was Spike Lee's *Do the Right Thing* (1989), a film about racial relations in the Bedford-Stuyvesant section of Brooklyn, which treated the topic of racial violence and questioned its necessity and appropriateness in various situations. The film became notorious because some white critics criticized it for its potential to incite black audiences to riot, while others, including Spike Lee himself, felt such commentaries themselves were racist in their assumption that black viewers could not contain themselves when confronted with filmic violence (see Wikipedia n.d.-b). Both Kent Ono (2008) and Sylvia Chin Huey Chong (forthcoming) chronicle the history of the representation of Asians and Asian-Americans in Hollywood cinema and other media.[8]

Others have turned the lens of racial critique on other media. Television has a long history of underrepresenting racial minority groups. An excellent summary of television's history in this regard is Marlon Riggs' powerful documentary film *Color Adjustment* (Riggs 1992), which explores the history of racial representations, or the lack thereof, on prime-time television during the rise and fall of the network era. Using images from the first few decades of television, and interviews with its actors, actresses, writers, and producers, Riggs asserts in this documentary that African Americans in particular have been both underrepresented and stereotyped throughout the history of television. This has occurred in ways analogous to their treatment in film and other media, and parallel active stereotyping that occurs in our culture in general. Riggs also notes the insidiousness of stereotypical modes of portrayal in the few images that did appear.

On early television, the very presence of African Americans was so rare that even the appearance of one was a big event for the African-American community, ensuring that a mass audience of African Americans would turn out together to enjoy the event. One memorable segment of *Color Adjustment* features African-American scholars and black actress Diahann Carroll speaking about a very early television show about African-American urban life, *Amos 'n' Andy*. While white and African-American critics alike have in retrospect judged this show to be extremely denigrating, stereotyped, and racist to its African-American characters, these interviews feature recollections of actual viewers of the show, recounting how important it was in the American 1950s to see any images at all of African Americans on prime-time television. bell hooks recounts a similar recollection of her trip to the movies in the 1930s to see the newly minted *Imitation of Life*, featuring beautiful young black actress Fredi Washington portraying Peola, a young woman who speaks out against the racism of American society. Many viewers found it liberating simply to watch media products that recognized their existence as minority members of society, rather than the typical media fare that erased and ignored African Americans.

Henry Louis Gates Jr. describes how important it was for him and his family growing up as African Americans in the South to watch the television show *Amos 'n' Andy*. He recollects,

> Seeing somebody colored on TV was an event. "Colored, colored on Channel Two," you'd hear someone shout. Somebody else would run to the phone, while yet another hit the front porch, telling all the neighbors where to see it. And *everybody* loved *Amos and Andy* – I don't care what people say today. For the colored people, the day they took *Amos and Andy* off the air was one of the saddest days in Piedmont. ... What was special to us about *Amos and Andy* was that their world was *all* colored, just like ours. Of course, *they* had their colored judges and lawyers and doctors and nurses, which we could only dream about having, or becoming – and we did dream about those things. (Gates 1994: 22)

In the same memoir Gates mentions that it was through television, and television only, that he became acquainted with white people. Clearly in the early age of television, the media were beginning to play a key role in acquainting segments of society isolated from one another with each other. In fact, media scholars have theorized that one of television's key social functions has been to introduce some social groups to the "backstage" activities of other social groups from which they are isolated in real life (Meyrowitz 1985).

Another memorable segment of the documentary *Color Adjustment* featured an interview with Esther Rolle, a principal character on the hit show *Good Times* (1974–9). She discusses how, when this show – about a black family in the Chicago housing projects – was pitched to her, she was to be a single mother. Only when she demanded a husband was the black family at the center of this show portrayed as intact. She was simply outraged at the stereotypic assumptions about the absence of black fathers made by the show's writers and producers in their initial conception of the show. Of course, this particular issue is complicated by the sharp rise, during the years the show was aired, of the percentage of black children living in families headed by single mothers.[9]

Rolle's criticism of the show for representing this reality illustrates how difficult it is to define the role of the media in a changing society as either primarily reflection or primarily influence. Other stereotypes that occurred on this and other shows featuring African Americans were that they were often made the butt of buffoon-like humor. This was particularly evident in the character of JJ on this show, who used physical humor to such an extreme that he often presented himself as an overly dumb, clumsy laughingstock, which many black viewers found embarrassing and objectionable.

Prior to the appearance of *The Cosby Show* (1984–92), most black family comedies had revolved around either poor (as in *Good Times* and *Sanford and Son*) or lower-middle-class families, often with missing fathers, as the fatherless black family was prominently featured in the news of the 1960s and 1970s. One notable exception was *The Jeffersons*, who despite their working-class background were, as explained, an intact family "moving on up" and had reached upper-middle-class status.

The Cosby Show reclaimed the black family quite literally and consciously, as seen in Bill Cosby's own statements about his purpose in creating the black family at the center of this show. Cosby explicitly sought to give America an image of an intact, successful, professional black family on prime time, even in an era in which the two-parent intact black family was in steep decline. The show featured the popular comedian Cosby playing himself as a dad in an upper-middle-class black family. Though the show was structured quite conventionally for a situation comedy, it broke new ground with the upper middle classness of its African-American representations.

Jhally and Lewis' influential study *Enlightened Racism*: The Cosby Show, *Audiences, and the Myth of the American Dream* (1992) similarly changed the way we think about the relationship between representation and effect vis-à-vis the issue of racial inequality. Jhally and Lewis turned the lens of the reception theorist on *The Cosby Show*, which topped ratings charts for many of the eight seasons it aired, partly because of its wild popularity with white and black viewers.

Critics speculated that the show would improve race relations in the United States and that it would make whites more sympathetic to their black neighbors. In fact, the Jhally and Lewis research, which sampled white viewer and black viewer opinions, somewhat surprisingly – and certainly counterintuitively, for most scholars – found rather the opposite.

Instead of being more sympathetic to blacks, white *Cosby* fans became more critical of African Americans in the United States, expressing opinions about their black neighbors like "Why can't they work hard, apply themselves, and make it?" like the Cosbys had done. What had widely been viewed as a show exerting a clearly progressive racial impact was shown to be much more complex, and much more mixed, in its actual impact on viewers, and this troubled our commonsense notions about what social impact departures from the norm of television representations would have. This was very similar to the research on *All in the Family*, which as we discussed above showed that viewers both sympathized with, and opposed, lead character Archie Bunker and his racist attitudes (Vidmar and Rokeach 1974).

While currently stereotypes persist on television, producers, writers, actors, and actresses have become much more aware of the pervasiveness of common stereotypes, and have made conscious attempts to subvert them with a proliferation of diverse representations of a variety of minority groups. Lucy Liu's character of Lin Woo, the assertive Asian-American attorney who appeared on prime time's *Ali McBeal* (1997–2002), is a clear departure for Asian Americans from the quiet, submissive Asian-American domestic Mrs. Livingston, played by Miyoshi Umecki from 1969 to 1972 on the hit series *The Courtship of Eddie's Father*. More currently, Ono (2005) delineates a new subfield entitled Asian American studies, which looks at the ways in which Asians' various immigrant identities have changed life for Americans of Asian descent, and also looks at the way that other Americans have discussed, stereotyped, and represented Asian Americans throughout their history in this hemisphere.

Valdivia (1995) and other scholars (Harrison, Projansky, Ono, and Helford 1996; Ono 2005) expand the universe of analyzing racial representations from a focus on African-American images on television to those of Latinas, Asians, and other racial groups. In one article, for example, Valdivia analyzes the stereotyped way in which the Latina film actress Rosie Perez is characterized in her films (Valdivia 1996). Her clothing, her jewelry, and her tough language all speak to stereotypes that have been commonly applied to Latinas in our culture. Valdivia discusses the area of Latina/o communication and media studies as a relatively new focus of study within the field of media studies as a whole (Valdivia 2004, 2008).

Hill Street Blues in the 1970s featured an African-American cop alongside the white cops as a major figure whose character was explored in depth in the course of the show. More current shows (*The Wire*, *Grey's Anatomy*, *CSI*, *The L Word*, and *ER*) also feature racial and ethnic minority characters as major figures on shows with mixed-race casts. Although stereotypes have not been eradicated, these representations have come a long way from *Amos 'n' Andy*'s extreme stereotypic portrayals of black characters in television's earliest days.

In the section that follows, we trace the history of the portrayal of alternative sexualities in the media, and similarly discuss recent changes in the way sexuality is portrayed.

Sexuality

Official Showtime plot summary for *The L Word*

Jenny Schecter (MIA KIRSHNER) is a gifted young writer of fiction who ... arrives in Los Angeles to begin her "adult life" with her boyfriend – soon to be fiancé – Tim Haspel (ERIC MABIUS), a women's swim coach at a large state university.

They reside in West Hollywood, next door to Bette Porter (JENNIFER BEALS), a museum director, and her partner Tina Kennard (LAUREL HOLLOMAN). Bette and Tina have been a couple for seven years and are trying to find the perfect sperm donor to help them to start a family. ...

Bette and Tina's close network of friends includes Shane McCutcheon (KATHERINE MOENNIG), a hairdresser and the resident heartthrob; Dana Fairbanks (ERIN DANIELS), a professional tennis player not yet out of the closet; bisexual journalist Alice Pieszecki (LEISHA HAILEY); and Bette's half-sister Kit Porter (PAM GRIER), who is a musician and a recovering alcoholic.

Source: Showtime (2009).

The L-Word, a recent Showtime television show, details the lives of a group of lesbian, bisexual, and some straight women residing in the Los Angeles area. Although most of the women on *The L-Word* appear glamorous in traditional Hollywood fashion, the treatment of lesbian sexuality, lesbian identity, and lesbian relationships is all explicit in the show, and this clearly breaks new ground in the area of the depiction of sexuality in prime-time television.

Although of course Showtime is a subscription channel and, as we've argued, is less constrained than network television in its depiction of sexuality, this show is emblematic of the long way we have come in depicting sexuality in the popular media. This section will discuss the way nontraditional sexualities have been depicted and studied in popular film and television, and recent changes in allowable images and themes.

Many have argued that there is a long history of the media contributing to the oppression of sexual minorities such as gays, lesbians, and bisexuals (Gamson 1998; Walters 2001). Walters (2001) in particular looks at the way gay hate crimes have been committed in tandem with specific portrayals of gays and lesbians in popular films or television shows. Yet Gamson (1998) has argued that the television talk show changed this tradition. He demonstrates that television talk shows in fact were liberating, representing a great step forward for gays in our culture in that they were one of the first places that the actual voices of gays and lesbians in our culture became visible to the heterosexual world.

Recent scholars have explicitly uncovered what is now seen as a long tradition in Hollywood film and in popular television of representing gay and lesbian sexuality in a sub-rosa manner (Doty 2000; Russo 1981). Russo argues in his influential book *The Celluloid Closet* that some of the most popular and influential Hollywood films of the studio era and beyond embedded images of and references to gays and lesbians in their characters. Describing the many key and influential Hollywood actors and actresses of the silent and classical eras who were known to be gay, lesbian, or bisexual, Russo shows how many of the most popular films featured characters whose sexualities are ambiguous. Once again, these images may be read as both constricting, in that they were perhaps hidden to most viewers, yet also liberating, in that they might have been read by some as giving quite explicit voice to gay and lesbian perspectives.

One film he mentions in particular is the heterosexual romantic farce *Bringing Up Baby* (1938), starring Cary Grant and Katharine Hepburn. Though in a surface reading of the film Cary Grant is an entirely heterosexual character, Russo argues that a comic scene, in which Grant emerges from a bathroom wearing Hepburn's white frilly bathrobe and announces, "I've suddenly gone 'gay'!" is actually a subaltern reference to gay culture that was read explicitly as such by the many gay and lesbian viewers of this film. (See Figure 5.9.)

Throughout the decades of Hollywood film, there have also been films explicitly detailing violence against gays and lesbians. Of particular interest in this regard is *The Children's Hour* (1961), adapted from a

Figure 5.9. "I've suddenly gone 'gay'!" Cary Grant in Katharine Hepburn's bathrobe in *Bringing up Baby* (1938).

Lillian Hellman play about two teachers at a girls' school who lose their social standing and their school when they are accused of having a lesbian relationship with one another. *The Killing of Sister George*, released in 1968, was the first film in the United States to be released with an "X" rating. This film provoked considerable controversy by depicting the complex relationship between two lesbian lovers, George and Childie, and contains scenes of sexual practice and scenes in lesbian bars extremely unusual for its time.

By the 1980s and 1990s, representations of gay and lesbian characters were becoming more common, if not exactly routine, in popular American film. The representation of a gay-bashing crime in the 1980 film *Cruising* marked an era in which even the presence of an out gay character was incendiary, and sparked violence inside and outside theaters showing this film.

By the 1990s gay characters were popping up as ordinary in popular films. Films like *My Best Friend's Wedding* (1997), starring Hollywood mega-star Julia Roberts, featured an out gay character as her best friend, with little fanfare or overt attention to the "gayness" of his character. Similarly out gay characters have appeared in a number of other recent films to the degree that they are no longer unusual or provoke comment. Recently the hit film *Brokeback Mountain* (2005) featured a relationship between two cowboys set in the 1960s and 1970s. This film explicitly detailed social prejudice against gays at the time, while presenting in universal terms a sensitive love story about two men who happen to be gay.

Television's history of alternative sexual representation has been briefer but followed a trajectory similar to that of Hollywood film. Most locate the first examples of these representations in the 1980s with the "out" gay character Steven Carrington on the prime-time soap opera *Dynasty* (Gripsrud 1995). Steven was featured in the first prime-time explicitly gay kiss on American television. Another important event in the history of televisual representations of gay and lesbian sexuality is the episode of *Ellen* on which the show's star, Ellen DeGeneres, came out as a lesbian, both as a character and in real life. This event, coupled with the on-air lesbian kiss that introduced the lesbian Ellen in this episode, caused a huge stir in the media, and brought the issue of lesbian representation to popular awareness.

More recent shows like *Will and Grace* (1998–2006), *Queer as Folk* (2000–5), and, as discussed above, *The L Word* have revolved around gay and lesbian characters and families, and have begun the process of naturalizing these representations. As mentioned above, there has been excellent work in media studies (Walters 2001) that documents the connection between noted filmic and televisual representations of gays and lesbians, and the occurrence of crimes against gays and lesbians in the culture. As these images become more numerous, we can only hope that this association will diminish. (See Figure 5.10.)

Although representations of alternative sexualities have been slow in coming to the dominant media of film and television, we are now in an exciting era in which these representations do exist, are continually being created, and are often incredibly progressive. As mentioned above, *The L Word* features a large group of young, lesbian women, whom the show follows through their relationships, family lives, work lives, and careers. For almost the first time on prime-time television, being lesbian is simply one quality of the women featured, and a wide panorama of lesbian characters have been portrayed. Although this is a subscription cable rather than network show, and therefore accessible to a smaller and more affluent

Figure 5.10. The glamorous women of Showtime's *The L Word*.

audience, this show is truly a move toward more democratic and egalitarian representation for lesbians on television.

Conclusion

This concludes our overview of issues of the representation, and the reception, of images of class, gender, race, and sexual identities in the popular media. We have traced the evolution of media scholarship about class, gender, race, and sexual identities throughout the evolution of media from "old" media to the new media environment. We have looked at scholarship that is focused on each one of these issues, and some that looks at the way gender and class, or gender and race, or race and class, work in tandem with one another. While this discussion has of necessity only scratched the surface of the vast amount of information media studies scholars have generated on these issues, what we hope we have accomplished is to orient the general reader to the centrality and importance of scholarship about difference and inequality in our media heritage.

In the chapter that follows, we carry these concerns into a look at issues of representation and reception occurring today in the new media environment, which retains some of the biases characterizing old media but introduces new issues pertaining to the relationship between media, inequality, and bias. Once again, we pay particular attention to the gendered, classed, and raced nature of new media and its reception. How does the rise of digital media and the Internet change the configuration of images to which we are exposed in the media? Are there discernable changes in the influence of media given the new technological developments we have witnessed over the last several decades? How have scholars studied these issues, and which concerns serve as ongoing foci in media research in the new media environment? These are the issues to which we turn in the coming pages.

Notes

1. See Barker (2008) for a good overview of the field of cultural studies.
2. See Wikipedia (n.d.-a) for a fuller discussion of the British New Wave cinema.
3. See Wikipedia (n.d.-c) for a good introduction to third-wave feminism. The term "third-wave" is often traced to a 1992 essay written by Rebecca Walker entitled "Becoming the Third Wave." She coined this term in the context of speaking about the multiple contradictions of the Anita Hill–Clarence Thomas hearings for feminists in the 1990s. In particular, she claimed that she was a "third-wave" feminist, rather than a "postfeminist," thereby asserting that there was still a need for feminism, though a new version that transcended some of the issues plaguing second-wave feminism, in particular the exclusion of women of color and lesbians. The essay was reprinted in Ryan (1997). See also Dicker and Piepmeier (2003); Howie, Gillis, and Munford (2004); Reger (2005); and Walker (1995) for further discussions of third-wave feminism.
4. There is debate in our literature about whether the industry's assumptions are accurate in this regard. Most scholars believe this industry belief to be a self-fulfilling prophecy, in that as more films are angled toward a young male audience, the potential female audience is alienated and drops out of film viewing.
5. See Jackson (2008). This work provides a history of the relations between southerners and motion pictures from the silent era to the World War II era, illustrating the parallels between the rise and fall of the studio system and the rise and fall of racial segregation, and their points of intersection and mutual influence.
6. In addition to this, many primarily white films included segments featuring African-American actors that were often omitted when the films were shown in the southern states. *Ziegfield Follies* (1945) and *Till the Clouds Roll By* (1946) are examples of films that featured two different versions, one for northern

audiences, which might include black viewers as well as white viewers, and one for southern movie theaters, which would never include both audiences. (See Everett 2001.)

7. I am extremely indebted to Donald Bogle (2001) for this discussion of the films of Oscar Micheaux.

8. See Chong (2005, forthcoming).

9. By the end of the 1970s, the majority of black children in the United States lived in families headed by single mothers. For documentation, see Casper and Bryson (1998, n.d.) and Casper and Fields (2000).

References

Adorno, T. W. 1954a. "How to look at television." *The Quarterly of Film Radio and Television* 3:23–25.

Adorno, Theodor W. 1954b. "Television and the patterns of mass culture." *The Quarterly of Film Radio and Television* 8:213–35.

Adorno, Theodor W., and Max Horkheimer. 1944. "The culture industry: Enlightenment as mass deception." www.marxists.org/reference/archive/adorno/1944/culture-industry.htm.

Alasuutari, P., ed. 1999. *Rethinking the media audience: The new agenda*. London: Sage.

Alasuutari, P. 2002. "Three phases of reception studies." In *McQuail's reader in mass communication theory*, edited by Denis McQuail. Thousand Oaks, C.A.: Sage.

Ang, Ien. 1985. *Watching Dallas: Soap opera and the melodramatic imagination*. London and New York: Methuen.

Appleson, Gail. 2006. "Women are spending more on footwear." *Knight-Ridder Tribune Business News*, May 5.

Barker, Chris. 2008. *Cultural studies: Theory and practice*. London: Sage.

Baron, James N., and Peter C. Reiss. 1985. "Same time, next year: Aggregate analyses of the mass media and violent behavior." *American Sociological Review* 50:347–63.

Baudry, Jean-Louis. 1974–75. "Ideological effects of the basic cinematographic apparatus." *Film Quarterly* 28:39–47.

Baudry, Jean-Louis. 1976. "The apparatus." *Camera Obscura* 1:104–26.

Benjamin, Walter. 1977. *Illuminations*. New York: Schocken.

Bogle, Donald. 2001. *Toms, coons, mulattoes, mammies, and bucks: An interpretive history of blacks in American films*. New York: Continuum.

Brashares, Ann. 2003. *The sisterhood of the traveling pants*. New York: Delacorte.

Brodkin, Karen. 1998. *How Jews became white folks and what that says about race in America*. New Brunswick, N.J.: Rutgers University Press.

BuffyWorld.com. N.d. "BuffyWorld." www.buffyworld.com.

Casper, L. M., and K. Bryson. 1998. *Household and family characteristics March 1998*. US Census Bureau. www.census.gov/prod/3/98pubs/p20-515.pdf.

Casper, L. M., and K. Bryson N.d. *Co-resident grandparents and their grand-children: Grandparent maintained families.* US Census Bureau. www.census. gov/population/www/ documentation/twps0026/twps0026.html.

Casper, L.M., and J. Fields. 2000. *Americas families and living arrangements: Population characteristics.* US Census Bureau. www.census.gov/prod/ 2001pubs/p20-537.pdf.

Centerwall, Brandon S. 1992. "Television and violence: The scale of the problem and where to go from here." *Journal of the American Medical Association* 267(22): 3059–63.

Chong, Sylvia Shin Huey. 2005. "Restaging the war: The *Deer Hunter* and the primal scene of violence." *Cinema Journal* 44(2): 89–106.

Chong, Sylvia Shin Huey. Forthcoming. *The Oriental obscene: American film violence and racial phantasmatics in the Vietnam era.* Durham, N.C.: Duke University Press.

Condit, Celeste Michelle. 1990. *Decoding abortion rhetoric: Communicating social change.* Urbana: University of Illinois Press.

Coontz, Stephanie. 1992. *The way we never were: American families and the nostalgia trap.* New York: Basic Books.

Dempsey, John. 2003. "Viewers turn out for 'sex.'" *Daily Variety*, June 25.

Dicker, Rory Cooke, and Alison Piepmeier. 2003. *Catching a wave: Reclaiming feminism for the 21st century.* Boston: Northeastern University Press.

Doty, Alexander. 2000. *Flaming classics queering the film canon.* New York: Routledge.

Elliott, Stuart. 2008. "'Sex and the City' and its lasting female appeal." *New York Times*, March 17.

Everett, Ann. 2001. *Returning the gaze: A genealogy of black film criticism.* Durham, N.C.: Duke University Press.

Fanpop. N.d. "Buffy the vampire slayer." www.fanpop.com/spots/buffy-the-vampire-slayer.

Fan-Sites.org. N.d. "It's about power: Buffy the vampire slayer." http://buffy. fan-sites.org.

Foster, Gwendolyn Audrey. 2005. *Class-passing: Social mobility in film and popular culture.* Carbondale: Southern Illinois University Press.

Gabler, Neal. 1988. *An empire of their own: How the Jews invented Hollywood.* New York: Crown Publishers.

Gamson, Joshua. 1998. *Freaks talk back: Tabloid talk shows and sexual nonconformity.* Chicago: University of Chicago Press.

Gates, Henry Louis. 1994. *Colored people: A memoir.* New York: Knopf.

Gill, Ross. 2003. "From sexual objectification to sexual subjectification: The resexualization of women's bodies in the media." *Feminist Media Studies* 3(1):100–5.

Gill, Ross. 2008. "Postfeminist media culture: Elements of a sensibility." *European Journal of Cultural Studies* 10:147–66.

Gill, R., and E. Herdieckerhoff. 2006. "Rewriting the romance: New femininities in chick lit?" *Feminist Media Studies* 6(4):487–504.

Gledhill, Christine. 1987. *Home is where the heart is: Studies in melodrama and the woman's film.* London: BFI Publishing.

Gramsci, Antonio, Quintin Hoare, and Geoffrey Nowell-Smith. 1971. *Selections from the prison notebooks of Antonio Gramsci.* London: Lawrence & Wishart.

Gripsrud, Jostein. 1995. *The Dynasty years: Hollywood television and critical media studies.* London: Routledge.

Grossberg, Lawrence. 1992. *We gotta get out of this place: Popular conservatism and postmodern culture.* New York: Routledge.

Grossberg, Lawrence, Cary Nelson, and Paula A. Treichler. 1992. *Cultural studies.* New York: Routledge.

Hall, Stuart. 1973. "Encoding and decoding in the television discourse." Centre for Cultural Studies, University of Birmingham.

Hall, Stuart, Charles Critcher, Tony Jefferson, John Clarke, and Brian Roberts. 1978. *Policing the crisis: Mugging, the state, and law and order.* London: Macmillan.

Harrison, Kristen. 2000. "The body electric: Thin-ideal media and eating disorders in adolescents." *Journal of Communication* 50:119–43.

Harrison, K., and J. Cantor. 1997. "The relationship between media consumption and eating disorders." *The Journal of Communication* 47:40–67.

Harrison, Taylor, Sarah Projansky, Kent A. Ono, and Elyce Rae Helford. 1996. *Enterprise zones: Critical positions on Star Trek.* Boulder, C.O.: Westview.

Haskell, Molly. 1974. *From reverence to rape: The treatment of women in the movies.* Chicago: University of Chicago Press.

HBO. 2009. *The Wire.* www.hbo.com/thewire/.

Hendershot, Heather. 1998. *Saturday morning censors: Television regulation before the V-chip.* Chapel Hill, N.C.: Duke University Press.

Hendershot, Heather. 2004. *Nickelodeon nation.* New York: New York University Press.

Herzog, Herta. 1941. "On borrowed experience: An analysis of listening to daytime sketches." *Studies in Philosophy and Social Science* 9:65–95.

Hoggart, Richard. 1998. *The uses of literacy.* New Brunswick, N.J.: Transaction Publishers.

Howie, Gillian, Stacy Gillis, and Rebecca Munford. 2004. *Third wave feminism: A critical exploration.* Basingstoke, UK: Palgrave Macmillan.

Jackson, Robert. 2008. "Fade in, crossroads: The Southern cinema, 1890–1940." PhD diss., Department of History, University of Virginia.

Jhally, Sut, and Justin Lewis. 1992. *Enlightened racism: The Cosby Show, audiences, and the myth of the American dream.* Boulder, C.O.: Westview.

Kellner, Douglas. 2006. "Cultural studies and philosophy: An intervention." In *A companion to cultural studies,* edited by T. Miller, pp. 139–53. Oxford: Blackwell.

Kolko, Beth E., Lisa Nakamura, and Gilbert B. Rodman. 2000. *Race in cyberspace.* New York: Routledge.

Lichter, S. Robert, Linda S. Lichter, and Stanley Rothman. 1994. *Prime time: How TV portrays American culture.* Washington, D.C.: Regnery.

Lichter, S. Robert, Stanley Rothman, and Linda S. Lichter. 1986. *The media elite.* Bethesda, M.D.: Adler & Adler.

Lipsitz, George. 1990. *Time passages: Collective memory and American popular culture.* Minneapolis: University of Minnesota Press.

Livingstone, Sonia. 2003. "Children's use of the Internet: Reflections on the emerging research agenda." *New Media Society* 5:147–66.

Livingstone, Sonia M., and Moira Bovill. 2001. *Children and their changing media environment: A European comparative study.* Mahwah, N.J.: Lawrence Erlbaum.

Lotz, Amanda D. 2006. *Redesigning women: Television after the network era.* Urbana: University of Illinois Press.

MacBeth, Tannis M. 1996. *Tuning in to young viewers: Social perspectives on television.* Thousand Oaks, C.A.: Sage.

McCabe, Janet, and Kim Akass. 2006. *Reading* Desperate Housewives: *Beyond the white picket fence.* London: I. B. Tauris.

McMillan, Terry. 1994. *Waiting to exhale.* New York: Pocket.

McMillan, Terry. 1997. *How Stella got her groove back.* New York: Penguin.

McRobbie, Angela. 1991. *Feminism and youth culture: From* Jackie *to* Just Seventeen. Boston: Unwin Hyman.

Metz, Christian. 1974a. *Film language: A semiotics of the cinema.* New York: Oxford University Press.

Metz, Christian. 1974b. *Language and cinema.* The Hague: Mouton.

Metz, Christian. 1976. "The fiction film and its spectator: A metapsychological study." *New Literary History* 8:75–105.

Metz, Christian. 1982. *Imaginary signifier: Psychoanalysis and the cinema.* Bloomington: Indiana University Press.

Meyrowitz, Joshua. 1985. *No sense of place: The impact of electronic media on social behavior.* New York: Oxford University Press.

Montgomery, Kathryn C. 1989. *Target prime time: Advocacy groups and the struggle over entertainment television.* New York: Oxford University Press.

Morley, David. 1980. *The nationwide audience.* London: British Film Institute.

Morley, David, with Charlotte Brunsdon. 1978. *Everyday television: Nationwide.* London: British Film Institute.

Mulvey, Laura. 1975. "Visual pleasure and narrative cinema." *Screen* 16:6–18.

Muscio, Giuliana. 1997. *Hollywood's new deal.* Philadelphia: Temple University Press.

Ono, Kent A. 2005. *A companion to Asian American studies.* Malden, M.A.: Blackwell.

Ono, Kent. 2008. *Asian Americans and the media*. London: Polity.

Packard, Lucile. 1991. *The future of children*. Los Altos, C.A.: Center for the Future of Children.

Pectora, Norma Odom, Mohn P. Murray, and Ellen Wartella. 2007. *Children and television: Fifty years of research*. Mahwah, N.J.: Lawrence Erlbaum.

Press, Andrea Lee. 1991. *Women watching television: Gender, class, and generation in the American television experience*. Philadelphia: University of Pennsylvania Press.

Press, Andrea L. In press. "Feminism? That's so seventies!" In *New femininities: Postfeminism, neoliberalism and subjectivity*, edited by C. M. Scharff and Ros Gill. London: Palgrave.

Press, Andrea Lee, and Elizabeth R. Cole. 1999. *Speaking of abortion: Television and authority in the lives of women*. Chicago: University of Chicago Press.

Press, Andrea Lee, and Terry Strathman. 1993. "Work, family, and social class in television images of women: Prime-time television and the construction of postfeminism." *Women and Language* 16:7–15.

Reger, Jo. 2005. *Different wavelengths: Studies of the contemporary women's movement*. New York: Routledge.

Riggs, Marlon. 1992. *Color adjustments: Black in prime time*. Motion picture, 86 min. San Francisco: California Newsreel.

Rogin, Michael Paul. 1992. "Blackface, white noise: The Jewish jazz singer finds his voice." *Critical Inquiry* 18:417–53.

Rogin, Michael Paul. 1996. *Blackface, white noise: Jewish immigrants in the Hollywood melting pot*. Berkeley: University of California Press.

Rosen, Marjorie. 1973. *Popcorn venues: Women, movies, and the American dream*. New York: Coward, McCann and Geoghegan.

Russo, Vito. 1981. *The celluloid closet: Homosexuality in the movies*. New York: Harper & Row.

Ryan, Alan. 1997. *John Dewey and the high tide of American liberalism*. New York: Norton.

Schwichtenberg, Cathy. 1992. *The Madonna connection: Representational politics, subcultural identities, and cultural theory*. Boulder, C.O.: Westview Press.

Showtime. (2009). *The L Word*. www.sho.com/site/lword/home.do.

Singer, Dorothy G., and Jerome L. Singer. 2001. *Handbook of children and the media*. Thousand Oaks, C.O.: Sage.

Spigel, Lynn. 1992. *Make room for television*. Chicago: University of Chicago Press.

Spigel, Lynn. 1995. "From the dark ages to the golden age: Women's memories and television reruns." *Screen* 36:16–33.

Spigel, Lynn, and Denise Mann. 1992. *Private screenings*. Minneapolis: University of Minnesota Press.

Taylor, Ella. 1989. *Prime time families: Television culture in post-war America*. London: University of California Press.

Tushnet, Rebecca. 2000. "Copyright as a model for free speech law." *Boston College Law Review* 42:1–79.

Valdivia, Angharad N. 1995. *Feminism, multiculturalism, and the media: Global diversities.* Thousand Oaks, C.O.: Sage.

Valdivia, Angharad N. 1996. "Rosie goes to Hollywood: The politics of representation." *Review of Education, Pedagogy, and Cultural Studies* 18:129–41.

Valdivia, Angharad N. 2004. "Latina/o communication and media studies today: An introduction." *The Communication Review* 7:107–12.

Valdivia, Angharad N. 2008. *Latina/o communication studies today.* New York: Peter Lang.

Vidmar, Neil, and Milton Rokeach. 1974. "Archie Bunker's bigotry: A study in selective perception and exposure." *The Journal of Communication* 24:36–47.

VIP Limited Partnership. 2002. "Buffy the vampire slayer official merchandise." www.thebuffyfanclub.com.

Walker, Rebecca. 1992. "Becoming the third wave." *Ms.*, January–February.

Walker, Rebecca. 1995. *To be real: Telling the truth and changing the face of feminism.* New York: Anchor.

Walsh, Andrea S. 1984. *Women's film and female experience, 1940–1950.* New York: Praeger.

Walters, Suzanna Danuta. 2001. *All the rage: The story of gay visibility in America.* Chicago: University of Chicago Press.

Watkins, S. Craig. 1998. *Representing: Hip hop culture and the production of black cinema.* Chicago: University of Chicago Press.

Wikipedia. N.d.-a. "Cinema of the United Kingdom." http://en.wikipedia.org/wiki/cinema_of_the_United_Kingdom.

Wikipedia. N.d.-b. "Do the right thing." http://en.wikipedia.org/wiki/Do_the_right_thing.

Wikipedia. N.d.-c. "Third-wave feminism." http://en.wikipedia.org/wiki/Third_Wave_feminism.

Williams, Raymond. 1958. *Culture and society, 1780–1950.* New York: Columbia University Press.

Williams, Raymond. 1961. *The long revolution.* New York: Columbia University Press.

Williams, Raymond. 1966. *Communications.* London: Chatto & Windus.

Williams, Raymond. 1976. *Keywords: A vocabulary of culture and society.* New York: Oxford University Press.

Williams, Raymond. 1991. "Base and superstructure in Marxist cultural theory." In *Rethinking popular culture: Contemporary perspectives in cultural studies,* edited by C. Mukerji and Michael Schudson. Berkeley: University of California Press.

Wilson, Leah. 2005. *Welcome to Wisteria Lane: On America's favorite desperate housewives.* Dallas, T.X.: BenBella.

Chapter 6

Studying Media Texts and Their Reception in the New Media Environment

In chapters 4 and 5, we discussed the history of the way different types of inequalities have been represented in the media, and introduced the theoretical tools media studies scholars have used for analyzing these issues. We also considered the probable social impact of these representations as we examined the research about their reception. These chapters followed on from the first three chapters of the book, which introduced the general issue of the new media environment and its impact on modern life (chapter 1), the political economy and patterns of ownership and control historically and in the new media environment (chapter 2), and considered the implications of new media for the democratic process (chapter 3). In this chapter, we focus on the reception of new media and its implications for democracy and inequality. We've moved from an era in which film and television have been the dominant media, to an age in which even these media are presented, and received, through the Internet, and in various technologically new, digital formats. What are the implications of these changes for the issues of democracy and inequality which we've been considering thus far? Here we offer a preliminary answer to this question, the investigation of which is ongoing in current media studies scholarship.

Suppose you were to decide that you were going to the movies one Sunday afternoon. You decided that, perhaps, you would see the new hit movie *Knocked Up*, to use our running example. To make this decision you turned on your computer to check the current movie locations and times. Finding that *Knocked Up* was showing nearby at a convenient time, you took a minute to "Google" its title. In a matter of seconds, you are presented with a screen full of referents. First, you are referred to the Internet Movie Database (IMDB), which provides all the following information:

- Flashes the entire cast and crew, and a plot synopsis
- Offers sneak-peak trailers
- Gives you a summary (you are warned that this summary may contain plot "spoilers")
- Tells you how many awards the film has been nominated for and has won
- Offers you a "MOVIEmeter," which tells you how popular the film was this week (whether it went "up" or "down" in popularity, and by how many percentage points)
- Offers an array of further links to the background of each member of the film's crew, and each star
- Tells you whether and when the film is upcoming on the television screen, information that might encourage you to cancel your outing to the movies altogether

Other sites offer even more detailed plot summaries (Wikipedia), detailed reviews, online viewer comments, a series of video clips, and a critical article entitled "When Chick Flicks Get Knocked Up" by Alissa Quart (2008) in *Mother Jones* magazine, which discusses the "dark" nature of the slew of new alleged comedies about fertility, and ruminates over their popularity and their particular slants.

You'll probably attend the film with one or two of your friends, and discuss it afterward. Perhaps one of them will have seen it reviewed on the *Ebert and Roper* television show, another will have read reviews in the local paper, and you will have the *Mother Jones* review, with its attendant online forum, fresh in your mind. All of these varied media exposures will be influential in the ensuing discussion you and your friends have about the film after you view it, and set the stage for (or "prime," in social science parlance) the way you think about the film in your own mind as well.

In the new media environment, your movie attendance, which was never an activity fully isolated from the rest of your life, has acquired the qualities of a multimedia event. This makes any assessment of how the media influence you a complex problem at best. For example, despite the relative proliferation of ideologically anti-abortion texts like *Knocked Up*, which we analyzed in chapter 4, opinions about abortion in the United States have remained relatively constant for the past 35 years, since the US Supreme Court legalized the act by declaring a woman's right to choose in the famous *Roe v. Wade* case of 1972.[1] Does this fact mean that media products like *Knocked Up* have no impact?

In fact, the problem of media influence was always complex. How do you assess the relative importance of your own interpretation of a film text vis-à-vis your friend's ideas, the newspaper review that you read, and the way the popular kids at school, the wealthy family down the street, or your boss at work discussed it with you prior, during, or after your own viewing? Add the new media environment to the mix, which as we've seen increases exponentially the number of reviews, video previews, discussion forums, critical analyses, and alternative formats for viewing that are available at your fingertips, in a matter of minutes or seconds, and the problem becomes even more difficult.

As we saw in chapters 4 and 5, ideas about how much the media affect us have shifted over the decades amongst media scholars. This is in response both to changing social ideas about the role of media in society, and to the development of the new interactive technologies that we consider the primary constituents of the "new media environment." The development of new media technologies make the enterprise of the analysis of media products and their influence even more complex, particularly given the increasingly intertwined nature of media production and media reception.

Analyzing media images themselves has also become a more complicated enterprise. With the breakdown of the studio era in Hollywood film, and the decline of the network era on television, we have witnessed a proliferation of images and perspectives in media products. There is in fact more diversity because there is more targeting of audiences. The age of the "mass" in "mass media analysis" has rapidly come to a close. Media images have not only proliferated but also diversified. More and more, creators consider particular segments of an increasingly fragmented media audience, rather than aiming at what used to be called the "lowest common denominator" of the mass audience (see Gitlin [1983] for a fuller explanation of this concept). The interesting and important question for scholars today is to assess whether audience fragmentation has actually increased, in a progressive way, the diversity of representations available to the average viewer or user of media. Some argue that, yes, diversity of representation has clearly increased, the evidence being the simply increased numbers of racial, ethnic, and sexual minorities on television, in Hollywood films, and so on, some of which we detail later in this chapter.

Others argue that given the increased concentration in patterns of ownership and control, which we've discussed extensively in chapter 2 above, we can expect, and in fact witness, a growing lack of diversity in media representations, particularly with regard to political and socioeconomic perspectives. Complicating matters is the fact, as we've pointed out previously, that the media environment is very different now, and is much more participatory as evidenced by the proliferation of phenomena such as blogs, Web pages, chat rooms, Twitter, and so on, all of which have become accessible to almost all segments of society.

For instance, returning to our example of popular media representations of abortion, there were systematic, identifiable, historic shifts in the dominant perspective on this issue that, in the case of television, the major networks took (Montgomery 1989; Condit 1990; Press and Cole 1999) as they produced entertainment programming. While initially abortion on prime-time television was presented as a noncontroversial option for pregnant women, protesters quickly shifted network television representation of abortion to the presentation of an avowedly "balanced" perspective (Montgomery 1989). "Balance," initially defined as presenting people on both sides of the choice issue, has slowly but unmistakably evolved into the unacceptability of presenting abortion in at all a sympathetic light, and the recent reluctance of any television networks to represent abortion at all (Press and Cole 1999; Pollitt 2008). While over the past two decades some cable television stations have created programming critical of this view, even that has dwindled recently.[2]

The history of these televisual and filmic representations of abortion indicates that although there are more television channels in the current era and a proliferation of images, nevertheless there are still overall, systematic slants in many of the images we confront, and these can be uncovered when certain basic properties of media representations are critically analyzed. It is the task of the media studies scholar to identify such media slants, even as some findings about media representations become more and more difficult to generalize in the age of a more fragmented media.

In this chapter, we'll briefly discuss recent innovative approaches to studying the new media environment, focusing on how the issues, and methods, central to new media and its study have transformed the field of media studies. In the course of our discussion we discuss the methodological perspectives we ourselves have employed in two new studies of our own, and present some preliminary findings from these studies.

Transformative Images in the New Media Environment

The study of representations on new media such as the Internet has posed some interesting possibilities and challenges for those interested in the study of gender and its images. While this is a vast literature, it is important to mention just a few of the issues raised in the new scholarship.

What the Internet makes possible is an endlessly malleable set of representations that are much more amenable to "gender bending" than are images on television (though digital filmmaking has created this same possibility for other media such as film and television). Haraway's important work notes that in the age of new media, the representation of women is finally freed from embodiment. She coins the term "cyborg" instead, a term indicating the hybrid of human and machine, to replace what she terms the essentializing concept of "woman" (Haraway 1991: 155; 1997; Bell 2007).

Nakamura's work initiated the study of the representations of race on the Internet (Kolko, Nakamura, and Rodman 2000; Nakamura 2002). She argues that the study of racial representations on the Internet is complex, as racial categories are inexorably tied to bodies in everyday life, yet on the Internet, representations are divorced from actual bodies. Therefore a whole plethora of new approaches to the representation of race becomes possible. She finds cyberspace to be "raced"; racial stereotypes, or "cybertypes" (2002: 3), persist and need further examination, even in the bodiless space of the Internet.

Nakamura examines the way that cybertypes replace normal stereotypes in online representations. Most interesting is her argument showing the way visual racial tropes are re-created in the iconography of various Internet images. Thus the images themselves, which would not necessarily have a quality defined as "racial," appropriate the norms of the "raced" representations common in our norms of body representation, main-taining these norms even in cyberspace. She talks specifically about the characters in various computer games that conform to Asian stereotypes of the "Oriental" male with a "sword," confirming the stereotype of the Asian male as potent, antique, exotic, and anachronistic (2002: 445; quoted in Silver and Massanari 2006: 135).

Jenkins (2006), Turkle (1996, 2005), and others have written about the way media "content" is presented; in fact, the very notion of what media "content" *is* is being redefined. For example, Jenkins' book *Convergence Culture: Where Old and New Media Collide* (2006) describes the proliferation of book-, television-, or film-induced texts that have emerged in new media locations like the Internet around such popular old-media phenomena as the *Harry Potter* books, the film *The Matrix*, or the hit reality television show *American Idol*. He documents the amount of fan activity and the creation of new fan-produced texts that are then made generally available through Web technologies (we return to Jenkins' important work later in the chapter). Others have documented similar excitement and activity around the television show *Lost* (Golumbia 2004).

Most of these discussions focus on the way new technologies facilitate a more interactive type of media text, one more easily amenable to the participation of a wide variety of people, and easily available as well to those who do not participate in its creation. This contrasts with, say, our discussion of earlier literature of *Star Trek* fans in chapter 4. While Jenkins (1992) and Bacon-Smith (1992) both investigated the creative activities of *Star Trek* fan cultures in the 1980s and 1990s, we are now witnessing a higher level of participation in these types of activities, given the increased ease of entry into the production process enabled by new media technologies. While once fans had to travel to conventions to obtain the books produced by others like themselves, or to communicate easily with them, now it is simple to turn on the computer and witness these productions, read them, use them, converse with other producers and users, and produce them for others in the online fan community.

While the questions raised concerning intellectual property are just beginning to be considered in the courts (Vaidhyanathan, 2001, 2004), in fact most industry executives agree that media content has entered a new era in which traditional media forms, texts, and modes of ownership will soon be unrecognizable. The intellectual property issues, the issues concerning the new forms of community made possible by online groups, and the issues concerning the new types of language used to facilitate online communication: all of these and many other questions pertaining to the new interactive environment now constitute a significant and growing area of study that is changing rapidly in media studies. This new area involves not only the Internet but also contemporary forms of older media such as television and film. Through their new media connections – the availability of film and television shows on the Internet, and the presence of official and nonofficial sites, blogs, discussion groups, and the like about these media products – older forms of media such as film and television have morphed into a more interactive format in recent years.

Globalization and the new shape of media identities

Although our book has focused on media in the US, the scholarship in media studies shows that it is no longer possible to consider nation-states in isolation from one another. Additionally, media produced in the United States have had influence and exposure far beyond national boundaries. There is now a long and established tradition in media studies looking at both nonwestern media industries such as the Indian film industry (Punathambekar 2005, 2006) and the Japanese film industry (Desser 1983, 1988) alongside other similar topics.

Much of the most interesting new work in media studies addresses these issues. Kraidy (2005, 2010) offers an authoritative study of what he calls the "cultural logic of globalization" that has been influential in the study of media. He offers a theory based on Homi Bhabha's notion of "hybridity," which argues that previously isolated identities must now be considered as intertwined with one another (see Bhabha 1994). What this means in terms of media is that there is no pure "western" media product, or pure "nonwestern" product, particularly once one begins to consider the context in which western products are received and understood in nonwestern national contexts, and by non-Westerners in diasporic locations. For example, in Kraidy's discussion of reality television as received in the Arab world (Kraidy 2010), he traces the way the Western-developed reality television format became popular in the Arab world, and the ways in which its reception galvanized public discussion of difficult political issues such as the position of women in society, religion, political power, individual achievement versus social harmony, and the meaning of modernity itself (Kraidy 2010: 193, 202). The Western form morphed fundamentally into a new form that combined the concerns of Western and Arab societies.

Even the American media products we've discussed earlier in this chapter have taken on a global life of their own. Although, as we discussed in chapter 2, there is nothing new about the globalization of media (see our discussion of Gitelman's [2006] work on recorded music), there are some new aspects to the shape of globalization in the current media environment. New media technologies have made it increasingly possible for film, television, and other media produced in the United States to be consumed internationally, and a calculation about the international audience is now a standard business consideration in all media production. In the case of film at least, the flow is beginning to move in the other direction as well, as production becomes less nationally situated and takes on an international character. Many popular films, as with media products in general (as we mentioned above), are conceived in one country, shot in another, and edited and distributed in a third. In fact, it's become increasingly difficult to assign a particular nation of origin to media products. We are living in an era of global transformation in which more and more media products will be increasingly less nationally located, with correspondingly weaker national identities. An international media community is becoming a more real possibility, with attendant ramifications for the diversity of values that its media products embody.

Some argue (Dorfman, Kunzle, Lawrence, and Mattelart 1986; Grossberg, Wartella, Witney, and MacGregor Wise 2006) that media products often carry the values of international capital, including a positive evaluation of hard work, competition, the sanctity of private property, nationalism, and a separation between the valued middle-class inhabitants of the western developed world and everyone else, the latter being generally devalued. Much analytic work in media studies supports these allegations of a western, cultural imperialist bias in many media products. Work analyzing racial and ethnic images in film, for example, reveals an overwhelming majority of white, western characters in positive roles. In addition, many mainstream films produced in the United States support the sanctity of the national security state, and assert the militaristic values that bolster it (Kellner 2005). The glamorous or at least upper-middle-class ambiance of many, possibly most, media products produced in the United States supports a plethora of mainstream, western capitalist values as well. In this sense, media globalization supports the global export of capitalist values from the West to nonwestern societies.

Media Reception Research in the New Media Environment

Media reception, even pertaining to older media like television or film, now takes place in the context of a media environment that includes a variety of interactive processes. As mentioned before, a quick Google search of *Knocked Up* yields pages and pages of critical reviews, movie trailers, and publicity materials, and even a site entitled "Knocked Up Celebrities" on which Brooke Burke "dishes about being a mom to four kids." This introduces a plethora of new information to the viewer of the film.

New forms of user-viewer participation are introduced as well. By the time you get to page 4 of the search, passing the "official fan listing" site for the film, you encounter interactive sites, displaying discussions by interested viewers. Some of these discussions engage the controversial issue of the notable *absence* of the discussion of an abortion for Katherine Heigl's character in the film, which we have pointed out above. Sites wherein Seth Rogen or Katherine Heigl actually discuss their reactions to this aspect of the film are easily located. For example, Rogen is quoted on the "beliefnet" site as saying he felt the film needed to bypass the decision-making process and simply get to the part *after* Heigl decides to keep the baby; Heigl is quoted in *Vanity Fair* as saying she knew the film was sexist in its treatment of women.

So, this Googling of *Knocked Up* blogs takes you into a more interactive media world than had been offered by traditional television or film. For pages and pages, fans and ordinary viewers offer their opinions of the film, and sometimes speak directly to the critical controversies over the film. On these pages, the interactive possibilities of the new media environment become apparent. The "reception" paradigm can no longer be accurately represented by a sole viewer, or even a family or other small group, staring passively and quietly at a glowing television or movie screen in the dark. Instead, reception in the new media environment involves considering a much more complex situation that takes into account the ability of media viewers and users to participate actively as they receive media content, in a process that generates new and different types of media products that others then receive.

Attempts to study reception and usage in the new media environment have been varied and remain largely experimental, as researchers are still searching to find the best methodologies suited to this task. We need to utilize a variety of methods to explore the multiple dimensions of reception in the new context. We have found in our own work on new media that a multimethodological approach works best, one that can tap into the creativity enabled by the new media environment as well as engage issues of its influence or effects (we discuss this in detail later in this chapter).

Earlier work pioneered some of these methods and topics. Scholars like Sherry Turkle (1996, 2005) and Henry Jenkins (2006) have looked closely at the activities of users of the Internet, focusing on the creative possibilities of those involved in multiplayer games (in the case of Turkle) or those involved in producing fan fiction of various kinds using a variety of new media technologies (in the case of Jenkins).

Jenkins, for example, looks at the type of media content produced by fans of *Star Wars* and other popular film, television, or games (2006). In a chapter of his 2006 book subtitled "Grassroots Creativity Meets the Media Industry," he details how "[f]an digital film is to cinema what the punk DIY culture was to music" (2006: 132), referencing the beginnings of punk music in the 1970s when the least produced music became the most popular. Jenkins goes on to discuss a fertile, creative climate in which fan filmmakers come up with ideas that are starting to make their way into the mainstream industry. Their ideas turn up in commercial media, a rich interchange facilitated by the new media environment, which places the means of production in the hands of ordinary media consumers. One example he uses here is that digital filmmaker Kevin Rubio, after producing the 10-minute, $1,200 film *Troops* in 1998 which spoofed *Star Wars*, was profiled in *Entertainment Weekly*. Rubio thereby captured the attention of *Star Wars* creator George Lucas, who hired him to write for *Star Wars* comic books (Jenkins 2006: 131–2).

Jenkins gives example after example of situations like this as he makes a case for what he calls the current "convergence culture": the place where old and new media collide. Increasingly, scholars find that the study of new media use and reception is in fact the study of old media as well. The new media environment is one in which all types of media are used simultaneously. Our *Knocked Up* example illustrated precisely this situation. It also illustrated some of its consequences: viewers of the film *Knocked Up* who receive the film in the context of the new media environment are often confronted much more directly with the controversies that these products provoke. In this case, the controversy about how the film represented abortion, commented on throughout the film critics' reception of the film, was made immediately accessible to viewers, and subject to their comments and to extensive debates, through the new media environment in online reviews and their connected commentaries, and in various blogs about the topic.

Fundamentally, the new media environment is one in which "reception" as a paradigm must be enlarged to include the creative participations and productions that this environment enables. Reception studies in this changing system highlight a variety of issues that were incipient in the "active audience tradition" but have now taken on a new shape. Scholars have examined everything from the role media production plays in the lives of young people (Radway 2008) to the forms of social networking and social spaces that new media technologies make possible (Boyd 2007, 2009), thus enabling new and evolving types of communications to take place between people, in new configurations of time and space.

For example, Turkle followed young adults who become lost in the identities they assume playing online games. One story she relates is that of a 13-year-old girl who says that she finds it easier to establish relationships online, and actually have sexual contact online, than in "RL" (real life) (1996: 227). She also relates the story of the married couple, Martin and Beth. Beth has decided to tolerate Martin's online "sexual" relationships, considering them as not really adulterous (1996: 224). But when Martin began playing a female character having sex with a "man," Beth felt her trust had been violated, a vignette that illustrates how difficult it has become to draw the line between virtual and "real" reality (Turkle 1996: 225), as well as how complicated is the process of assessing an individual's "real" gender or sexuality.

Boyd and Ellison (2008) examine in close detail the way young people use social-networking sites like Facebook and MySpace. Interviewing many young Americans who use social-networking sites, they found that these sites have transformed processes of self-presentation, socializing with peers, and negotiating adult society for many young people. They argue that social-networking sites should be understood as networked publics that are simultaneously imagined communities and actual, technological spaces. Boyd and Ellison describe in some complexity the way new networked publics differ from the unmediated in terms of publics; their properties (persistence, searchability, replicability, and sociability); and, in terms of their dynamics, how they consist of invisible audiences. They argue that they have blurred the traditional way we think about the boundaries between the public and the private.

Others have focused their investigations more on the limitations that the new media environment places on some groups. Norris (2001), Mosco (2004), and Compaine (2001) have examined the new media environment and have noted the differential access, and differential types of competencies, experienced by various racial minority and ethnic groups, by women, and by older users. As cited above, Hargittai (2003b; Hargittai and Walejko 2008; see also Zillien and Hargittai 2009) and Dimaggio,

Hargittai, Neuman, and Robinson (2001) have amply documented gender, social class, and racial difference – in terms of both skill and access – amongst users of new media. Some scholars (Warschauer 2003) argue that the notion of the digital divide is becoming outmoded, in the sense that in industrialized nations, those who want or need computer technologies in fact can afford them, and those who don't have them don't need them. Others, however, argue that although some gaps may have been erased (that between women and men, for example), others persist, such as the gap between different racial and ethnic groups, between single-parent and other families, between the old and the young, and between high-income versus low-income individuals (Servon 2002). In all, the research shows that new media overwhelmingly both reinforce and reproduce social inequalities, in direct contradistinction to the idea that the new media environment would expedite liberation from these inequities. We illustrate this point with some examples from our own research below.

Livingstone (2008; Livingstone and Bober 2006a, 2006b) examines the way that children develop a different type of media "literacy" given the possibilities and limitations of the new media environment. How, she asks, are literary skills – for example, the mechanics of writing and reading – affected, and transformed, by the increasing number of hours spent by children and others on computers, and by their participation in new communicative formats like instant messaging, e-mail, Facebook, and other types of interactive virtual environments?

The results are inconclusive, in that some competencies are enhanced, and others diminished, by the possibilities and potentials provided. For example, there is some evidence that children now write more, and more easily, given new media technologies that encourage and facilitate written communications. But the research also shows that this writing conforms less to formal rules of grammar, spelling, and sentence structure. Are our competencies breaking down? Or are we developing new languages of communication? These are the questions being raised by media studies scholars now, and the jury on these issues is still out.

Global reception in the new media environment

Finally, the issue of the global or transnational nature of media is a fixture of the new media environment, and has implications for how we study media reception. More and more, it is difficult to pin down the national home of various media productions. To rephrase the example we gave above, a production might be financed globally, written by writers in Los Angeles, filmed in Vancouver or Australia, acted by Europeans, and distributed worldwide. The global nature of many media products is compounded, of course, by the new sense of place created by the World Wide Web. As Boyd's work established, participation in social-networking sites – and, by extension, other activities enabled by Web access – creates a sense of a global space, located nowhere physically but achieving a status in the universe of cyberspace that is real nonetheless.

Gillespie (1995) studied teenagers of Indian heritage and their families in London. She writes about how television and video are used to re-create cultural traditions amongst this diasporic community. She argues that these youth use media to create a new pluralist, hybrid cultural form of expression that is neither entirely Indian nor entirely British. She offers as an example the popularity of the feature film *Wild West*, which follows the story of a country-and-western band consisting of three Muslim brothers and their Sikh and Hindu friends. While the hero's mother wishes to return home to the Punjab, he wishes to fly to the United States to pursue a recording contract (1995: 5). The story melds the heroes' attachment to cultural forms indigenous to their own culture and to western musical traditions and business opportunities.

Some of the literature about global media and its reception examines the consumption of these nonwestern products in their country of origin, such as Juluri's study of the meaning of music television among young viewers in India (2003), where he argues that the reception of popular western music television is part of a major rethinking of common sense, which begins to look different in the context of a global culture. Some look at the consumption of western products in nonwestern contexts, such as Abu-Lughod's examination of the viewing of American television in Egypt (1998). Discussed in more detail in chapter 4, Liebes and Katz (1993) examined the reception of the American television show *Dallas* in Israel, where it was received differently by Jewish and Arab viewers, and in Japan, where Japanese citizens rejected the show. While many themes were common to all groups—for example, the theme that the rich are unhappy—there were differences in emphasis when comparing discussions of the show by the different groups interviewed. The Arabs emphasized primarily kinship roles and norms, the kibbutznicks and the Arabs mentioned the moral dilemmas posed by the show, but only the Americans made the business relations of the show a primary topic of discussion (Liebes and Katz 1993: 154).

A series of other studies of new media examines the global context of its influence and reception. Miller and Slater (2000) study the Internet in Trinidad, paying particular attention to the way Internet use facilitates the development of national identity in a global context for Trinidadians whose families are confronting various forms of westernization and immigration. Fung (2009) studies the case of Internet use in Hong Kong, focusing specifically on gaming and its influence on ideas about "real life" versus "cyberlife." Gajjala (2004) looks at the way the Internet builds communities amongst south Asian women, and how important it is in facilitating and creating diasporic identities in various south Asian communities. She specifically interrogates ideas of feminism and how these ideas become appropriated through the Internet, and how problematic the translation from western feminism is to these communities. All of these studies emphasize the central role of new media in any examination of changing national, gender, sexual, ethnic, and racial identities in our global society.

Gender, Race, Sexuality, and Social Class Inequality in New Media Reception: A New Study

The issue of media representations of inequality, and the reception of these representations, changes fundamentally in the age of new media. In an era where the promise of the Internet is to increase democracy and participation in our lives, new media forms hold out the potential of increased participation and influence, and decreased inequality, potentials that are particularly important for minorities who have felt, and been, ignored in the history and governance of this nation.

Early experience with the new media environment illustrates that this potential truly is there. The 2004 presidential election was the first to actually include a new level of widespread political participation by small donors, who contributed in much larger numbers than ever before in the Internet campaign of Democratic primary candidate Howard Dean (Shirky 2007; see our discussion below of the importance of new media in the 2004 election). The election of Barack Obama to the presidency in 2008 cemented the fact that new media have become big players in the American political scene. Obama's campaign utilized the Internet to organize an enormous number of smaller donors and supporters that previous election campaigns had been unable to tap – in particular the lower middle class,

African Americans, and the young (Trippi 2008). In addition to extensive e-mail lists, the campaign made great use of Facebook and other social-networking sites. Many credit his victory in large part to this successful online organizing, by which he was able to mobilize groups traditionally disempowered by their typical underrepresentation in our voting booths.

In other examples of the significance of new media technologies, we see more response and interactivity than ever before as viewers of all social classes, races, genders, and sexual orientations can actually communicate with networks, film companies, and each other about the media products they receive. So, a show like *The L Word* (already discussed in chapter 5), which represents lesbian life in the United States, can become a focal point of discussion amongst lesbians, and about lesbians by those of other sexual orientations, all of whom have access to the online forums that discuss this show in detail. Similar forums arose around *The Wire*, a TV show that portrayed ghetto life in Baltimore. There were many online discussions of the problems of the poor, and of poor minority communities, facilitated by the online forums organized around this show. The home websites of the networks that produce these shows are the locations for many of these forums, so that viewer feedback and commentary are now immediately accessible to producers on a much larger scale than was possible prior to the new media environment.

Finally, the means of producing media are available to more of us than ever before. Almost every college student now has the capability to produce short films, using equipment available to more segments of the population than ever before. In this context, scholars have posed the question: who benefits? Will the cause of democracy be furthered by these potentials and uses of the new technologies that constitute our new media environment? On a scholarly level, what this means is that the study of media production has become merged with the study of media reception: it is increasingly difficult to separate the two.

Another area of concern is the impact of new media technologies on the lives of young people. Scholars have always voiced concern about the impact of media on the young. In the 1930s, the Payne Fund financed a series of studies examining the impact of movies on children and teenagers (Blumer 1932; Charters 1933). These studies found that the impact of violence and romance in film was dependent on the age of the child, which affected the ability of children to understand what was presented on screen. Many others have extensively studied the impact of television on children (Himmelweit 1958; Livingstone 1990, 2002), generating a plethora of data with sometimes conflicting conclusions. Some argue that television has been harmful to children, and others that it increases their horizons in some ways. The literature on the impact of television on children is extensive, and the issues complex.

The new media environment introduces a new set of considerations in the issue of children's and adolescents' use of the media. One concern is the way gender, race, class, and sexuality morph into different categories in the new media environment. Adolescents freely post their profiles on such Internet sites as YouTube and MySpace and can create identities with much more freedom than they were able to do before the advent of such tools and practices. Identities seem no longer tied to the actual, physical reality of bodies.

One example of the dangers this poses for adolescents can be found in examining the court case regarding Megan Meier's suicide. This tragic incident serves as a good example of the gender bending made possible by new media – in fact it was easy, in this case, for an older woman to assume the online identity of an adolescent male. Unfortunately, in this instance she did this explicitly for the purpose of harassing a young woman who subsequently committed suicide as a result of this harassment.

The woman, Lori Drew, mother of another teenaged girl who was a social rival of Megan's, pretended to be an adolescent suitor of Megan. In the guise of her adolescent male persona, she then insulted, criticized, and harshly rejected Megan, who committed suicide as a direct result of this feigned rejection. The courts were nonplussed by the case, due to the legality of this process of "posing" online, despite its tragic consequence in this unusual instance. Although doing nothing technically illegal, this mother was able to drive her daughter's nemesis to suicide through the use of new media. What made the case even more complicated was that the mother's younger employee had acted as her technical assistant in the case, facilitating her ability to accomplish this online posing. Who, if anyone, was at fault for the adolescent's death? (See Wikipedia [n.d.] for a fuller explanation of this tragic incident.)

One of the disturbing findings regarding the use of new media by children and adolescents is that, as we've discussed above, gender, race, and class differences persist in the expertise required to use particular media skills. Joiner et al. find that male college students used the Internet more than female students; in particular, they were more likely to use game websites, to use other specialist websites, and to download material from the Internet (Joiner, Gavin, Duffield, Brosnan, Crook, Durndell, et al. 2005). The differences were relatively small, however, and gender differences in Internet use seem to be decreasing, although some particular usage differences persist (Bimber 2000; Hargittai 2003b, 2008). Walkerdine raises an interesting set of questions concerning how gender differences may begin at the earliest levels in games that are designed differently to appeal to young girls and boys, and involve developing different skills for each (2007).

Some of the most important work in gender and new media involves the increasing participation in the production of new media, particularly by young women and girls (Kearney 2006; Radway 2008). The participation in the production of new media by young people and adolescents, which exists and is growing, is a key factor in changing the notion of media reception, which now takes a different form given the increasingly interactive nature of the technologies. Kearney (2006) examines, in historical context beginning with studies predating the existence of the Internet, the activities and products of young women as media makers. She argues, in a reference to Mulvey's theory of the sexism of classical Hollywood cinema, that such productions have "developed the girl's gaze" (2006: 189). While extensively documenting the fact that Hollywood is still run by men, Kearney nevertheless offers a plethora of examples of women-produced media that differ significantly from the mass-produced, commercial, male-dominated Hollywood products, and indeed explicitly challenge the norms of female activities and beauty assumed in conventional media products. Increased access to the means of media production made possible by new media technologies is a key democratizing element helping young women to develop alternative images that challenge the sexism in dominant media. On the other hand, much of the woman-produced media does not in fact differ in fundamental ways from other media products. Female-controlled media products are not always more sensitive to the needs and situations of women.

Finally, there is a substantial and still growing literature about social class and racial differences in new media skills and use, popularly referred to in the scholarly literature as the "digital divide." Many researchers have uncovered inequalities in access to the Internet and in particular to broadband and high-speed Internet, and in skills relating to its use, amongst racial and ethnic minorities, lower income populations, rural residents, and those with less education (Hargittai 2003b). Researchers disagree as to whether the divides amongst groups are increasing or decreasing. Hargittai (2003a) notes that the same statistical data can be interpreted in several ways, giving rise to confusion about whether over time the divides between groups will simply disappear without intervention, or whether concrete differences exist that must be directly addressed to level the digital playing field.

In general, much of the research points to the distinctions between access and skill: access alone does not ensure equality between groups, and the measurement of Internet skills is a complex business but does seem to show that to some extent women, older people, ethnic and racial minorities, and members of low-income groups lag in particular skills necessary for successful Internet use (DiMaggio, Hargittai, Neuman, and Robinson 2001; Robinson, DiMaggio, and Hargittai 2001; Hargittai 2008), though in most cases – in particular, in the cases of age and gender – these differences seem to be shrinking (Joiner, Gavin, Duffield, Brosnan, Crook, Durndell, et al. 2005). As we mentioned at the conclusion to chapter 3, the key remedy to these inequalities is a widespread media literacy suited to the demands of the new media environment. This is central if we are to minimize these differences in media use and capacities, and if we are to minimize the ways these differences contribute to overall inequality in our society.

New Studies: Gender and Social Class Identities in the New Media Environment

Press' recent study, which we discuss in some depth here, focuses on both the possibilities and limitations of media effects and usage in the new media environment. In a longitudinal study of adolescent girls and boys using the Internet, which focuses on children of different social classes and races using the Internet for schoolwork as well as leisure activities, Press (2004, 2005a, 2005b) used ethnographic methods to look contextually at how the impact of computers in both the work and leisure realms varied for girls across social classes. A brief presentation of some of her findings serves as emblematic of the important issues scholars are facing, studying, and discussing in current media studies work.

In the study, Press discusses the case of Rebecca, a working-class girl who became a computer "addict" given the long absences of her single mother and her relatively long, unsupervised hours on the computer. Rebecca serves as an interesting case given that her long hours on the computer did develop a certain sort of competence in that she writes extensively on the computer and has learned rudimentary computer skills. Although this might have translated into better research skills facilitating her homework and concomitant progress in school, in actuality it did not. Instead, as a teen Rebecca used her time on the computer to basically avoid doing homework by communicating with her friends, often far into the night, and to avoid reading required books by relying on the book notes readily available online.

Although middle-class adolescents were observed in the study using the computer similarly, often they were supervised more closely by parents steering their computer use into directions more directly favorable to their progress in school. For example, one middle-class boy, Isaac, was encouraged to be creative and constructive in his computer use by the close supervision and involvement of his mother. He was able to create CDs of his own music, market them, and copyright them, aided closely by his facility with the Internet.

Rebecca and Isaac are two of the young people whom Press followed for several years in this longitudinal study. In this time she discovered that, indeed, these differences had influenced the future directions of their lives. Rebecca, for example, who was 14 at the time of her first interview, by the age of 22 had dropped out of community college to marry a serviceman. She continued working at the kind of minimum-wage jobs, in supermarkets, which she had begun during her high school years. In a pattern typical for working-class girls, marriage interrupted Rebecca's educational plans, and she had yet to regain her momentum. She was thinking, very vaguely, about continuing her education, as she maintained her interest in computers. Her new experience as a military wife, however, had given rise to an alternative plan to enlist in the military and follow a career parallel to her husband's. This, she reasoned, would give her some college benefits, and some maternity and health benefits, unlike the temporary position she currently held, as well as yield her a higher salary. Rebecca had been unable to turn her interest in computers into a skill that would translate into an advantage on the job market. Her new environment following her marriage, however, had given her some new ideas for her future direction, and she still harbored hopes of working with computers, and receiving computer training, in the military.

Isaac, on the other hand, also 14 at the time of his first interview, by the age of 22 had been able to do precisely this. His interest in music production continued throughout his college years, during which he studied some music and continued playing in a local band. After college his mother supported his desire to find employment in a recording studio by taking him on a trip to Los Angeles, during which he investigated firsthand the opportunities available in studios in that area. Deciding that an internship in Chicago offered him superior employment, Isaac moved there with the full financial and emotional support of his parents, who kept in touch as he tried to launch his career in the area of musical technology, remained available to advise him on graduate programs, and so on.

The contrast between these two cases is interesting for several reasons. First, Isaac's case validates the findings of educational scholars like Lareau (2003) and others, who demonstrate that parental involvement in the lives of middle-class children is much more extensive than for working-class kids, and opens many doors and opportunities for their future lives. Isaac's mother is planning future trips with him as well to help him become situated in his new career, and perhaps in a new graduate program that will facilitate this. This extensive attention from his parents helped to limit some of the impact of media, in his case helping him to transform his contact with the media in creative, productive ways that have ultimately turned into a promising career.

Rebecca, on the other hand, grew up with very little parental involvement from her single mother, who was forced to work extensive overtime, limiting their contact. Having little education herself, Rebecca's mother, though extremely concerned about her daughter's future direction, was unable to give her much guidance vis-à-vis her education or future career. Rebecca's use of media, therefore, did not develop in the promising and ultimately productive ways experienced by Isaac. This study, though preliminary, nevertheless illustrates the growing importance of studying media consumption in the context of the user's life, as we mentioned in chapter 3.

What is particularly interesting about the contrast between Rebecca and Isaac in the context of digital divide literature is the fact that it illustrates that early and extensive access to the Internet, and extensive use of Internet technologies, did not significantly widen Rebecca's horizons or increase her educational or employment opportunities, contrary to the assumptions of some scholars of the digital divide. While she did participate in Internet dating, she ultimately met her husband through mutual friends. When she was enrolled in community college, she specifically elected *not* to take online courses, as she knew that being online distracted her from her studies, rather than enhanced them. Despite having developed an interest in work on computer technologies, she had been unable to follow through on this interest and turn it into any sort of practical, marketable skill, or even a skill that was beneficial to her educational endeavors.

Isaac, in contrast, followed a very different path. In his case, an early interest in computers and digital technologies translated directly into the facility that is currently enabling him to break into a very competitive field, the technical production of audio recordings, although he remains at the entry level. The resources available to him in his middle-class household – not only access to the Internet, but also the close counsel and advice of his highly educated parents (his mother is a successful artist and special education teacher, and his dad an architect) – enabled him to train for this career, largely on his own, and to find an entry-level position. Currently his parents are helping advise him as to what the next step will be: will he pursue a graduate degree related to his interest, will he continue to work his way up in the Chicago company that currently employs him, or will he move to Los Angeles or New York to pursue possibly richer employment opportunities in these environments? His mother is currently planning a trip to New York City to explore this last option with Isaac.

These findings, showing social class differences in the way computers benefit children and young people, both echo and supplement statistical research now being published. This research indicates that skill level in the digital environment is a complex issue, is difficult to measure, and certainly differs between the genders and social classes (Hargittai 2003a, 2003b). As we saw with our discussion of the two hurricanes in chapter 1, it is clear that changes in our media environment have not either erased or always directly reinforced the significance and impact of membership in different gender, race, and class groups in our society, but must be considered as a part of a larger, complex set of variables affecting these distinctions. There are no easy conclusions from Press' (admittedly small) and other, larger studies. For example, in some (though very few) cases, Press found working-class girls and their families who did derive direct benefit from the presence of the Internet in their homes.

For instance, the case of Betty Jo illustrates a working-class family able to harness computer use in the interests of their daughter's progress in school. In this case, a stay-at-home mom closely supervised her daughter's use of the Internet, severely curtailing its more social uses and encouraging its primarily educational uses. A more skilled reader than Rebecca, in part due to her extensive use of the library, again under her mother's supervision and encouragement, Betty Jo was able to use Internet research much more critically to produce advanced research papers relying on library as well as online sources, and she was able to critically appropriate the online sources she did find, relying on library materials to develop a critique of information she found to be flawed in the case of some of her research papers. This was an example of the Internet directly and markedly enhancing rather than restricting literary skills.

Betty Jo's position at the age of 22 reaffirms these fundamental differences between her experience and Rebecca's. Betty Jo is pursuing her associate's degree while working in computer technologies at the local community college. With her parents' full support, she is continuing to develop her Internet technology skills through her employment while investigating the best types of programs available to help her develop them further. She is interested in composing music and in developing software that can be used to enhance music composition. She is both sophisticated and realistic in her interests, and has been able to use her familiarity with the Internet, and with technology, to gather the kind of information about these issues that was not available in her immediate environment. Betty Jo serves as an excellent example of someone who, although from a working-class background, was able to use the opportunities that the Internet brought to expand her horizons significantly.

Press' study has raised questions about some of the more simplistic assumptions made by scholars of the digital divide, who look at the impact of new media on members of different social class and racial groups. These two young women illustrate two different possibilities for the impact of the introduction of new media into the lives of lower class children. Others in the study increase the complexity of the findings. One mother, for example, uses the Internet to home-school her young daughter for religious reasons. Yet the mother's own limited education constrains her ability to effectively educate her daughter; in this case the presence of the Internet, with its promise of easy access to information and ideas, in many ways masks these limitations.

The Internet certainly affords children ready access to creative means of production of products of all kinds. Yet it is the middle-class kids in this study who are better positioned to make use of these resources. They, and their parents, have access to the external help and information that allow the most extensive and creative use of Internet resources. So for example Isaac, the middle-class boy discussed earlier, was able, on his own, to copyright his own songs; he then placed his CD for sale online. And while some middle-class children were able, like the working-class Betty

Jo, to use the Internet to enhance their ability to research school assign-ments, often its usage was not so clearly beneficial. Like Rebecca, many middle-class children at times used the proximity of Internet resources and technology to shirk their schoolwork, by cribbing summaries of books they were supposed to read, IMing during homework time, or otherwise avoiding the rigors of school assignments.

A segment of the study that underscores the class differential in the impact of the Internet is the online community college teens Press studied. Sitting with members of the study who entered the local community college, which was a leader in pioneering online education, Press observed them as they experienced online education. Many of them were the first in their families to attend college. The online educational experience was fragmented at best due to the lack of real-time and real-space proximity to teachers. Their lack of engagement illustrated that the college experi-ence was being fundamentally altered, and fundamentally diluted, by the increasing popularity and cost-effectiveness of online education, particu-larly for working-class students.

The findings of this study point to the necessity of studying new media use in context. They also highlight the importance of ethnographic, inter-viewing, and observational methods that help scholars contextualize media reception and use, and supplement other, more large-scale statistical methods. While there are many isolated examples in the emergent litera-ture on this issue of Internet use enhancing children's creativity, we've yet to produce systematic studies that look across gender, social class, and racial divides at the impact of Internet use on children's learning, achieve-ment, and social class mobility, though this literature is beginning to emerge (Hargittai 2003a, 2003b). We now report on another study in which, together, we attempted to use multiple methodologies for contex-tual study of the use of the Internet by adults for political information during the American presidential election.

Politics, Media Impact and Use, and the New Media Environment

Together we have recently been involved in a large study of the use of the new media environment in the United States during a presidential election (Press, Williams, Moore, and Johnson-Yale 2005a, 2005b, 2006a, 2006b). In this study, again we find that there is no simple answer to the question of how the new media environment affects the quality and amount of information actually accessed and used by American citizens. Using a sociological perspective that allowed us to focus on individuals and their media worlds, our method enabled us to enlarge the traditional media studies focus on merely one medium by looking at media use in context. As a result, we report on the relative attention that citizens pay to a variety of different media at any given time. We also get a sense of the relative importance that citizens give to a variety of different media when seeking information on the political process, or when pursuing civic engagement.

The data used for this research consist of in-depth interviews and media diaries collected from 32 individuals from Champaign County, Illinois, during a three-month period from October to December 2004.[3] In the diaries, subjects recorded what media they used on a daily basis and how this media use intersected with other aspects of their public and private lives, including conversations about sports with coworkers, discussions of religion and politics with friends, and personal time with the family at home. Before the diary process was begun and after it had ended, in-depth interviews were conducted with subjects to understand their perspectives on a variety of issues, as well as explore major themes that emerged in their diaries. In sum, the diaries and interviews allow a detailed understanding of how media are used in everyday lives, as well as the implications of this for understanding the relationship between media use and civic engagement.

We do not claim that our participants constituted a representative random sample. Nevertheless, subjects' socioeconomic characteristics varied widely, and the pool included both media-rich and media-poor households and the range in between. Our various subject groups included secular and religious individuals, US citizens and immigrants, students and retired individuals, and members of a diverse spectrum of racial and ethnic groups. Subjects in the study used a broad range of new media – including cable, satellite and digital television, DVDs, cellular telephones, and the Internet. In the study we also included their use of old media such as radio, broadcast television, and print media (e.g., newspapers, magazines, books, newsletters, and direct mail). Attention to both diversity and context of media use is, we argue, a key aspect of any examination of the role that new media play in the lives of citizens today.

In our study, we defined the new media environment as we do in the rest of this book. It means the evolving media system that includes both new and old media; cable, satellite and digital television; DVDs; videos; cellular telephones; and the Internet. It also means radio, broadcast television, and print media such as newspapers, magazines, books, newsletters, direct mail, and so on. In media studies, the tradition has been explorations that focus on just one medium – such as television, the Internet, telephones, cell phones, DVDs, or VCRs – and there is a vast literature on each of these media separately. What we did here, by contrast, is something rather different, which we argue is more suited to the new media environment. Rather than focusing on merely one of these media, we explore how this new and varied complex of media becomes part of the lived experience of individual citizens in our society.

Our study spanned the three months surrounding the 2004 US presidential election. By tracking subjects both before and after the presidential election, we were able to investigate how citizens used both old and new media during a very particular time in American political life. We argue that the months preceding and following a presidential election are perceived by many as a time when it is particularly important to have access to political information, so that citizens can make an informed decision at the polls. We were interested to see whether citizens' use of media, particularly their use of new media, differed in the weeks leading up to the election, when this need was crucial, as opposed to the weeks following the election, when it might be seen as less so. Similarly our media diaries span these two types of time periods in the American political process – one during the period of frenzied political excitement before the election, and one after the election in a more "typical" moment of democratic life.

Our media diaries yielded a vast amount of data concerning the way American citizens engage in the political process. Citizens used the diaries to record their conversations about politics, about issues they read in the media, and about their own thoughts about the meaning of citizenship and civic engagement. The diaries are an example of citizens' conscious thoughts and reflections on the media system, their encounters with it, and the nature of their public involvement in US society. Perhaps most interesting, they are an example of what people say – and how they say it – when specifically asked to reflect on their use of media, their beliefs more generally, and their encounters with the public world. Citizens' own reflections on these key issues make an important addition to the data we have about new media and its use, as they provide some early examples of the importance of new media in their political and cultural lives. While these phenomena have been studied in the political and media literatures, few researchers have gathered citizens' own words in direct response to a request for reflection on these issues about the media and public life.

Our data indicate that the issues of new media's influence on fragmentation and connection are complex. Our data demonstrate that both increased integration and increased fragmentation occur partly as a function of Internet use. Citizens interested in bolstering a particular worldview can use the Internet as a filter, which facilitates their isolation from individuals holding opposing perspectives, and reinforces their own beliefs. Given the new and increasing variety and complexity of media sources, isolated citizens with an interest in an issue must develop more expertise in filtering information in sophisticated ways.

By contrast, citizens motivated to seek out actual diversity of opinion, to have their prior opinions challenged and their beliefs developed, can also take advantage of the new media environment in complex ways that facilitate these goals. The sophisticated use of (particularly high-speed) Internet makes it possible for users motivated to seek a diversity of perspectives to uncover almost any idea or perspective. An online discussion site, for example, might facilitate the exchange of oppositional opinions, or online news can be sought from sources with which one normally disagrees.

Our data indicate most pointedly that new media can be used in extremely disparate ways. Our clearest finding is the idea that the media environment and its effect on community and public connection is extremely variable in its impact, dependent in part on the political orientation of the particular person being examined. It is possible, we argue, for citizens to create their own media environment, constituted by a complicated mix of old and new media, and familiar or oppositional political perspectives.

Old and New Media in the Individualized Media Environment: The New Media Environment Is Never *Just* New Media

One insight from our attempt to study media in context is that old and new media are both used simultaneously, in fact at times interchangeably, in the everyday lives of individuals. Also, both are combined with a series of interpersonal interactions and involvements. As we discussed earlier,

Jenkins argues this about entertainment media (2006). We take his arguments one step further and assert that these same conditions and the same set of usages shape the quest for political information in the new media environment.

To isolate the impact of one or another medium in this environment, therefore, becomes almost an impossible task. As laid out in the canonical text *Personal Influence* by Elihu Katz and Paul Lazarsfeld (1964), information garnered from television and other old media; from the Internet and other new media; and from personal conversations with relatives, neighbors, coworkers, and friends all interact seamlessly in the daily lives of those in our study (a point we have already noted in chapter 3). This complex lived reality, composed of a series of intertwined factors, is the actual arena in which individuals develop and maintain their beliefs, opinions, and biases; think their thoughts; and live their lives. The qualitative interviews, observations, and diaries that comprised our method in this study have been developed particularly to investigate this aspect of human social life. It is a messy method, but it is suited to the messy environment in which human life is conducted, in which isolating the influence of particular variables is often impossible.

We found that citizens moved seamlessly between old and new media with ease, supplementing their consumption of newspapers and television with current, "up-to-the-moment" information from digital sources. Often, when participants learned about an issue or event from television or from reading newspapers, this led them to go "online" to check the facts or get more information. The Internet seemed to occupy a particularly important position for those seeking the most up-to-date information during the time of the election. Consider the comment of one of our participants, an administrator in his late forties who wanted to learn more about the election: "I checked CNN's Web page for the latest presidential vote tallies. This seemed easy, gave me control, and will surely be the way of the future." Two other participants, a retired schoolteacher and a florist, after seeing a program on television that had portrayed presidential candidate John Kerry in a negative light, turned to the Internet to look up the political affiliation of Sinclair Broadcasting Company, the station owners.

Bias in old media and new

Individuals also spoke differently about old and new media when they reflected on the truth content and the relative degree of bias in each.

Entries in our diaries indicated that the participants placed a significant emphasis on "fair and balanced" coverage from media sources. This seemed particularly true, to their minds, during the time leading up to the presidential election, as their responsibilities as citizens seemed to many to be particularly dependent on their ability to receive true and timely political news.

In one diary, an informant emphasized this thinking: "I've tended to go to 'AP Newswire' because I appreciate it. ... I appreciate it as kind of like a 'Switzerland' of news." Associated with the desire for unbiased information was an emphasis on personal neutrality. As one individual, an Indian-Arab student named Sam, stated, "I'm still forming my opinion ... that's one of the big things. I want to be unbiased so that I can form a free opinion. Not be forced to any one side."

Many informants were concerned about "bias" in the news they read and heard. Not only was the Internet seen as avoiding the biases of old media, but also participants expressed the sense of empowerment that the Internet gave them. They felt it gave them control over the information they sought. These expressions of power and control were not matched in any way by how individuals reacted to and commented upon more traditional news sources. These qualities of new media seemed particularly important to individuals when the election came under discussion. Those in our study prized the ability to garner the latest "impartial" news relevant to their coming vote, as these comments indicate:

[Television news] doesn't necessarily give me the information I want. ... [It] has to limit itself. ... [S]ee, I can click on the headline I want to on the Internet, view that information, scan past information that I might not be interested in, and zero in on what I am interested in. (Troy, university researcher, 36)

[O]n the Internet, oftentimes there's access to different news outlets, different news sources ... and so the Internet is useful because, at least when you get your news off the Internet, even if you do go to a source that has limited or skewed information, there are still other sources out there. (Andre, educator, 35)

For many of the citizens in our study, the Internet occupied a special role in their daily lives, we think because it was seen as the source of "unbiased," up-to-date news. According to Mark, a young law student, "I think the Internet is the first thing I turn to and the last thing I check before I go to bed. You know, whether it's my mail or the news. I check it constantly throughout the day." What becomes clear through analysis of the data is that the Internet was seen by many of the participants as being an essential tool to being well informed on political and social issues, a key role that media play in the relationship between free access to information and civic engagement.

Civic engagement in the new media environment

Over and above their political comments, and despite the fact that these dropped off following the election, many of our participants were integrally involved in public civic activities during the time our research was conducted. Some wore contentious political T-shirts in public, others participated in local grassroots groups, and still others ran for student government offices; served as campaign volunteers for state representatives; donated money for campaigns; worked as election judges; voted; and got into spirited political arguments with family, friends, coworkers, church members, strangers, and colleagues, both online and "offline."

We had a high voting rate amongst our diary participants – overall, 22 out of the 30 participants (approximately 75 percent) eligible to vote recorded in their diaries they that did vote.[4] Of course, the fact that these percentages significantly exceed the national average of 64 percent potentially calls into question either the representativeness or the veracity of our sample. However, the representative nature of our sample is bolstered by the fact that this higher than average voter turnout is supported by US Census Bureau data, which indicate that individuals in the US Midwest, where the study was located, are more likely to vote than Americans elsewhere in the nation.[5] Specifically in the last election, in the Midwest region where our study was based, voter turnout was a high 76 percent. This number closely approximates our own figures. Our findings indicate that when the circumstances call for it, as in the case of a contentious election, Americans can be extremely politically active and engaged.

Americans and Political Discussion: How the New Media Environment Is Changing the Civic Landscape

Scholars such as Eliasoph (1998) have noted Americans' avoidance of public political discussion and debate. In this light, our findings of high civic engagement and political discussion are interesting, and counter some of the literature about these questions. In addition, the majority of conversations chronicled by our participants do not fit neatly with the model of American citizens as shunning collective political debate, especially in public talk with strangers. In our sample, 23 out of the 32 participants (almost 72 percent) reported having discussions about politics with people outside of their immediate family members. Often, these conversations occurred in spaces that approximate public space, rather than the simply private spaces of home and family. Very few participants in our study actively avoided political talk – only three diarists fell into this category. Most instead found public debate comfortable and, indeed, enjoyable, even when such discussion might clearly make uncomfortable some of the others involved:

> It always makes my Mom and [my husband] Patrick happy when we have political talks at dinner, NOT! They both … have their views on politics but they keep it quiet   in the family setting, where I don't keep it quiet. (Terry, real estate agent, 25)

> My friend and I were talking about the election and how politics is a very sensitive subject among some people. I really do not like for people to come up and directly ask "who are you going to vote for?" (Katherine, cosmetics salesperson, 38)

Of course, such findings raise the possibility that our sample might be self-selected, with our study attracting political "extroverts" who were comfortable expressing their views on politics in the environment of a contentious election.

In our study, participants most vocal in their criticisms of the bias in the media were some of the most civically engaged as well. In one instance, Nadine was someone who attended political groups, participated in door-to-door political campaigns, and voted. Yet her diary and inter- views were filled with numerous criticisms of the biases in the media she consumed. Mark, while citing his "deep mistrust of the media," was already very involved in public activities and discussion before the election. He commented after the election, "I think the ultimate outcome of this election has motivated me to get more involved in some way if I can. I will not sit idly by and let moral … hicks dictate the policy of this country." In his case, his criticisms of the media did not lead him to conclude that a civically uninvolved course was the best response for him.

This finding countered the results of the parallel British study, in which criticisms of media objectivity translated into decreased civic engagement and political participation for many respondents (Couldry, Livingstone, and Markham 2007).[6]

In fact, participants in our study were more critical of old media than new media. While many seemed self-aware and critical of the sources of political information defined in the Golden Age of Broadcast News, overall they were much less self-conscious about new media. To assess this, we counted the space individuals used in their media diaries (measured by word count) to make what we coded as negative and positive comments about old versus new media. We found that old media were mentioned more often and much more negatively than new media, as our counts indicate:

- Old media negative comments = 11,435
- Old media positive comments = 4,922
- New media negative comments = 1,470
- New media positive comments = 1,630

Additional analysis of the actual comments led us to conclude that our subjects were aware of the limits of older forms of media and adjusted their understanding of the information it supplied accordingly. Yet when it came to new media, they were much less critical and sophisticated when it came to evaluating the information they received.

As we've discussed briefly above, recent studies just beginning to come out concerning the 2008 presidential election indicate that the Internet is now overtaking traditional news organs as the source of news for most people (Pew Research Center 2008). Indeed, the very process of the election itself was shaped by Internet communications, as many scholars and news organs have reported (Todd, Gawiser, Arumi and Evans Witt 2009; Gueorguieva 2008; Dube 2009; Greengard 2009). In part because the Obama electoral team was so skilled at using new sources of information, young people were mobilized for this election in much greater numbers than we've seen previously, and many political analysts believe that this participation radically influenced the outcome of this contest. It could be that Obama had a particular appeal that will not translate into the next election; or it could be that we have entered an era in which the sources and shape of information of all sorts, including political information, have changed radically . These changes raise questions concerning the future shape of community, politics, and collective action in the United States and worldwide.

Conclusion

The study of media reception in the new media environment is a complex process that has only just begun to be attempted by media studies scholars. In this chapter, we have laid out a series of issues central to current media studies debates about the way the new media environment has changed the media landscape. We've discussed the way the analysis of texts and their reception has changed, and the implications of this for the way media portray race, class, gender, and sexuality, and the social impact media have on these social identities; the evolving importance of globalization to understanding new media production and reception; and the way the current media environment facilitates participation, both politically and culturally, in new and ever evolving ways. We've examined media convergence – convergence between media types, between old media and new media, and between old environments and new ones.

We've examined the way this complicated situation has encouraged the use of ethnographic methods suited to studying media use in context. The authors of this volume have been involved in two recent studies employing these methods: one that focuses on new media use amongst adolescents in the private, family environment, and the other amongst citizens in the public environment during the presidential election, a particularly politicized time in American life. Both studies reinforce the notion that media in their complex, integrated forms have become an integral part of our culture, and that their impact is central to the experience of modern life. Our concluding chapter will expand on this notion as we reflect on what media studies has to tell us about this modern experience.

Notes

1. See, for example, Finer et al. (2005).
2. See HBO's made-for-television movie *If These Walls Could Talk* (1996) for an example of an attempt to balance the increasing pro-life bias of network television during the 1990s.
3. This research was funded by a grant from the National Science Foundation, DST IIS–0438803 in the Digital Societies and Technologies Program (Press and Williams 2004).
4. This rate was higher than that of the national average in the United States for the 2004 election (64 percent) but approximated the rate in the Midwest, the

region from which our sample was derived, which was 76 percent. See the numbers at US Census Bureau (2006).
5. National figures indicate that 65 percent of women voted in the 2004 election, as compared to 62 percent of men, and more women are registered to vote than men (US Census Bureau 2006: 1). This number does seem to be a bit high, as compared to the national voting rate of 64 percent in 2004, according to US Census Bureau numbers, and prompts the question, as we discuss, of whether our sample was self-selecting for highly active, engaged individuals. Again, however, the US Census Bureau reports that people in the Midwest are more likely to vote than other Americans – 76 percent versus 64 percent nationwide (2006: 8) – a pattern that fits our study data.
6. This discussion of our NSF findings is indebted to several earlier conference papers coauthored with Ellen Moore and Camille Johnson-Yale; see Press, Williams, Moore, and Johnson-Yale (2005a, 2005b, 2006b).

References

Abu-Lughod, Lila. 1998. *Remaking women: Feminism and modernity in the Middle East*. Princeton, N.J.: Princeton University Press.
Bacon-Smith, Camille. 1992. *Enterprising women: Television fandom and the creation of popular myth*. Philadelphia: University of Pennsylvania Press.
Bell, David. 2007. *Cyberculture theorists*. New York: Routledge.
Bhabha, Homi K. 1994. *The location of culture*. London: Routledge.
Bimber, Bruce. 2000. "Measuring the gender gap on the Internet." *Social Science Quarterly* 81.
Blumer, Herbert. 1932. *Movies and conduct*. New York: Macmillan.
Boyd, Danah. 2007. "Why youth (heart) social network sites: The role of networked publics in teenage social life." In *MacArthur Foundation series on digital learning: Youth, identity, and digital media volume*, edited by D. Buckingham. Cambridge, M.A.: MIT Press.
Boyd, Danah. 2009. "Taken out of context: American teen sociality in networked publics." Berkeley: Information Management Systems, University of California.
Boyd, Danah M., and Nicole B. Ellison. 2008. "Social network sites: Definition, history, and scholarship." *Journal of Computer-Mediated Communication* 13:210–30.
Charters, William. 1933. *Motion pictures and youth*. New York: Macmillan.
Compaine, Benjamin M. 2001. *The digital divide: Facing a crisis or creating a myth?* Cambridge, M.A.: MIT Press.
Couldry, Nick, Sonia M. Livingstone, and Tim Markham. 2007. *Media consumption and public engagement: Beyond the presumption of attention*. Basingstoke, UK: Palgrave Macmillan.

Desser, David. 1983. *The samurai films of Akira Kurosawa*. Ann Arbor, M.I.: UMI Research Press.

Desser, David. 1988. *Eros plus massacre: An introduction to the Japanese new wave cinema*. Bloomington: Indiana University Press.

DiMaggio, Paul, Eszter Hargittai, W. Russell Neuman, and John P. Robinson. 2001. "Social implications of the Internet." *Annual Review of Sociology* 27:307–36.

Dorfman, Ariel, David Kunzle, John Shelton Lawrence, and Armand Mattelart. 1986. *How to read Donald Duck: Imperialist ideology in the Disney comic*. New York: Internat. General.

Dube, William. 2009. "The effect of new media on political advertising: Television ads and internet ads in the 2008 presidential primary." Available at http://hdl.handle.net/1850/9697

Eliasoph, Nina. 1998. *Avoiding politics: How Americans produce apathy in everyday life*. Cambridge: Cambridge University Press.

Finer, Lawrence B., Lori F. Frohwirth, Lindsay A. Dauphinee, Susheela Singh, and Ann M. Moore. 2005. "Reasons U.S. women have abortions: Quantitative and qualitative perspectives." *Perspectives on Sexual and Reproductive Health* 37:110–18.

Fung, Anthony Y. H. 2009. "Online games, cyberculture and community: The deterritorization and crystallization of community space." In *Embedding into our lives: New opportunities and challenges of the Internet*, edited by Louis Leung, Anthony Y. H. Fung, and Paul S. N. Lee, 189–208. Hong Kong: Chinese University Press.

Gajjala, Radhika. 2004. *Cyber selves: Feminist ethnographies of South Asian women*. Walnut Creek, C.A.: AltaMira Press.

Gillespie, Marie. 1995. *Television, ethnicity, and cultural change*. London: Routledge.

Gitelman, Lisa. 2006. *Always already new: Media, history, and the data of culture*. Cambridge, M.A.: MIT Press.

Gitlin, Todd. 1983. *Inside prime time*. New York: Pantheon.

Gitlin, Todd. 1998. "Public sphere or public sphericules?" In *Media, ritual, and identity*, edited by Tamar Liebes and James Curran, pp. 168–75. London: Routledge.

Golumbia, David. 2004. "What is LOST?" *Flow* 3:2005.

Greengard, Samuel. 2009. "The first internet president." *Communications ACM* 52: 16–18.

Grossberg, Lawrence, Ellen Wartella, D. Charles Witney, and J. MacGregor Wise. 2006. *Mediamaking: Mass media in a popular culture*. Thousand Oaks, C.A.: Sage Publications.

Gueorguieva, Vassia. 2008. "Voters, MySpace, and YouTube." *Social Science Computer Review* 26:288–300.

Haraway, Donna. 1991. *Cyborgs and women: The reinvention of nature*. New York: Routledge.

Haraway, Donna. 1997. *Modest_Witness@Second_MilleniumFemaleMan_Meets_OncoMouse*. New York: Routledge.

Hargittai, Eszter. 2003a. "The digital divide and what to do about it." In *New economy handbook*, edited by D. C. Jones, pp. 822–41. San Diego, C.A.: Academic Press.

Hargittai, Eszter. 2003b. "How wide a web? Inequalities in accessing information online." Ann Arbor, M.I.: Proquest Information and Learning.

Hargittai, Eszter. 2008. "The digital reproduction of inequality." In *The digital reproduction of inequality*, edited by D. Grusky, pp. 936–44. Boulder, C.O.: Westview.

Hargittai, Eszter, and Gina Walejko. 2008. "The participation divide: Content creation and sharing in the digital age." *Information, Communication & Society* 11:239–56.

Himmelweit, Hilde T. 1958. *Television and the child: An empirical study of the effect of television on the young*. London: Published for the Nuffield Foundation by the Oxford University Press.

Jenkins, Henry. 1992. *Textual poachers: Television fans and participatory culture*. New York: Routledge.

Jenkins, H. 2006. *Convergence culture: Where old and new media collide*. New York: New York University Press.

Joiner, Richard, Jeff Gavin, Jill Duffield, Mark Brosnan, Charles Crook, Alan Durndell, Pam Maras, Jane Miller, Adrian J. Scott, and Peter Lovatt. 2005. "Gender, Internet identification, and Internet anxiety: Correlates of Internet use." *CyberPsychology & Behavior* 8:371–8.

Juluri, Vamsee. 2003. *Becoming a global audience: Longing and belonging in Indian music television*. New York: Peter Lang.

Katz, Elihu, and Paul Felix Lazarsfeld. 1964. *Personal influence: The part played by people in the flow of mass communications*. New York: Free Press.

Kearney, Mary Celeste. 2006. *Girls make media*. New York: Routledge.

Kellner, Douglas. 2005. *Media spectacle and the crisis of democracy: Terrorism, war, and election battles*. Boulder: C.O.: Paradigm.

Kraidy, Marwan M. 2005. *Hybridity, or the cultural logic of globalization*. Philadelphia: Temple University Press.

Kraidy, Marwan M. 2010. *Reality television and Arab politics*. Cambridge: Cambridge University Press.

Lareau, Annette. 2003. *Unequal childhoods: Class, race, and family life*. Berkeley: University of California Press.

Liebes, Tamar, and Elihu Katz. 1993. *The export of meaning: Cross-cultural readings of Dallas*. Cambridge: Polity Press.

Livingstone, Sonia M. 1990. *Making sense of television: The psychology of audience interpretation*. Oxford and New York: Butterworth/Heinemann.

Livingstone, Sonia M. 2002. *Young people and new media: Children and the changing media environment*. Thousand Oaks, C.A.: Sage Publications.

Livingstone, Sonia. 2008. "Engaging with media: A matter of literacy?" *Communication, Culture and Critique* 1:51–62.

Livingstone, Sonia, and Magdalena Bober. 2006a. "Regulating the Internet at home: Contrasting the perspectives of children and parents." In *Digital generations: Children, young people, and new media*, edited by D. Buckingham and R. Willett. Mahwah, N.J.: Lawrence Erlbaum.

Livingstone, Sonia, and Magdalena Bober. 2006b. "UK children go online: A child-centered approach to the experience of using the Internet." In *Information and communications technologies in society: E-living in a digital Europe*, edited by B. Anderson, Malcolm Brynin, J. Gershuny, and Yoel Raban, pp. 104–18. London: Routledge.

Miller, Daniel, and Don Slater. 2000. *The Internet: An ethnographic approach.* Oxford: Berg.

Mosco, Vincent. 2004. *The digital sublime: Myth, power, and cyberspace.* Cambridge, M.A.: MIT Press.

Nakamura, Lisa. 2002. *Cybertypes: Race, ethnicity, and identity on the Internet.* London: Routledge.

Norris, Pippa. 2001. *Digital divide: Civic engagement, information poverty, and the Internet worldwide.* New York: Cambridge University Press.

Pew Research Center for the People and the Press. 2008. "Internet overtakes newspapers as news outlet." http://people-press.org/reports/pdf/479.pdf.

Pollitt, Katha. 2008. "Maternity fashions, junior style." *The Nation*, January 3.

Press, Andrea Lee. 2004. "Teens online: Tracing the everyday nature of the digital divide." Invited speaker, Colloquium Series, University of Maryland, Department of Communication, April.

Press, Andrea Lee. 2005a. "Digital divide? Young women, the Internet, and inequality." Invited lecturer, Women's Studies Program and Sociology Department, University of New Hampshire.

Press, Andrea Lee. 2005b. "What digital technologies mean for public life." Paper presented at the annual meeting of the American Sociological Association, Philadelphia, August.

Press, Andrea Lee, and Elizabeth R. Cole. 1999. *Speaking of abortion: Television and authority in the lives of women.* Chicago: University of Chicago Press.

Press, Andrea Lee, and Bruce Williams, co-principal investigators. 2004. [Raw data.] National Science Foundation Grant no. DST IIS-0438803, Digital Societies and Technologies Program.

Press, Andrea Lee, Bruce Williams, Ellen Moore, and Camille Johnson-Yale. 2005a. "Connecting the private to the public: Media and the future of public life." Paper presented at the annual meeting of the American Political Science Association, Washington, D.C., September.

Press, Andrea Lee, Bruce Williams, Ellen Moore, and Camille Johnson-Yale. 2005b. "Re-envisioning civic life: Normative and critical lessons from the Blackwell Companion to the Sociology of Culture." Paper presented at the annual meeting of the American Sociological Association, Philadelphia, August.

Press, Andrea Lee, Bruce Williams, Ellen Moore, and Camille Johnson-Yale. 2006a. "Media and the structuring of public discourse: The ethnographic study." Paper presented at the annual meeting of the International Communication Association, Dresden, Germany, June.

Press, Andrea Lee, Bruce Williams, Ellen Moore, and Camille Johnson-Yale. 2006b. "Political Uses of the Internet and Other Media." Paper presented at the annual meeting of the National Communication Association, San Antonio, T.X., November.

Punathambekar, Aswin. 2005. "Bollywood in the Indian-American diaspora: Mediating a transitive logic of cultural citizenship." *International Journal of Cultural Studies* 8:151–173.

Punathambekar, Aswin. 2006. "Between ROWDIES and RASIKAS: Rethinking fan activity in Indian film culture." In *Fandom: Identities and communities in a mediated world*, edited by J. Gray. New York: New York University Press.

Quart, Alissa. 2008. "When chick flicks get knocked up." *Mother Jones*, May 15. www.alissaquart.com/articles/2008/05/when_chick_flicks_get_knocked. html.

Radway, Janice A. 2008. "Girls, zines, and the limits of the body." Paper presented at the 2009 Meeting of the International Communication Association, Chicago, November.

Robinson, John, Paul DiMaggio, and Eszter Hargittai. 2001. "New social survey perspectives on the digital divide." *IT&Society* 1:1–22.

Schudson, Michael. 1997. "Why conversation is not the soul of democracy." *Critical Studies in Media Communication* 14:297–309.

Servon, Lisa J. 2002. *Bridging the digital divide: Technology, community, and public policy.* Malden, M.A.: Blackwell.

Shirky, Clay. 2007. *Here comes everybody: The power of organizing without organizations.* New York: Penguin.

Silver, David, and Adrienne Massanari. 2006. *Critical cyberculture studies.* New York: New York University Press.

Sunstein, Cass R. 2006. *Infotopia: How many minds produce knowledge.* Oxford: Oxford University Press.

Todd, Chuck, Sheldon R. Gawiser, Ana Maria Arumi, and G. Evans Witt. 2009. *How Barack Obama won: A state-by-state guide to the historic 2008 presidential election.* New York: Vintage Books.

Trippi, Joe. 2008. *The revolution will not be televised: Democracy, the Internet and the overthrow of everything.* New York: Harper.

Turkle, Sherry. 1996. *Life on the screen: Identity in the age of the Internet.* London: Weidenfeld & Nicolson.

Turkle, Sherry. 2005. *The second self: Computers and the human spirit.* Cambridge, M.A.: MIT Press.

US Census Bureau. 2006. *Voting and registration in the election of November 2004.* March. www.census.gov/prod/2006pubs/p20-556.pdf.

Vaidhyanathan, Siva. 2001. *Copyrights and copywrongs: The rise of intellectual property and how it threatens creativity.* New York: New York University Press.

Vaidhyanathan, Siva. 2004. *The anarchist in the library: How the clash between freedom and control is hacking the real world and crashing the system.* New York: Basic Books.

Walkerdine, Valerie. 2007. *Children, gender, video games: Towards a relational approach to multimedia.* Basingstoke, UK: Palgrave Macmillan.

Warschauer, Mark. 2003. *Technology and social inclusion: Rethinking the digital divide.* Cambridge, M.A.: MIT Press.

Wikipedia. N.d. "Suicide of Megan Meier." http://en.wikipedia.org/wiki/Suicide_of_Megan_Meier.

Zillien, Nicole, and Eszter Hargittai. 2009. "Digital distinction: Status-specific types of Internet usage." *Social Science Quarterly* 90:274–91.

Chapter 7

Conclusion

We hope that readers will take away at least three insights about how to understand media from this book.

We Are Living in a Mediated Age

First, and most generally, we live in a mediated age. The emerging discipline of media studies starts from the observation that media now permeate almost every moment of our existence. There is almost nothing that we do that escapes mediation. In each of the preceding chapters, we have shown how media are central to every aspect of our lives. Yet, the impact of media is not static. The rapidly changing media environment in which we live requires dynamic and flexible approaches if we are to understand the new communication technologies that have emerged in the last two decades.

Some argue that the increasing presence of media technologies in the lives of young people (and, indeed, in the lives of everyone) has transformed the face of everyday life, and the place of media technology in it. They point, for instance, to the way people use social-networking sites like Facebook to meet, reunite with, and stay in touch with others, or constantly Twitter to alert others of their every thought, thus altering the very fabric of interpersonal relations. Others argue that new media technologies are simply assimilated into patterns of social life that already exist, without radically transforming these patterns. Let's take the classroom as an example.

Education is one of the fundamental institutions of US society, and colleges have existed here since the 1600s. From the kindergarten classroom to the university lecture hall, media are everywhere. In many high schools of today, every classroom has a video projector. In lectures, professors often have a computer hooked up to the Internet. Videos are commonly shown. Also, look at the students listening to (and watching) the lecture. Many of them have their laptops on, many of these connected to the Internet. Some are taking notes or researching issues related to the lecture. Others are twittering each other, or shopping online. Any way you look at it, you cannot understand education in the United States today, from the first time you go to preschool to the time you get an advanced degree, without seeing that media make up an important presence in education.

While once controversial when used in an educational setting, the current, widespread acceptance of media as an integral part of the educational process has influence far beyond the classroom. It is yet another reinforcement that media comprise an essential part of almost any part of life, and we now expect to be entertained and/or enlightened by some sort of screen or by references to media, whether we are attending a church service in a megachurch, walking to class, exercising, or waiting for an airplane or doctor appointment. The very notion that media would be excluded from *any* aspect of our lives seems quaint.

We're sitting writing this in a coffeehouse, an institution that goes back to the eighteenth century, when people sat in them discussing the important issues of that time. Yet we're sitting here in part because it's a wifi hotspot, listening on headphones to music streamed through these connections. So, we are participating in the coffeehouse tradition, but the coffeehouse tradition with a twist. As in the past, we *might* participate in a debate over the issues of the day. Indeed, given our access to the Internet, we might engage in conversations that both are more informed (i.e., it might draw on the many websites providing information about almost any subject imaginable) and include many more people (both those in the café itself and those reachable online). At the same time, given the ability to plug ourselves into headphones, ignore the people sitting around us, and just listen to music, we might also use new media to avoid any conversation or interpersonal contact.

To understand modern life, you have to understand the role of the media. Media are everywhere. But media must be understood in context: media are "placed" in the contexts in which we already function, socially, technologically, and culturally. As we saw in the previous chapter, the influence of new media in the lives of the adolescents we studied was always conditioned by the specific family situation in which our subjects lived. As well, we found in our study of media use around the 2004 election that citizens rely on a complex diet of both old and new media, as well as interpersonal communication with friends, relatives, and coworkers, making few distinctions between television and newspapers, on the one hand, and the Internet or e-mail, on the other.

The Complexity of Our Relationship With the Media

Our second point is that no simple conclusions can be drawn from these developments. The relationship between the media, and the other dimensions of social life, is complicated. A sophisticated student of media studies understands that two kinds of claims that are often made about media are both wrong. First, there are those who claim that changes in media can transform and change almost anything in society. In fact, however, media don't directly "cause" developments in society, culture, or even personalities. As we noted above, with respect to the influence of media on children, or its use in political campaigns (discussed below), there is a complicated interaction between the media and other dimensions of our lives.

That said, we cannot understand how any of the institutions of modern life work unless we develop a sophisticated understanding of media. Those who argue that there have "always" been new technologies, that there is nothing new under the sun, are missing the point about the fundamental transformation our society has undergone over the past several decades. They dismiss the independent role of media in their explanations of political, social, psychological, and economic life. An understanding that the recent media transformation has ushered in a new era for the intertwined relationship between media technologies and social, political, psychological, and economic life is the raison d'être of media studies as a new discipline. While media studies draws on other disciplines, it is distinct in making the media environment its central focus and insisting that media are a primary feature of modern society and integral to any informed analysis of life in the twenty-first century.

As an example of the insights that media studies offers into the complex effects of a changing media environment, consider Wikipedia. Many professors forbid students from using this online, user-created encyclopedia as a source in papers and other class work. In our view, this exclusion is often based on the professor's own knee-jerk rejection of the role of new media as a potential facilitator of innovative models for the creation of knowledge. A more sophisticated approach, rooted in media studies, would recognize that, as we saw in chapter 1 with respect to the transition from oral to print cultures, changes in the dominant form of communication always affect the way societies understand what counts as reliable knowledge.

Wikipedia is based on a model of knowledge that depends on the collective judgment of the many users who create, review, and edit any particular entry, rather than relying on a single expert, as in the more traditional model of academic knowledge. James Surowiecki (2004) calls the former "the wisdom of crowds" and argues that large groups are often able to arrive at better decisions than any single individual. In the case of Wikipedia, this collective approach to knowledge is made possible by the interactivity of Web 2.0, and is not necessarily less reliable than other sources that students regularly consult, such as textbooks or print encyclopedias. The articles in Wikipedia are usually extensively footnoted (with footnotes often connected through hyperlinks to the source material, making them easily accessible), and entries are flagged when they are inadequately sourced or are contested. In many (but not all) areas of knowledge, Wikipedia provides rapidly updated information that is impossible to duplicate in print sources like textbooks or most academic writing. Rather than universally dismissing new forms of information, we must be self-conscious and critical about any source of information.

The history of research on media and its impact is a constant tale of finding that the impact of media on institutions and people is subtle and complicated. Movies, for example, do not have any one clear impact on people, and in order to develop a real understanding of the impact of media on people, a complex, contextual study must take place. How a film like *Knocked Up* actually affects people is not necessarily related to changing in some measurable way the mentality of pro-choice individuals: we must understand more about the way people assess and use a fictional film, in their social and cultural context, and about the processes of making meaning and forming beliefs, in order to attain a depth knowledge of its impact.

This is no less true for older forms of media such as books. As we saw in Radway's (1984) pioneering study of media reception, she found that while many critics saw romance novels as reinforcing weak and subservient images of women, actual fans of these books instead interpreted the heroines in them as uplifting, strong, and independent, and liked particular romances that stressed these qualities.

Media have occupied this complex and important place in our society for decades, even before the spread of television as a mass medium in the second half of the twentieth century. Yet we argue that the present moment is a particularly important one for the media. We live in a time when the dominant characteristics of the mediated environment in which we live are changing rapidly. If the past is any predictor of the future, these media changes will exercise significant and profound influences on almost everything in our society, from its institutions to the very idea of what it means to be human. In short, although it might once have been possible to discuss the relationship between the "media system" and other "systems," scholars increasingly are seeing the media as an ever-present dimension of every aspect, every system, every institution, indeed every dimension of life in an age that is increasingly being defined as "mediated."

Human Agency in Media Decisions and Directions

Our third point is that there is nothing inevitable about the impact of changing media technologies, or the impact they have on a particular society. Human agency, especially in the form of political action, plays a key role in determining the ways in which new media are deployed (with lasting consequences that can sometimes make these characteristics *seem* to be inevitable and determined by the technology itself). We saw in chapter 2 the significance of the political struggles in 1930s America over whether the new mass medium of radio (and later television) would be operated by private corporations for profit or run as a publicly funded trust with a dominant public service orientation. The significance of these political decisions is illustrated by the vast differences even now in the media systems of Canada and the United Kingdom, where the public service model was adopted, and the United States, where the commercial model triumphed.

One of the reasons why it is so important to understand the significance of human agency in the development of new media technologies is that it is contingent policy decisions, and not something inherent in new technologies, that determine the impact of media on the broader society. So, right now there are fierce debates in Washington over whether to preserve the norm of network neutrality (which we discussed in chapter 2) or to allow Internet service providers (ISPs) to charge for different levels of service – if you pay more, your information packets travel and load faster on users' computers. If network neutrality survives, if there is one standard of service for all information packets, then it will foster an Internet environment encouraging the leveling of the media playing field as individual users are able to disseminate their blogs and videos much the same as well-financed elites, large corporations, or Hollywood studios. On the other hand, if tiered service is allowed, it will advantage those who can pay for it, especially large media corporations that see the Internet ultimately as the primary medium for distributing high-quality (and copyright-protected) audio and video. At the same time, the media made and distributed by those who cannot pay for improved speed will seem frustratingly slow and glitchy by comparison. Over the long term, this might well lead to a future Internet much like Neil Postman's prediction of "cable television on steroids." In short, two vastly different futures for the Internet depend not on anything inherent in the medium's technology, but rather on the outcome of political struggle.

Not all decisions affecting the contingent future of the media environment are determined by policy makers in Washington. Returning to the institution of higher education, an interesting example is the online rating of university professors. In the 1970s, when course evaluations began they were rather controversial, resisted by many professors, students, and administrators as inappropriate ways to judge the quality of teaching and learning. In fact, many universities eschewed them entirely. Now when students register at many universities, all they do is click on the course and all the professor ratings for the past five years come up.[1]

Yet, the widespread dissemination of faculty ratings and the increasing ease with which students can fill out evaluations have changed the way universities evaluate faculty and, inevitably, the way professors behave in the classroom. So, as tenure and promotion decisions increasingly rely on the quantitative tallying of answers to a few evaluation questions, professors tend to alter their classroom behavior to score higher on these scales. Reducing class workloads, increasing the number of "fun" activities, and giving higher grades are generally thought (sometimes correctly, sometimes not) to improve a professor's evaluations. While this may improve evaluations and be popular with students, it is not at all clear that it improves the quality of education.

Issues of ownership and control, which we raised in chapter 2, are also relevant. If students want to pursue a nonuniversity source for professor ratings, they can sign on to RateMyProfessor.com online. They may think that these ratings are more democratic, and a more "authentic" reading of student opinion, because they take advantage of the much-touted interactivity of the Internet where anyone at all can post their ratings, unedited and uncensored by the university or the professor.

Yet RateMyProfessor.com is owned by Viacom, one of the nine largest media conglomerates in the world. This opens the door to clear conflicts of interest as RateMyProfessor.com becomes a vehicle for not only providing students with information about their teachers, but also furthering Viacom's economic interests. As the website becomes a platform for advertisements for MTV, another Viacom holding, the temptation grows to increase viewership by providing more flamboyant and attention-getting features (e.g., icons and questions rating whether professors are "hot" or "not hot").

A focus on the significance of human agency directs our attention to whether or not the media system fosters an informed public that can then, in turn, effectively participate in the decisions that shape the future of the media environment. For example, the media audience has fragmented and is continuing to fragment, as we've illustrated particularly in our discussion of political economy in chapter 2 and inequalities in chapter 5. As the audience continues this process of fragmentation, individuals have more and more choice about the media they consume, and more and more control over it. Concomitantly, the media environment affords more and more detailed choices to individuals for alternative individual products to consume.

Yet in contrast, our discussion of political economy indicates that it is important to understand that the mere diversity of media outlets does not necessarily indicate an increasing diversity in the viewpoints or content that those outlets carry. The dynamic that's running counter to audience fragmentation is concentration and conglomeration. So, for instance, although there are hundreds of radio stations on the dial, FCC relaxation of the limits on how many stations a single corporation can own in 1996 allowed Clear Channel to acquire 900 stations and become far and away the largest owner of radio stations in the United States (in addition to substantial holdings in television stations and concert promotion). This concentrated ownership has resulted in less local programming, centralized control over playlists, and much less diversity in content across the 900 stations. The question of Clear Channel's effect on content became especially controversial in 2004 when the company was accused of censoring viewpoints critical of the Bush administration, including a ban on the music of the Dixie Chicks and a refusal to run ads critical of the Iraq War. Overall, then, while our choices as consumers of media seem to have grown, those choices are being provided by fewer and fewer companies – thus leaving open the question of how much true diversity the media actually provide.

In the political realm, media fragmentation has made it more difficult than ever to assemble everyone as a single audience for political events or issues – we've definitely left the Age of Broadcast News, where as many as three out of every four television sets were tuned into one of the nightly network news broadcasts. This makes the rare times when we do all focus on the same issue – media events – even more significant than they were in the past. A national presidential election, which galvanizes a mass public in the United States, becomes an even more unusual and noteworthy event than it had been in the age of broadcast news. The example of Barack Obama's inauguration illustrates this phenomenon. The inauguration was the second most watched inauguration in television history. But, it was the largest Internet event in history, measured by the number of hits on sites that were streaming the inauguration, and many other factors.

In addition, the inauguration was a global as well as national event, illustrating how important it is to understand the degree to which media have become global. This is important because the global nature of media creates new ways for people to bind together as communities. At one time, the nation was the primary point of identification. We could take it for granted that people were citizens of nation-states, responded to their government, and so on. In the new media system, because citizens can become directly connected to each other across national boundaries, the bonds of nationality may be weakened. This makes it more difficult, for example, to convince people that they have more in common with people of different social classes and ethnicities in their own country than they have with people of the same social class and ethnicities in other states.

Running counter to this idea is that the global reach of a small number of media corporations that are not necessarily connected to any one state or another is dramatically increasing. Current work on the Indian film industry, one of the world's biggest, indicates that the influence of Hollywood, on many dimensions, is still terribly important to the way movies are financed, made, and distributed (Punathambekar 2008). But what does it mean when we say "Hollywood" has changed significantly in this global era? "Hollywood" itself is not spatially locatable in southern California anymore; instead, with regard to the location of its moviemaking, "Hollywood" is a system and an idea that exists in many places, such as India and China, where multinational corporations are replacing more local sources of capital.

Reflecting the significance of human agency and the contingency of the future of media, the growing reach of global media and its homogenizing effect is being challenged by local, indigenous media that often use new media to win wider audiences than formerly possible (Barber 1996). The mediated resurgence of the local takes many forms with a wide range of political, social, and cultural impacts. On the one hand, there is a growing audience for "world music," which is easily available on the Internet. On the other hand, resisting globalization are the messages of fundamentalist Muslims hostile to the West that are circulated through websites, DVDs, and other forms of new and old media.

Finally, a focus on human agency and the potential role that citizens might play in shaping the future of media makes critical media literacy and how (and whether) it is taught in schools as important as print literacy a century and a half ago. Only if citizens have acquired basic media literacy can we have an enlightened democratic dialogue over the vital political, economic, and social decisions that face our local, national, and global communities. We believe that the insights of media studies can inform the development of such literacy.

In Closing: The Case of the RFID

We close with an example of a new technology, the impact of which is not yet clear, for you to think about as you close our book. Radio frequency identification (RFID) uses tiny chips, placed in objects or implanted in animals and humans, which broadcast radio waves that allow their identification and tracking. Many large corporations, Walmart for example, already use RFIDs to track and control their inventories, but the chips can also be made small enough that researchers have glued them to ants. Still in its infancy, there are many possible uses for RFIDs. In the health field, RFIDs (if implanted on patients) might track their location and provide information on their health and habits. In the area of security,

RFIDs implanted in identification cards can monitor the location of individuals to make sure they are not in places they should not be. Yet some of the most far-reaching uses for RFID would involve combining their tracking potential with information available from other databases.

Imagine that you buy a sweater with an RFID at Walmart. When you pay for the item with a credit card, you can be identified, and now you and your purchase might be tracked. Where else do you go, what else do you buy, and what do you watch on television? All these pieces of information might be combined to allow a complete picture of what you do, where you go, who else you see, and so forth. Advertisers see the potential of this sort of information to tailor specific commercial messages directly at you. So, once your location, identification, and product purchases are known, it might be possible for you to receive television advertisements aimed directly at you – which would not be seen by your neighbors. Governments also see the potential of such information to track criminals, terrorists, and so forth.

But whether such a future comes to pass depends not simply on the development of RFIDs and associated technologies, but also on the decisions that policy makers reach about privacy; access to information; the rights of individuals to opt out of the system; the limits, if any, on the right of government officials to compile and use such information; and so forth. The specific answers to these policy questions will be determined by the interests sitting around the table at the FCC, Federal Trade Commission, or Justice Department when they come up. The representatives of organized interests, from advertisers to chip makers to the government agencies affected, will surely be present in these policy debates. Whether the public is represented at all depends on their critical media literacy, which would allow them to see what is at stake for fundamental issues like privacy, surveillance, corporate and government power, and so on.

Cartoonist David Farley (1996) captures the challenge for individual citizens when it comes to RFID and other intrusive technologies as he echoes the argument of Neil Postman's *Amusing Ourselves to Death*. In the first cell, labeled "The Wrong Way" to gain acceptance for RFID, there is a vaguely threatening corporate type in a suit saying, "We want to implant this RFID tag into you." A sweating and fearful young man answers, "That violates my rights!" In the second cell, labeled "The Right Way, the same corporate representative says, "We want to implant this

RFID tag in you, and it's also a cell phone, digital camera, and MP3 player." The same young man, now smiling and excited, answers, "Cool!" What do you think about RFIDs?

Note

1. Now the RateMyProfessor.com site is used by *Forbes* magazine to help establish the rankings of various institutions, when they publish their rankings.

References

Barber, Benjamin. 1996. *Jihad vs. McWorld: How globalism and tribalism are reshaping the world*. New York: Ballantine Books.

Farley, David. 2006. *Doctor fun*. January 16. http://biblio.org/David/drfun. html.

Gitelman, Lisa. 2006. *Always already new: Media, history and the data of culture*. Cambridge, M.A.: MIT Press.

Marvin, Carolyn. 1988. *When old technologies were new: Thinking about electric communication in the 19th century*. Oxford: Oxford University Press.

Punathambekar, Aswin. 2008. "We're online, not on the streets': Indian cinema, new media, and participatory culture." In *Global Bollywood*, edited by Anandam P. Kavoori and Aswin Punathambekar, New York: New York University Press.

Radway, Janice A. 1984. *Reading the romance: Women, patriarchy, and popular literature*. Chapel Hill: University of North Carolina Press.

Surowiecki, James. 2004. *The wisdom of crowds*. New York: Anchor.

Index

ABC: The Alphabetization of the Western Mind (Illich and Sanders), 10–11
ABC network, 18, 94, 108*n*, 114, *135*
abortion
  American views on, 93, 107*n*, 157
  Fast Times at Ridgemont High movie, 95–6
  Knocked Up movie, 92–4, 98, 101, 118, 157, 164, 165
  representation in movies, 67, 92–4, 95–6, 98, 101, 118, 122, 157, 164, 165
  representation on television, 106, 120, 121, 159, 187*n*
Abu-Lughod, Lila, 168
"active audience" tradition, 103–6, 166
Adams, John, 68, 69
Adorno, Theodor, 116
Advance Publications, 40, 58*n*
Advanced Research Projects Agency Network, 58*n*
advertisements
  financing of media, 9, 34, 35, 115
  on Google, 30
  impact on public opinion, 70, 75
  impact of RFID, 203
  news channels, 23*n*

political campaigns, 64, 65, 76, 82, 83, 102, 105
  on radio, 37
  revenue decline, 55
  on television, 18, 23*n*, 101–2
  as threat to democracy, 75
Akass, Kim, 135
Al-Jazeera TV, 48
Alasuutari, P., 108*n*
Ali McBeal, 133, 143
Alice, 106
All in the Family, 99–100, 123, 143
Allor, Martin, 101
Amazon, 40
Ambrose, bishop of Milan, 11–12
American Aurora (Rosenfeld), 68
American Idol, 161
Amos 'n' Andy, 140, 141, 144
Amusing Ourselves to Death (Postman), 13, 203
Ang, Ian, 104, 108*n*
Annan, Kofi, 51, 58*n*
Ansolabehere, Stephen, 82
anthropology, 9
anti-Semitism, 121, 137
AOL, Chinese government censorship, 31
AOL e-mail services, 57*n*
AOL search engine, 41
AP Newswire, 183

Apatow, Judd, 91
Appleson, Gail, 126
Arab world
  reality television, 162
  reception of *Dallas*, 105, 168
Arnaz, Desi, *125*
ARPANET, 58n
Arsenio Hall program, 66
Arumi, Ana Maria, 186
Asians
  Internet studies, 169
  media representation, 137, 140,
    143
  stereotyping in computer games,
    160
  study of Indian teenagers, 168
audiences
  "active audience" tradition, 103–6,
    166
  attentive vs. inattentive, 82, 84
  fragmentation of, 7–8, 18–19, 84,
    124, 158, 200
  network television, 7, 13, 17–18
  popular culture, 6, 117
  television news channels, 18, 64,
    81, 84–5
  textual analysis, 92–100, 118
  see also reception studies
Augustine, St., 11–12
Aurora, 68–9
Austen, Jane, 93

Bache, Benjamin Franklin, 68
Bacon-Smith, Camille, 105, 161
Bagdikian, Ben H., 37, 39, 40, 53
Baker, C. Edwin, 38, 39, 50, 52–3,
    58n
Ball, Lucille, 124, *125*
Barber, Benjamin, 202
Barker, Chris, 120, 149n
Barnes and Noble, 40, 49
Barnet, Richard J., 47

"Base and Superstructure in Marxist
    Theory" (Williams), 118
Baudry, Jean-Louis, 129
BBC *see* British Broadcasting
    Corporation (BBC)
Beals, Jennifer, 144
"Becoming the Third Wave"
    (Walker), 149n
Beijing, Google search results, 26–31
The Beijing Guide, 27, 29
beijingtrip.com, 28
Bell, David, 160
Benjamin, Walter, 116
Bennett, W. Lance, 79
Berelson, Bernard, 76, 102
Bergman, Ingrid, 129
Berlusconi, Silvio, 50–2, 53, 59n
Bertelsmann, 37
Bewitched, 122
Bhabha, Homi K., 162
Bimber, Bruce, 172
bin Laden, Osama, 72
Bird, Elizabeth, 108n
Birmingham School, 117–19
Birth of a Nation, 136, *137*, 138
Birthright, 139
bisexuals, representation in media,
    144, 145
blogs
  challenge to broadcast news, 85
  growth of, 20, 159, 199
  Knocked Up movie, 164, 165
  political process, 20, 63, 66, 85
  Twittering of Obama's address, 32
Blumer, Herbert, 170
Bober, Magdalena, 167
Bogle, Donald, 137–8, 150n
book publishing, ownership and
    control, 40
Borat, 100
Borders, 40, 49
Boulton, Clint, 20

Boutell.com, 38
Bovill, Moira, 136
Boyd, Danah M., 166, 168
The Brady Bunch, 122, *123*, 133
Brady, Matthew, 23*n*
brand loyalty, 18
Brashares, Ann, 131
Bridget Jones's Diary, 131, 132
Bringing Up Baby, 145, *146*
British Broadcasting Corporation
   (BBC), 27, 29, 35–6, 37, 58*n*
British Gramophone Company, 47
Brodkin, Karen, 137
Brokeback Mountain, 147
Brosnan, Mark, 171–2, 173
Brown, Mary Ellen, 104
Brunsdon, Charlotte, 117, 119
Bryson, K., 150*n*
Buffy the Vampire Slayer, 133–4
BuffyWorld.com, 134
Burke, Brooke, 164
Burkeman, Oliver, 85
Burns, Ed, 113
Bush, George H. W., 64
Bush, George W., 73, 85

C-SPAN, 64
cable news channels, 18, 38, 48, 53,
   64
cable television
   abortion issue, 159, 187*n*
   competition, 50
   emergence of, 39, 40, 115
   gender issues, 133
   niche markets, 49, 115
   ownership and control, 40, 49, 50
   political coverage, 63, 64, 66
Cafferty, Jack, 5
call centers, 47
Callender, James, 69, 88*n*
campaign advertising *see* political
   advertising

Canada
   health care systems, 58*n*
   public ownership of media, 35, 37,
      198
   television broadcasting system, 33
Cantor, J., 129
capitalism, 22*n*, 116, 120, 163
Carey, James, 13, 96
Carroll, Diahann, 123, 140
Casper, L. M., 150*n*
CBS Evening News, 23*n*, 79, 85
CBS network, 18, 114
celebrities, 20
cell phones
   election information, 9, 63
   numbers in USA, 17
   uploads to Internet, 20–1
The Celluloid Closet (Russo), 145
Centerwall, Brandon S., 136
Charters, W. W., 170
chat groups, 20, 86, 159
"chick lit", 99
childhood socialization, 80
children
   influence of movies, 170
   influence of television, 103, 136,
      170–1
   media experience, 1–2
   media literacy, 167
   television programs, 80
   use of Internet, 171, 173–8
The Children's Hour, 145–6
China
   Google search results, 26–31
   government Internet censorship,
      21, 31, *32*
chinavista.com, 27
Chong, Sylvia Shin Huey, 137, 140,
   150*n*
ChristusRex.org, 27, 30
Cisco Systems, Chinese government
   censorship, 31

Citigroup, 58*n*

civic engagement, new media environment, 179, 180, 184–6

civic life, effects of television, 33, 84

civic responsibilities, 74–5, 87

"civic retardation", 71

civil rights movement, 123

Clarke, John, 117

class
  cultural studies, 117, 118–19
  cultural works, 117
  Florida Hurricane (1928), 2–3, 5–6, 7
  hegemonic ideology, 118–19
  Hurricane Katrina (2005), 5, 6
  Internet use, 167, 170, 173–8
  interpretation of television, 120–1
  Knocked Up movie, 118
  media representations, 106–7, 112, 115–16, 118–19, 121–2, 167
  new media skills, 171–3
  popular culture, 6
  representation in movies, 118, 121–2
  representation on television, 106–7, 114–16, 118–19, 120–1, 122

Clear Channel, 200–1

Clinton, Bill, 66, 69

Clinton, Hillary, 66

CNBC, 46

CNN, 45–6, 182
  Americans trust in, 58*n*
  average age of viewers, 18
  Gulf War (1991) coverage, 49
  ownership, 41

Cohen, Sacha Baron, 100

The Colbert Report, 65, 88*n*

Colbert, Stephen, 69

Cold War, end of, 17, 89*n*

Cole, Elizabeth R., 106, 120, 121, 159

Colmes, Alan, 53

Color Adjustment, 140, 141

Columbia Journalism Review, 51

Compaine, Benjamin M., 38, 58*n*, 59*n*, 166

computer games, 19, 160, 166

computers
  compared to memory, 10–11
  "dumbing down" concept, 11
  importance in modern life, 1
  literary skills, 167
  sales in USA, 17
  significance to corporations, 47
  social class differences, 173–8
  see also Internet

Condit, Celeste M., 159

conglomerations, 40–6, 48, 49, 52, 56, 200

"convergence culture", 165

Convergence Culture (Jenkins), 161

Coolidge, Calvin, 22*n*

Coontz, Stephanie, 114, 133

Cosby, Bill, 142

The Cosby Show, 106, 142–3

"couch potatoes", 19

Couldry, Nick, 186

The Courtship of Eddie's Father, 133, 143

Crawford, Joan, 128, 131

crime, social impact, 117

Critcher, Charles, 117

Cronkite, Walter, 79

Crook, Charles, 171–2, 173

Cruising, 146

CSI, 66, 144

cultural creativity, and media concentration, 52–3

cultural studies, 9–10, 116–19

culture, potential of new media, 55–6

Curran, J., 58*n*

"The Culture Industry" (Horkheimer and Adorno), 116

"cybertypes", Nakamura's concept of, 160

"cyborg", Haraway's concept of, 160

Daily Kos, 5, 65
The Daily Show, 32, 52, 53, 65, 66
Daley, Suzanne, 107*n*
Dallas, 104–5, 168
Daniels, Erin, 144
Davis, Bette, 128, 130
Dayan, Daniel, 86
Dean, Howard, 169
The Deceit, 139
DeGeneres, Ellen, 147
Delli Carpini, Michael X., 23*n*, 67, 74, 80, 89*n*
democracy
  changing media environments, 68–84
  Dewey's critique, 74–5
  empirical research, 75–9
  Lippmann's critique, 69–71, 72, 73, 74, 75, 76, 77, 79, 80, 82–3, 87
  and media concentration, 52–5
  propaganda campaigns, 69–70, 71–4, 79
demonization, 72
Dempsey, John, 126
Desperate Housewives, 133, 134–5, 135
Desser, David, 162
Dewey, John, 74–5, 79, 80, 87–8, 88*n*
Diana, Princess, death as media event, 5, 86
Dicker, Rory Cooke, 149*n*
digital divide, 47, 167, 172–3, 175–7
digital video recorders (DVRs), 19
DiMaggio, Paul, 166–7, 173
discussion groups online, 20, 86, 170, 181
Disney, 37, 38
Dixie Chicks, 201
Do the Right Thing, 140
The Donna Reed Show, 132
Dorfman, Ariel, 163

Doty, Alexander, 145
Douglas, Stephen A., 16
Douglas, Susan J., 94
Downie, Leonard Jr., 55
Drew, Lori, 171
Drudge Report, 48, 65, 69
Duane, William, 68–9
Dube, William, 186
Duffield, Jill, 171–2, 173
Dukakis, Michael, 64
"dumbing down" concept, 11
The Dungeon, 139
Durndell, Alan, 171–2, 173
DVD players, 17, 19
Dynasty, 147

East Side West Side, 122
Ebert and Roper, 157
economic liberalism, 54
economic structures, 8
  new communications technology, 33, 34–5, 57, 78
economics, 8, 9
Edelman, Benjamin G., 31
Edison National Phonograph Company, 47
Edison, Thomas, 57*n*
education
  media presence, 194–5
  online rating of professors, 199–200
elections
  "horse race" aspect, 83, 88*n*
  Iran, 21
  media influence on voting decisions, 76–9, 82, 83, 103, 105
  political advertising, 65, 76, 82, 83, 102, 105
  role of Internet, 9, 39, 63–4, 169–70, 178–84, 186
  role of journalists, 39, 65, 83, 88*n*
  role of newspapers, 9, 63, 64, 65
  role of television, 9, 63, 64–5, 66–7, 82, 83

elections (*cont'd*)
United States, 9, 39, 59*n*, 63–5,
66–7, 76–9, 169–70, 178–86
use of cell phones, 9, 63
electronic media
emergence of, 12–16
see also movies; radio; telegraph;
television
Eliasoph, Nina, 184
elite democracy, 71
elites
challenge of new media, 20–1, 29,
86, 87, 195
cultural works, 117
political, 68, 75, 84, 85, 86
Ellen, 147
Elliott, Stuart, 126
Ellison, Nicole B., 166
EMI, 40
empirical research, 75–9
"Encoding and Decoding in the
Television Discourse" (Hall),
119
encyclopaedias *see* Wikipedia
English studies, 9
Enlightened Racism (Jhally and
Lewis), 142
Entertainment Weekly, 165
Entman, Robert M., 80
epistemology, 13
ER, 144
ethnicity
American soap operas, 104–5
new media skills, 166, 172–3
popular culture, 6
representation in movies, 137, 163
representation in new media, 166,
167
representation on television,
114–15, 122, 144
ethnographic methods
gender and class identities on
Internet, 173–8

politics and new media study,
178–86
Everett, Ann, 150*n*
Everyday Television (Morley and
Brunsdon), 119
"Examine the Home Computers", 17

face-to-face interaction, 64, 70, 77,
78
Facebook, 166, 170, 194
Faludi, Susan, 95
families
media experience, 1–2
representation in movies, 94, 95,
118
representation on television, 106,
114–5, 122, 127, 141–2
Famous Players theatres, 46
fan cultures, 105, 134, 161, 165
Fan-Sites.org, 134
Fanpop, 134
Farley, David, 203
Fast Times at Ridgemont High, 95–6
Father Knows Best, 122
FCC (Federal Communications
Commission), 59*n*, 199, 200, 203
Federal Trade Commission, 203
feminism
I Love Lucy show, 125
impact on society, 123
interpretations of Madonna, 104
Knocked Up movie, 92–4, 95, 97,
98, 118, 132
romance novels, 99, 104
"second-wave", 99, 127, 132
Sex and the City, 127
south Asian communities, 169
television norms, 121
"third-wave", 127, 132, 149*n*
women's role in movies, 128
Fey, Tina, 67
Fields, J., 150*n*
film production *see* movie production

film studies, 9
films *see* movies
Finer, Lawrence B., 187*n*
Fiske, John, 86–7, 104
Florida Hurricane (1928), 2–4, 5–7, 8, 17
Forbes, 58*n*
Forbes magazine, 204*n*
Ford Foundation, 41–5
Foster, Gwendolyn Audrey, 121
Fox network, 18
Fox News, 41, 52, 53, 58*n*, 65
Frank, Thomas, 54
Frankfurt School, 116, 117
Franklin, Benjamin, 68, 69
FreeRepublic.com, 23*n*, 89*n*
fundamentalist Islam, 202
Fung, Anthony Y. H., 169

Gabler, Neal, 137
Gajjala, Radhika, 169
Galveston Hurricane (1900), 3
Gamson, Joshua, 145
Gary, Brett, 71
Gates, Bill, 58*n*
Gates Jr., Henry Louis, 141
Gattuso, James, 48–9, 59*n*
Gaudet, Hazel, 76, 102
Gavin, Jeff, 171–2, 173
Gawiser, Sheldon, 186
gays
  changing status, 17
  representation in media, 145–7
Gazette of the United States, 68
gender
  cultural studies, 117
  Internet use, 166, 167, 171–2, 173–8
  interpretation of television, 120–1
  media representations, 92–5, 112, 123–36, 160
  popular culture, 6
  production of new media, 172

representation on Internet, 160
representation in movies, 92–5, 128–32
representation on television, 123–7, 132–6
gender bending, 160, 171
gender roles, effects of television, 33
General Electric, 37, 41
Gentleman's Agreement, 121
Germany, propaganda campaigns, 71
Gettysburg Address, 16
Gill, Ross, 108*n*, 132
Gillespie, Marie, 168
Gillis, Stacy, 149*n*
Gingrich, Newt, 58*n*
Gitelman, Lisa, 46–7, 57*n*, 162
Gitlin, Todd, 105–6, 158
Gledhill, Christine, 130
globalization, 17, 46–8, 162–3, 167–9, 201–2
God's Stepchildren, 139
The Goldbergs, 114, 115, 122
Golumbia, David, 161
Gone with the Wind, 138, *139*
Good Times, 141–2
Goodman, Ellen, 93
Google
  advertisements, 30
  Chinese government censorship, 31
  dominance of Internet, 20, 21, 38, 41
  privacy issues, 30
  public obligations, 30–1
  purchase of YouTube, 23*n*
  revenue generation, 30
Google search engine
  dominance of, 41
  Tiananmen Square results, 26–31
Gore, Al, 58*n*
governments
  hurricane response, 2, 4, 6
  Internet censorship, 21, 31, *32*
  Internet policies, 36

governments (*cont'd*)
 manipulation of public opinion,
  72–3
 media development role, 54
 media ownership, 35
 media regulations, 8, 9, 31, 50
 new media environment, 34
 radio regulation, 34
 RFID technology, 203
 support for markets, 54
Graber, Doris, 49, 59*n*
Gramsci, Antonio, 117, 118, 120
Grant, Cary, 145, *146*
Greenberg, Bradley S., 103
Greengard, Samuel, 186
Grey's Anatomy, 133, 144
Grier, Pam, 144
Griffith, D. W., 136, *137*
Gripsrud, Jostein, 147
Grossberg, Lawrence, 120, 163
Gueorguieva, Vassia, 186
Gulf War (1991), 49
Gutierrez, Miren, 46

Hailey, Leisha, 144
1/2 Hour News Report, 65
Hall, Stuart, 108*n*, 117, 119
Hallin, Daniel C., 9, 14
Hamilton, Alexander, 69
Hamilton, James T., 50
Hannity, Sean, 53
Haraway, Donna, 160
Hardball, 53
Hargittai, Eszter, 166, 167, 172, 173,
  176, 178
Harrison, Kristen, 129
Harrison, Taylor, 143
Harry Potter books, 161
Hartley, John, 104
Haskell, Molly, 128
Havelock, Eric, 10
HBO, 112–14, 115, *126*, 134, 187*n*

Headline News, 18
health care systems, 58*n*, 85
Hearst, 40, 58*n*
Heckerling, Amy, 95
Hedren, Tippi, 129
hegemonic ideology, 118–19, 120–1
Heigl, Katherine, 91, 164
Helford, Elyce Rae, 143
Hellman, Lillian, 146
Hemings, Sally, 69
Hendershot, Heather, 136
Hepburn, Katharine, 128, 145, *146*
Herdieckerhoff, E., 108*n*
Heritage Foundation, 48
Herzog, Herta, 128
Hill, Anita, 87, 149*n*
Hill Street Blues, 143–4
Himmelweit, Hilde, 103, 170
Hitchcock, Alfred, 129, 130, *130*
Hitwise, 46
Hoare, Quintin, 118
Hodge, Bob, 103
Hogeland, L. M., 108*n*
Hoggart, Richard, 117
Holloman, Laurel, 144
The Honeymooners, 115, 122
Hong Kong, Internet use study, 169
hooks, bell, 141
Horkheimer, Max, 116
How Stella Got Her Groove Back, 131
Howie, Gillian, 149*n*
Huckabee, Mike, 66
human agency, new media
  environment, 198–202
hurricanes
  Florida (1928), 2–4, 5–7, 8, 17
  Galveston (1900), 3
  Katrina (2005), 3, 4, 5, 6, 8, 17, 86
Hurston, Zora Neale, 6, *7*
Hussein, Saddam, 72
"hybridity", Bhabha's notion of, 162
hypodermic needs theory, 101–2

I Love Lucy, 124–5, *125*
I Remember Mama, 114
ideology, 92–8
  and culture, 117, 118
If These Walls Could Talk, 187*n*
Illich, Ivan, 10–11
image analysis, 121–4
IMDB (Internet Movie Database),
  156–7
Imitation of Life, 141
India
  film industry, 162, 201–2
  meaning of music television, 168
inequalities *see* class; gender; race;
  sexuality
intellectual property, 161
international law, 73
Internet
  book-induced texts, 161
  challenge to broadcast news, 85–6
  children's use of, 171, 173–8
  creation of new information
    models, 29
  election information, 9, 39, 63–4,
    169–70, 178–84, 186
  emergence of, 16, 19–21
  fan groups, 134
  film-induced texts, 161
  government censorship, 21, 31, *32*
  government policies, 36
  government role, 54
  household access in USA, 17, 19
  impact of, 33, 34
  international websites, 20, 86
  Iraq invasion (2003), 48
  media reception research, 163–9
  movie information, 156–8, 161–2,
    164, 165
  net neutrality, 33–4, 36, 55, 199
  nonmainstream websites, 20, 86
  numbers of web sites and pages, 38
  ownership and control, 36, 38, 41

  perceived lack of bias, 183–4
  political information, 78
  political and social activists, 86
  privacy issues, 30, 36
  representations of inequality,
    169–73
  television-induced texts, 161
  top news websites, 46
  transformative images, 160–3
  transformative properties, 39
  use by class, 167, 170, 173–8
  use by gender, 166, 167, 171–2,
    173–8
  see also blogs; chat groups; digital
    divide; Google; online
    discussions; social networking
    sites; Twitter; Wikipedia; Yahoo;
    YouTube
Internet Movie Database (IMDB),
  156–7
Internet search engines
  AOL, 41
  Google, 26–31, 41
  Yahoo, 41
Internet service providers (ISPs), 2,
  36, 50, 199
"invisible hand theory", 49, 59*n*
Iran, 21
Iraq invasion (2003)
  media coverage, 14, 48
  as media event, 5
  propaganda campaigns, 72–3, 74,
    79
Islam, 202
ISPs *see* Internet service providers
  (ISPs)
Israel, reception to *Dallas*, 105, 168
Italy, "Berlusconi" effect, 50–2
Iyengar, Shanto, 81, 82

Jackson, Robert, 136, 149*n*
Jamieson, Kathleen Hall, 82

Japan
  film industry, 162
  public ownership of media, 35
  reception to *Dallas*, 105, 168
Al-Jazeera TV, 48
The Jazz Singer, 138
Jefferson, Thomas, 55, 68, 69
Jefferson, Tony, 117
The Jeffersons, 142
Jenkins, Henry, 56, 105, 160–1, 165,
  181–2
Jhally, Sut, 142
Johnson, Clark, 113
Johnson-Yale, Camille, 39, 178, 188*n*
Joiner, Richard, 171–2, 173
Jon Stewart Show, 53
journalism
  agenda setting, 80, 81, 84, 85, 86
  bias of, 75
  challenge from bloggers, 20, 85
  concentration of media control, 51
  crisis in, 55
  criticisms of, 39
  Hurricane Katrina (2005), 5
  priming role, 81–2, 85
  reflection of American values, 49
  role in political campaigns, 39, 65,
    83, 88*n*
Julia, 123
Juluri, Vamsee, 168

Kaplan, E. Ann, 93, 107*n*
Kate and Allie, 133
Katrina, Hurricane (2005), 3, 4, 5, 6,
  8, 17, 86
Katz, Elihu
  active audience theory, 104–5
  Dallas TV program, 104–5, 168
  interaction of information sources,
    182
  limited media impact, 79
  media events, 86
  "opinion leaders", 102

television superceded by Internet,
  22*n*
two-step flow theory, 78, 102
Kearney, Mary Celeste, 172
Keen, Andrew, 29
Keeter, Scott, 74, 80
Kellner, Douglas, 117, 163
Kelly, Grace, 129
Kennedy, John F., 14, 86
Kerry, John, 182
The Killing of Sister George, 146
Kinder, Donald R., 81
Kirshner, Mia, 144
Klapper, Joseph T., 101, 103
Klawans, Stuart, 100
Kleinberg, Eliot, 6, 22*n*
Knocked Up, 197
  abortion issue, 92–4, 98, 101, 118,
    157, 164, 165
  blogs, 164, 165
  feminism, 92–4, 95, 97, 98, 118,
    132
  influence on teen viewers, 102
  Internet information, 156–7, 164,
    165
  magic bullet theory, 101
  social class factor, 118
  text analysis, 118, 119
Kolko, Beth, 160
Kraidy, Marwan M., 162
Ku Klux Klan, 136, *137*
Kunzle, David, 163
Kurtz, Howard, 18, 88*n*, 94, 108*n*

The L Word, 124, 144–5, 147–8, *148*,
  170
L.A. Law, 133
Lareau, Annette, 175
Lasswell, Harold D., 71–2, 73, 74,
  75, 79, 92
Latinas, media representation, 137,
  143
Lawrence, John Shelton, 163

Lawrence, Regina, 79
Lazarsfeld, Paul
  "active audience" tradition, 105
  interaction of information sources,
      182
  media influence on politics, 75–7,
      78, 79, 81, 82, 102
  opinion leaders, 102
  "two-step flow" theory, 78, 102
Lear, Norman, 99–100, 123
Leather Boys, 122
Leave It to Beaver, 132
lectures, impact of television, 15
Lee, Spike, 139–40
Leigh, Janet, 129
Leigh, Vivian, *139*
lesbians, representation in media, 115,
      124, 133, 144–6, 147–8, 170
Lessig, Lawrence, 34
Lewinsky, Monica, 69
Lewis, Justin, 142
Lewis, Lisa L., 105
Leys, Colin, 54
Lichter, Linda S., 132, 133
Lichter, S. Robert, 132, 133
Liebes, Tamar, 104–5, 168
The Life of Riley, 122
Lifetime network, 18
Limbaugh, Rush, 65, 69
Lincoln, Abraham, 16
Lippmann, Walter, media and
      democracy, 69–71, 72, 73, 74,
      75, 76, 77, 79, 80, 82–3, 87
Lipsitz, George, 6, 114, 121, 122
literacy, effects of television, 33
literary skills, 167
Liu, Lucy, 143
Livingston, Steven, 79
Livingstone, Sonia M., 101, 104,
      108*n*, 136, 167, 170, 186
Lohan, Lindsey, 20
Longhurst, Brian, 40
Lost, 161

Lott, Trent, 85
Lotz, Amanda D., 108*n*, 133, 134
Lucas, George, 165

Mabius, Eric, 144
MacBeth, Tannis M., 103
McCabe, Janet, 135
McCain, John, 66
McChesney, Robert Waterman, 9, 36,
      37, 40, 41, 50, 55, 80
McCombs, M. E., 81
McDaniel, Hattie, 138, *139*
MacGregor Wise, J., 163
McHugh, Josh, 30
MacLeish, Archibald, 71
McLuhan, Marshall, 10
McMillan, Terry, 131
McRobbie, Angela, 108*n*, 117
Madonna, 104
magazines
  cultural studies, 117
  election information, 63
  niche markets, 49
  ownership and control, 40
magic bullet theory, 101–2
Mama, 122
The Man in the Gray Flannel Suit,
      121
Mancini, Paolo, 9
Manguel, Alberto, 11–12
Mann, Denise, 122
market failure, 50, 55
market outcome, 50, 59*n*
"market populism", 54–5
market substitutability, 38–9, 58*n*
MarketingVOX, 41
markets
  government support, 54
  media ownership and control, 9,
      34–5, 36–7, 48–56, 83, 198
  see also niche markets
Markham, Tim, 186
Marshall, John, 76

Marshall, Joshua, 85, 89*n*
Marx, Karl, 116
The Mary Tyler Moore Show, 123, 133
mass media
  as elitist and antidemocratic, 55
  emergence of, 67, 75
  impact on democracy, 75, 76–9,
    82, 83
  impact on public opinion, 70
  "magic bullet theory", 101
  origin of the term, 76
  ownership and control, 34, 35
  social harms, 105
  see also Internet; magazines; movies;
    newspapers; radio; television
Massanari, Adrienne, 160
The Matrix, 161
Mattelart, Armand, 163
Maude, 123
meanings
  reception studies, 98–100, 101–7
  television texts, 119
  of texts, 92, 97, 99–100
media diversity, 38–9, 49, 50, 53, 79,
    158–9, 200
media environment
  changes in, 10–16
  defined, 8–10
  market substitutability, 38–9, 58*n*
media event, concept of, 4–5, 86–7,
    201
media literacy, 32, 88, 92, 167, 173,
    202, 203
media mergers, American concern,
    45
The Media Monopoly (Bagdikian), 37
media ownership and control
  alternative models, 35–7
  cable television, 40, 49, 50
  concentration of, 9, 35, 37–46,
    48–56, 158–9, 200–1
  conglomerations, 40–6, 48, 49, 52,
    56, 200

of the Internet, 36, 38, 41
market-driven, 9, 34–5, 36–7,
    48–56, 83, 198
patterns of, 26–32
public service model, 9, 35–6, 37,
    198
radio, 36–7, 198, 200–1
television, 33, 40, 83, 198
US newspapers, 39–40
media representations, 96–8
  bisexuals, 144, 145
  class, 106–7, 112, 115–16, 118–19,
    121–2, 167
  ethnicity, 114–15, 122, 137, 144,
    163, 166, 167
  families, 94, 95, 106, 114–15, 118,
    122, 127, 141–2
  gays, 145–7
  gender, 92–5, 112, 123–36, 160
  lesbians, 115, 124, 133, 144–6,
    147–8, 170
  race, 112, 115–16, 123–4, 136–44,
    160, 163, 166, 167
  sexuality, 112, 121, 144–8
  women, 92–5, 123–7, 128–36,
    160, 166, 167
"media in use", 39
Mediaset, 50, 51
Meier, Megan, 171
memory, 10–11
Metz, Christian, 128, 129
Meyrowitz, Joshua, 33, 141
Michaels, Meredith W., 94
Micheaux, Oscar, 138–9, 150*n*
Microsoft, 21, 37
Mildred Pierce, 131
Miles, Vera, 129
Miller, Daniel, 169
Miller, Dennis, 65
Moennig, Katherine, 144
Moneyline with Lou Dobbs, 45–6
Montgomery, Kathryn, 159
Moore, Ellen, 39, 178, 188*n*

Moore, Michael, 58*n*, 69
Morley, David, 108*n*, 117, 119–20, 121
Mosco, Vincent, 166
Mother Jones, 157
motherhood, impact on careers, 94–5
mothers
  in literature, 93
  in movies, 92–3
Moveon.org, 6, 23*n*, 89*n*
movie production
  independents, 58*n*
  India, 162, 201–2
  influence of Hollywood, 201–2
  international character, 163
  Japan, 162
  ownership and control, 40
  United Kingdom, 122
movie studios, as conglomerates, 40–1
movies
  abortion issue, 67, 92–4, 95–6, 98, 101, 118, 122, 157, 164, 165
  development of, 15
  Frankfurt School criticism, 116
  gender issues, 92–5, 128–32
  "ideological work", 92–8
  impact on children/teenagers, 102, 170
  impact on people, 197
  interactive format on Internet, 156–8, 161–2, 164, 165
  Internet information, 156–8, 161–2, 164, 165
  propaganda campaigns, 71
  representation of class, 118, 121–2
  representation of families, 94, 95, 118
  representation of gender, 92–5, 128–32
  representation of race, 136–40, 141, 163
  representation of sexuality, 121, 145–7
  representation of women, 92–5, 128–32
  studio era, 129
  textual analysis, 92–100
  women's film, 130–1
MSNBC network, 18, 41, 53, 59*n*, 65
msnbc.com, 59*n*
MTV, 200
Müller, Ronald E., 47
multiculturalism, 89*n*
Mulvey, Laura, 128–30, 131, 132, 172
Munford, Rebecca, 149*n*
Murdoch, Rupert, 41
Murray, John P., 103, 136
Muscio, Giuliana, 121
Museum of Broadcast Communications, 14
music publishing, ownership and control, 40
Muslim fundamentalists, 202
My Best Friend's Wedding, 146–7
My Three Sons, 133
MySpace, 166, 171

Nakamura, Lisa, 160
National Committee on Education by Radio, 37, 55
The National Enquirer, 69
National Public Radio, 1
Nationwide, 120
The Nationwide Audience (Morley), 119
NBC network, 37, 46, 59*n*, 114
NBC news channel, 18
Nelson, Cary, 120
neoliberalism, 54
nervous liberals, 71, 73
net neutrality, 33–4, 36, 55, 199
Neuman, W. Russell, 167, 173

new media environment, 156–9
  bias, 182–4
  challenge to elites, 20–1, 29, 86,
    87, 195
  civic engagement, 179, 180, 184–6
  gender and class identities, 173–8
  human agency, 198–202
  media reception research, 163–9
  political information, 84–7,
    178–86, 201
  potential of, 55–6
  relations with old media, 181–4
  representations of inequality,
    169–73
  skills requirements, 166–7, 171–3
  transformative images, 160–3
  see also cable television; cell phones;
    DVD players; Internet; satellite
    television
The New Media Monopoly (Bagdikian),
  37
New Orleans, Hurricane Katrina
  (2005), 3, 4, 5, 6, 8, 17, 86
New York Times, 1, 4, 69
  website, 28, 29
news channels *see* television news
  channels
News Corporation, 37, 38, 41
newspaper websites, 58*n*
newspapers
  bias, 183
  election information, 9, 63, 64, 65
  Florida Hurricane (1928), 4
  impact on public opinion, 70
  ownership and control, 39–40
  source of political information, 70
  Twittering of Obama's address, 32
  in United States, 39–40, 58*n*
niche markets, 49, 115
Nichols, John, 55
Nixon, Richard, 14
Norris, Pippa, 166
Novak, Kim, 129, *130*

Now, Voyager, 130–1
Nowell-Smith, Geoffrey, 118

Obama, Barack, 32, 63, 66–7, 85,
  169–70, 186, 201
"Obama Girl" video, 63
Olbermann, Keith, 65
online discussions, 20, 86, 170, 181
Ono, Kent, 137, 140, 143
opinion leaders, 102
oral communication, impact of
  television, 15
oral cultures, 10–12
O'Reilly, Bill, 69
Our Miss Brooks, 116, 133
Out of Order (Patterson), 82–3

Packard, Lucile, 136
Palin, Sarah, 52, 67
Patterson, Thomas, 82–3, 88*n*
Payne Fund, 170
PBS *see* Public Broadcasting System
  (PBS)
Pecora, Norma Odom, 103, 136
People magazine, 41
The Peoples' Choice (Lazarsfeld,
  Berelson and Gaudet), 102
Perez, Rosie, 143
Personal Influence (Katz and
  Lazarsfeld), 102, 182
Peters, Clarke, *114*
Peters, John Durham, 13
Pew Internet and American Life
  Report, 19
Pew Project for Excellence in
  Journalism, 40, 58*n*
Pew surveys, 48, 58*n*, 59*n*, 107*n*, 186
Phalen, Patricia, 18
Pham, Vincent, 143
The Phantom Public (Lippmann), 71
phonograph, 57*n*
photography, 14–15, 23*n*
Piepmeier, Alison, 149*n*

Plato, 11
Polanyi, Karl, 54
political advertising, 64, 65, 76, 82, 83, 102, 105
political culture, effects of television, 33
political elites, 68, 75, 84, 85, 86
political science, 8, 9
political socialization, 77, 79, 80
political structures, 8
  new communications technology, 33, 34–5, 57, 78
politics
  changing media environments, 68–84
  citizens limited capacities, 67, 70–1, 74–5
  impact of blogs, 20, 63, 66, 85
  journalist role, 39, 65, 83, 88n
  media influence, 50–4, 66–7, 70, 76–9, 103, 105
  in new media environment, 84–7, 178–86, 201
  potential of new media, 55–6
  television coverage, 14, 63, 64–5, 66–7, 79–84
  television news programs, 63, 64–5, 83, 84–5
  see also elections
Pollitt, Katha, 93, 159
popular culture
  cultural studies, 116–19
  effects of television, 33
  Frankfurt School, 116, 117
  small specialist audiences, 6, 117
portable digital assistants (PDAs), numbers in USA, 17
post office, government role, 54
postfeminism, 99
Postman, Neil
  Amusing Ourselves to Death, 13, 203
  political debate, 14, 16, 68

television, 13, 15–16, 20, 33, 83, 199
pregnancy, impact on careers, 94–5
presidential debates, television, 14
presidential elections, United States, 9, 39, 59n, 63–5, 66–7, 76–9, 169–70
Press, Andrea Lee
  abortion issue, 159
  active audiences, 104, 106
  gender and class identities on Internet, 173–8
  gender issues, 125
  hegemonic ideology, 119
  politics and new media study, 39, 178, 187n, 188n
  television and class, 120, 121, 122
print cultures, 10–12
  impact of television, 15
printing press, societal impact, 34
Prior, Markus, 68, 80, 87
private sector
  new communications technology, 34
  ownership of media, 9, 34–5, 36–7, 48–56, 83, 198
Projansky, Sarah, 143
propaganda
  and democracy, 69–70, 71–4, 79
  invasion of Iraq (2003), 72–3, 74, 79
  segmenting, 73
  slicing and dicing, 73
  wars, 69–70, 71–4, 79
  World War I, 69–70, 71–2, 79
Propaganda Technique in World War I (Lasswell), 71–2
Prouty, Olive Higgins, 131
Pruitt, Gary, 18
psychics, 13
psychoanalysis, 128–9
public broadcasting models, 9, 35–6, 37, 198

Public Broadcasting System (PBS), 28, 29
Public Opinion, 70
public relations, 70, 75
public sphere, 29, 56
Punathambekar, Aswin, 162, 202
punk music, 165
Putnam, Robert D., 33, 84

Quart, Alissa, 157
Queer as Folk, 147

race
　changing status, 17
　cultural studies, 117
　Florida Hurricane (1928), 2–3, 5–6, 7, 17
　Hurricane Katrina (2005), 5, 6, 17
　media representations, 112, 115–16, 123–4, 136–44, 160, 163, 166, 167
　new media competencies, 166
　new media skills, 166, 172–3
　popular culture, 6
　representation on Internet, 160, 166, 167
　representation in movies, 136–40, 141, 163
　representation on television, 115–16, 123–4, 140–4
racism
　All in the Family, 100, 123, 143
　Amos 'n' Andy, 140
　Birth of a Nation, 136
　Hollywood film industry, 136–7, 138
radio
　advertising in USA, 37
　audiences, 88n
　election information, 9
　Florida Hurricane (1928), 4, 7, 8
　government control, 34
　government role, 54

media ownership and control in USA, 36–7, 198, 200–1
propaganda campaigns, 71
soap operas, 128
societal impact, 34
radio frequency identification (RFID), 202–4
Radway, Janice, 99, 104, 166, 172, 197–8
Rai, 51
Rainie, Lee, 59n
RateMyProfessor.com, 200, 204n
rational-legal society, 22n
reading
　decline in, 11
　impact of television, 15
　in silence, 11–12
Reading the Romance (Radway), 99, 104
reality
　media representation, 7, 12, 96–8, 122
　structured by communication mode, 12
　transition from oral and written culture, 10
reality television, 106–7, 161, 162
Rear Window, 129
reception studies, 98–100, 101–7
　new media environment, 163–9
　television, 119–21
recorded sound industry
　competition, 50
　globalization, 46–7
　ownership and control, 40
RedState, 65
Redstone, Sumner, 41
Reed, Donna, 132
Reger, Jo, 149n
remote controls, growth of, 19
representations *see* media representations
republic.com (Sunstein), 57n

RFID (radio frequency identification), 202–4
Rich, Matty, 139–40
Riggs, Marlon, 140
Roberts, Brian, 117
Roberts, Julia, 147
Robinson, John P., 167, 173
Rockefeller Foundation, 76
Rodman, Gilbert B., 160
Roe v. Wade (1972), 157
Rogan, Seth, 91, 164
Rogin, Michael Paul, 136, 137, 138
Rokeach, Milton, 100, 143
Rolle, Esther, 141–2
romance novels, 99, 104, 197–8
Roosevelt, Franklin D., 76
Rosen, Marjorie, 128
Rosenfeld, Richard N., 68–9
Rosengren, Karl Eric, 103
Rothman, Stanley, 132, 133
Route 66, 122
Rubin, Alan, 103
Rubio, Kevin, 165
Ruby Gentry, 121
Russo, Vito, 145
Rutenberg, Jim, 18
Ryan, Alan, 88*n*, 149*n*

Saddam Hussein, 72
Safire, William, 88*n*
Sanders, Barry, 10–11
Sanford and Son, 123, 142
satellite television
    competition, 50
    election information, 63
    emergence of, 39, 40
    niche markets, 49
    ownership and control, 40, 49, 50
Saturday Night Live (SNL), 66, 67, 88*n*
Scandalmonger (Safire), 88*n*
Schiller, Dan, 31
Schroder, Kim, 103, 108*n*

Schudson, Michael, 55, 88*n*
Schwichtenberg, Cathy, 120
search engines *see* Internet search engines
segmenting, 73
Seinfeld, 18
September 11
    Iraqi connections, 73
    as media event, 5, 8, 86
serendipity, 29
Servon, Lisa J., 167
Sesame Street, 80
Sex and the City, 126–7, *126*, 130, 131–2, 133
sexism, 172
    All in the Family, 100
    Hollywood film industry, 164, 172
    romance novels, 104
sexuality
    and clothing, 99
    interactivity on Internet, 170
    interpretations of Madonna, 104
    media representations, 112, 121, 144–8
    representation in movies, 121, 145–7
    representation on television, 144–5, 147–8
    "third-wave feminism", 127, 132, 149*n*
    see also bisexuals; gays; lesbians
Shaw, D. L., 81
Shirky, Clay, 33, 58*n*, 169
Showtime, 144, 145
Silver, David, 160
Silverstone, Roger, 108*n*
Simon, David, 113
Simpson, O. J., 87
The Simpsons, 66
Sinclair Broadcasting Company, 182
Singer, Dorothy G., 136
Singer, Jerome L., 136
The Sisterhood of the Traveling Pants, 131

60 Minutes, 94
Skeggs, Bev, 106
Slater, Don, 169
slicing and dicing, 73
Smith, Aaron, 59*n*, 63, 64
Smith, Adam, 54, 59*n*
soap operas, 104–5, 128
social boundaries, effects of television, 33
social coercion, 118
social networking sites, 64, 166, 168, 170, 194
social structures, 8
  new communications technology, 33, 57, 78
sociology, 8–9
Sohn, Sonja, *114*
Sontag, Susan, 47–8, 58–9*n*
Sony/BMG, 40
sound bites, 14, 22*n*
Soviet Union, propaganda campaigns, 71
Speaking of Abortion (Press and Cole), 120, 121
Spears, Britney, 20
spectator theory, 128–9, 132
Spigel, Lynn, 114, 115, 122
Standage, Tom, 34
Stanwyck, Barbara, 131
Star Trek, 105, 161
Star Wars, 165
Statistical Abstracts of the United States, 23*n*
Steel, Ronald, 69, 71
Stella Dallas, 131
Stewart, James, 129, *130*
Stewart, Jon, 52, 53, 69
Stille, Alexander, 51, 59*n*
Stone, Brad, 2
Stowe, Harriet Beecher, 138
Strathman, Terry, 121
subcultures, 117
A Summer Place, 121

Sunstein, Cass, 7, 29, 55, 57*n*
Surowiecki, James, 197

Tapscott, Don, 29
A Taste of Honey, 122
Taylor, Ella, 114
technological determinism, 33, 39
teenagers
  impact of movies, 102, 170
  London study, 168
  magazines, 117
  use of Internet, 171, 178
telegraph
  emergence of, 12–13, 16
  government role, 54
  societal impact, 34
Telemundo, 46
telephone
  Florida Hurricane (1928), 4, 7, 8
  significance to corporations, 47
  world penetration, 47, 58*n*
television
  advertisements, 18, 23*n*, 101–2
  changes in, 17–19
  children's programs, 80
  coverage of politics, 14, 63, 64–5, 66–7, 79–84
  "dumbing down" concept, 11
  election information, 9, 63, 64–5, 66–7, 82, 83
  emergence of, 13–16
  Frankfurt School criticism, 116
  growth of remote controls, 19
  households with multiple TVs, 19
  image analysis, 122–4
  influence on children, 103, 136, 170–1
  influence of, 15–16
  influence on women, 104, 106–7
  interactive format on Internet, 161–2
  mass audiences, 7, 13, 17–18
  as mass medium, 13, 103, 198

negative social consequences, 33
"network era", 114–15, 133, 158
number of channels received, 17–18
ownership and control, 33, 40, 83,
    198
presidential debates, 14
reality shows, 106–7, 161, 162
reasons for watching, 103
reception studies, 119–21
representation of abortion, 106,
    120, 121, 159, 187*n*
representation of class, 106–7,
    114–16, 118–19, 120–1, 122
representation of ethnicity, 114–15,
    122, 144
representation of families, 106, 115,
    122, 127, 141–2
representation of gender, 123–7,
    132–6
representation of race, 115–16,
    123–4, 140–4
representation of sexuality, 144–5,
    147–8
representation of women, 123–7,
    132–6
soap operas, 104–5
talk shows, 145
textual analysis, 119
as visual medium, 13–14
see also ABC network; British
    Broadcasting Corporation (BBC);
    cable television; CBS network;
    NBC network; satellite television
television journalists, as primary
    gatekeepers, 81
television news channels
agenda setting, 81, 84, 85, 86
audiences, 18, 64, 81, 84–5
bias, 183
changing content, 50
competition, 50, 64
cultural studies, 117
"Age of Broadcast News", 79–84

political information, 63, 64–5, 83,
    84–5
priming role, 81–2, 85
reception research, 119–20
see also cable news channels; *CBS
    Evening News*; Fox News
terrorism *see* September 11
That Girl, 123, 133
Their Eyes Were Watching God
    (Hurston), 6, *7*
Thomas, Clarence, 87, 149*n*
Thumim, Nancy, 106
Thurmond, Strom, 85
Tiananmen Square, Google search
    results, 26–31
Till the Clouds Roll By, 149–50*n*
Time Warner
    Chinese government censorship, 31
    global ranking, 58*n*
    holdings, 42–5
    magazine ownership, 40
    media domination, 37, 38, 40
    music publishing, 40
    ownership of news websites, 41
TiVo, 19, 64
The Today Show, 108*n*
Todd, Chuck, 186
transportation, and communication,
    12–13
travelchinaguide.com, 27
Treichler, Paula A., 120
Trinidad, Internet study, 169
Tripp, David, 103
Trippi, Joe, 33, 170
Troops, 165
Turkle, Sherry, 160, 165, 166
Turow, Joseph, 7, 18
Tushnet, Rebecca, 136
TV Dimensions 2004, 23*n*
Twain, Mark, 16
Twitter, 32, 57*n*, 159, 194
"two-step flow" theory, 77–8, 79, 81,
    84, 102

Umecki, Miyoshi, 143
Uncle Tom's Cabin, 138
Underworld, 139
United Kingdom
  control of empire, 47
  film industry, 122
  health care systems, 58*n*
  Indian teenagers, 168
  public ownership of media, 35–6,
    37, 198
  public trust in BBC, 35–6, 58*n*
  television broadcasting system, 33
United States
  Americans' political capacities, 67,
    70–1, 74–5, 80
  Civil War photographs, 23*n*
  concentration of media, 37–46,
    200–1
  crisis in journalism, 55
  education sector, 194–5
  election campaigns, 9, 39, 59*n*,
    63–5, 66–7, 76–9, 169–70,
    178–86
  health care reforms, 58*n*, 85
  hurricanes, 2–4, 5–7, 8, 17, 86
  local news media, 38–9
  news distortion, 52
  newspapers, 39–40, 58*n*
  political conflict and partisanship,
    84
  private ownership of media, 34–5,
    36–7, 83, 198
  public political discussion, 184–6
  radio ownership and control, 36–7,
    198, 200–1
  television broadcasting system,
    33
  trust in news channels, 58*n*
  urbanization, 22*n*
  views on abortion, 93, 107*n*, 157
  voting turnout, 184, 187–8*n*
  written Constitution, 12

university lectures, impact of
  television, 15
US Census Bureau, 184, 188*n*
US Justice Department, 203
uses and gratifications tradition, 103

Vaidhyanathan, Siva, 30, 161
Valdivia, Angharad N., 143
Vanity Fair, 164
Vargas, Elizabeth, 94, 108*n*
VCRs, numbers in USA, 17
Vertigo, 129, *130*
Viacom, 37, 38, 41, 46, 200
video game players, 19, 160, 166
Vidmar, Neil, 100, 143
Vieira, Meredith, 94, 107–8*n*
Vietnam War, 49
VIP Limited Partnership, 134
"Visual Pleasure and Narrative
  Cinema" (Mulvey), 128–9
Vivendi Universal, 40
voting decisions, 76–9, 82, 83, 103,
  105
voting turnout, 184, 187–8*n*

Waiting to Exhale, 131
Walejko, Gina, 166
Walker, Rebecca, 149*n*
Walkerdine, Valerie, 172
Walmart, 58*n*, 202, 203
Walsh, Andrea S., 130
Walters, Suzanna Danuta, 93, 107*n*,
  145, 147
The War of the Worlds (Wells), 102
wars, propaganda campaigns, 69–70,
  71–4, 79
Warschauer, Mark, 167
Wartella, Ellen, 103, 136, 163
Washington, Fredi, 141
Washington, George, 68–9
The Washington Post, 1, 88*n*
  website, 28, 29

Watkins, S. Craig, 139
WB network, 18
weapons of mass destruction
    (WMDs), 72, 73
Web logs *see* blogs
Weber, Max, 22*n*
WebSiteOptimization.com, 23*n*
Webster, James, 18
Welles, Orson, 102
Wells, H. G., 102
West, Dominic, *114*
West Side Story, 121
"When Chick Flicks Get Knocked
    Up" (Quart), 157
"Who Owns What"?, 42–5
Who's the Boss?, 133
Wife Swap, 106–7
Wikipedia, 27, 29, 140, 149*n*, 157,
    171, 196–7
Wild West, 168
Wilentz, Sean, 68
Wilhelm II, King of Germany, 72
Will and Grace, 147
Williams, Anthony D., 29
Williams, Bruce A., 23*n*, 88*n*,
    89*n*
  politics and new media study, 39,
    67, 178, 187*n*, 188*n*
Williams, Raymond, 108*n*, 117–18,
    119, 120
Willkie, Wendell, 76
Wills, Gary, 16
Wilson, Leah, 135
The Wire, 66, 112–14, 115, 118–19,
    123–4, 144, 170
Witney, D. Charles, 163

women
  changing status, 17
  influence of television, 104, 106–7
  interpretation of television, 120–1
  in literature, 93, 99, 104, 197–8
  new media competencies, 166
  production of new media, 172
  radio soap operas, 128
  representation on Internet, 160,
    166, 167
  representation in movies, 92–5,
    128–32
  representation on television, 123–7,
    132–6
  television reality shows, 106–7
  television soap operas, 104
  see also feminism
Women Watching Television (Press),
    120
Wood, Helen, 106
Woods, Tiger, 20
"world music", 202
World War I, propaganda, 69–70,
    71–2, 79
Wresch, William, 47
written cultures *see* print cultures

Yahoo
  dominance of Internet, 21, 38, 41
  Internet portal, 19–20, 23*n*
Yahoo search engine, 41
YouTube, 21, 23*n*, 63, 171

Ziegfield Follies, 149–50*n*
Zillien, Nicole, 166
Zittrain, Jonathan, 31, 36